PENGUIN BOOKS

THE POST-AMERICAN WORLD

'Measured, erudite, thrilling in its breadth of reference'
Kenny Hodgart, *Herald*

'A minor masterpiece full of pragmatic, informed
intelligence . . . He brings a sharp mind and an eye for
detail, example and anecdote to his task in his new
book . . . readable and succinct'
Jason Burke, *Observer*

'Sharply observed . . . he is on to important stuff'
Stanley Reed, *Business Week*

'Mature, interesting and thankfully non-partisan' *Time Out*

'Zakaria is illuminating and right'
Peter Berkowitz, *New York Sun*

'Judicious, reasonable, smooth, intelligent'
Ian Buruma, *New Yorker*

'An important reality check for a nation whose sense of place
in the world is largely outdated' Paddy Smyth, *Irish Times*

D1392184

ABOUT THE AUTHOR

Fareed Zakaria is the editor of *Newsweek International* and writes a weekly column on international affairs. His previous book was the *New York Times* bestseller *The Future of Freedom*. He lives in New York City.

The Post-American World

And the Rise of the Rest

Fareed Zakaria

PENGUIN BOOKS

PENGUIN BOOKS

Published by the Penguin Group
Penguin Books Ltd, 80 Strand, London WC2R 0RL, England
Penguin Group (USA), Inc., 375 Hudson Street, New York, New York 10014, USA
Penguin Group (Canada), 90 Eglinton Avenue East, Suite 700, Toronto, Ontario, Canada M4P 2Y3
(a division of Pearson Penguin Canada Inc.)
Penguin Ireland, 25 St Stephen's Green, Dublin 2, Ireland (a division of Penguin Books Ltd)
Penguin Group (Australia), 250 Camberwell Road, Camberwell, Victoria 3124, Australia
(a division of Pearson Australia Group Pty Ltd)
Penguin Books India Pvt Ltd, 11 Community Centre, Panchsheel Park, New Delhi – 110 017, India
Penguin Group (NZ), 67 Apollo Drive, Rosedale, North Shore 0632, New Zealand
(a division of Pearson New Zealand Ltd)
Penguin Books (South Africa) (Pty) Ltd, 24 Sturdee Avenue, Rosebank, Johannesburg 2196, South Africa

Penguin Books Ltd, Registered Offices: 80 Strand, London WC2R 0RL, England

www.penguin.com

First published in the United States of America by W. W. Norton & Company, Inc., 2008
First published in Great Britain by Allen Lane 2008
Published in Penguin Books with a new Preface 2009

3

Copyright © Fareed Zakaria, 2008, 2009

Printed in Great Britain by Clays Ltd, St Ives plc

A CIP catalogue record for this book is available from the British Library

978-0-141-03805-6

www.greenpenguin.co.uk

Penguin Books is committed to a sustainable future
for our business, our readers and our planet.
The book in your hands is made from paper
certified by the Forest Stewardship Council.

For
Arshad Zakaria

Growth takes place whenever a challenge evokes a successful response that, in turn, evokes a further and different challenge. We have not found any intrinsic reason why this process should not repeat itself indefnitely, even though a majority of civilizations have failed, as a matter of historical fact.

Arnold J. Toynbee
A Study of History

Contents

Preface to the Paperback Edition   xiii

1   The Rise of the Rest   1

2   The Cup Runneth Over   6

3   A Non-Western World?   49

4   The Challenger   87

5   The Ally   129

6   American Power   167

7   American Purpose   215

Notes   261

Acknowledgments   269

Index   273

The
Post-American
World

Preface to the Paperback Edition

The Fastest Race Car in the World

Every golden age comes to a close. The more glittering the era, the more fiery the end. The crash of 2008 was the world's worst financial collapse since 1929 and has ushered in the worst economic slowdown since the Great Depression. Every event in the last year has been unprecedented: the destruction of approximately $40 trillion in equity value in the global economy; the nationalization of America's largest mortgage lenders; the largest bankruptcy in history (Lehman Brothers); the disappearance of the investment bank; bailouts and stimulus packages around the world adding up to trillions of dollars. We are living through times that will be recounted and studied for generations.

How did we get here? I would argue that, ironically, the fundamental cause for this collapse has been—success. The last quarter-century has been one of extraordinary growth. The size of the global economy doubled every ten years or so, going from $31 trillion in 1999 to $62 trillion in 2008, and inflation stayed surprisingly and persistently low. Economic growth reached new regions. While Western families moved into bigger homes and bought laptops and cell phones, subsistence farmers in Asia and Latin America found new jobs in rapidly growing cities. Even in Africa, people were able to tap into a global market to sell their goods. Everywhere, the prices of goods fell, while wealth in the form of stocks, bonds, and real estate soared. Macroeconomic indicators reveal the story at a glance. In 2006 and 2007, the years that marked the high tide of the golden age, 124 of the world's countries—roughly two-thirds of the total—grew faster than 4 percent annually.

What caused the age of global growth? As I lay out in detail in this book, it was a combination of political, economic, and technological forces.

Politics. The Soviet Union's demise ushered in a generation of relative political stability. During the Cold War, there had been dozens of civil wars, armed insurgencies, and small guerrilla groups that the Soviets had funded—and in most of these cases the West had funded their counterparts. Without great power competition, there were fewer wars and those that broke out were smaller in scale. There were exceptions, such as the brutal bloodletting in Congo in the 1990s and, of course, terrorism like that unleashed by Al Qaeda, but on the whole the world enjoyed greater peace and stability than it had in centuries. The number of deaths caused by political violence continued to decline.

Economics. Communism's collapse left free-market capitalism the only viable way to run an economy, which gave governments everywhere an enormous incentive to become a part of the international economic system. New agreements and institutions like the World Trade Organization worked to lower trade barriers and integrate the world. Governments from Vietnam to Colombia realized they couldn't afford to miss out on the global race to prosperity. They adopted sound policies, lowering debt levels and eliminating distorting subsidies—not because people like Bob Rubin or Hank Paulson forced them to do so, but because they could see the benefits of moving in that direction (and the costs of not doing so). Those reforms encouraged foreign investment and created new jobs.

At the same time, central bankers were learning to control and moderate the business cycle, preventing the volatile swings that can destroy jobs and savings and lead to unrest and revolution. To use the United States as an example: Between 1854 and 1919, recessions struck once every four years and lasted nearly two full years when they came. Over the last two decades, the United States experienced eight years of uninterrupted growth between recessions, and the downturns, when they hit, lasted only eight months. This period of stability was a spoil of the decades-long assault on inflation. Starting with Paul Volcker in the early 1980s, central bankers waged war on inflation, wielding the blunt tools of monetary policy to keep the price of goods relatively stable. The tactics honed in that war became one of America's most successful exports. By 2007, just twenty-three countries had an inflation rate higher than 10 percent, and only one—Zimbabwe—suffered from hyperinflation.

Technology. The information revolution accelerated the rise of a single global economy. Communications costs plummeted, information became accessible everywhere, and integration became easier. Suddenly, a Nebraskan sporting goods store could source from China, sell to Europe, and have its checkbooks balanced by accountants in Bangalore.

But the major side effect of all this success—low inflation, global growth, swift technological advancement—was arrogance, or more technically, the death of risk. During the nineties and the naughts, businessmen kept a wary eye out for political risk—the danger to economic growth from coups, terrorist attacks, and social turmoil. But there was little political risk to be found. A coup simply brought in a new regime that still faced all the constraints and opportunities of the global economy. And despite terrorism and the occasional calamity, the basic political stability of the post–Cold War world endured.

These same businessmen paid little attention to a much more familiar problem closer to home: economic risk. Like Alan Greenspan, they assumed that the growth of complex financial products actually reduced risk by spreading it around. They believed that levels of debt that were once considered dangerous were now manageable given what they assumed were permanently changed conditions. As a result, investors became willing to accept relatively little reward in return for what would, under normal circumstances, be considered dangerous investments. Credit spreads—the difference in yield between a U.S. treasury bond, considered the world's safest investment, and the bonds of companies with limited track records—hit historic lows. Volatile countries like Ecuador and teetering companies like Chrysler could borrow almost as cheaply as the U.S. government. (By 2009, of course, Ecuador had defaulted on its debt and Chrysler had averted bankruptcy only because of a last-minute government bailout.) And since debt was cheap, financiers and homeowners used it to excess, spending beyond their means. The banks and investors who supplied all the cheap cash were reassured by fat corporate coffers—with profits that rose at a double-digit clip for eighteen consecutive quarters between 2002 and 2006—and bankruptcy rates that were well below normal. The good times seemed never-ending.

The world economy had become the equivalent of a race car—expensive, with incredible range, and capable of performing at breathtaking speed. For the last decade everyone rode it and experienced the adrenaline rush and the highs. There was only one problem: it turned out that nobody really knew how to drive a car like this one. Over the last ten years, the global economy had become something no one had ever seen—an integrated system of about 125 countries, all participating and all going at speeds unheard of before. It was as if that race car was being driven by 125 different drivers—and no one remembered to buy shock absorbers.

The Problem of Debt

There were those who wanted shock absorbers. They were seen as naysayers during the boom years. They asked why packages of subprime mortgages should be rated as highly as bonds from General Electric. But each successive year ended with another eye-boggling earnings report or billion-dollar payday for the hedge fund manager of the moment, the much-promised correction failed to materialize, and the naysayers grew quieter and quieter. A kind of reverse natural selection occurred on Wall Street. As Boykin Curry, a managing director at Eagle Capital, said, over the last twenty years "the DNA of nearly every financial institution had morphed dangerously. Each time someone at the table pressed for more leverage and more risk, the next few years proved them 'right.' These people were emboldened, they were promoted, and they gained control of ever more capital. Meanwhile, anyone in power who hesitated, who argued for caution, was proved 'wrong.' The cautious types were increasingly intimidated, passed over for promotion. They lost their hold on capital."

Warren Buffett explained that the heart of the problem was ever-rising levels of leverage—the fancy Wall Street word for debt. It is "the only way a smart guy can go broke," Buffet said. "You do smart things, you eventually get very rich. If you do smart things and use leverage and you do one wrong thing along the way, it could wipe you out, because anything times zero is zero. But it's reinforcing when the people around you are doing it successfully, you're doing it successfully, and it's a lot like Cinderella at the ball. The guys look better all the time, the music sounds better, it's more and more fun, you think, 'Why the hell should I leave at a quarter to 12? I'll leave at two minutes to 12.' But the trouble is, there are no clocks on the wall. And everybody thinks they're going to leave at two minutes to 12." And that, in a nutshell, is the story of how we arrived at the calamity of 2008.

At some level, debt is at the heart of the whole story. Since the early 1980s, Americans have consumed more than they have produced—and they have made up the difference by borrowing. This happened at every level of society. Household debt mushroomed from $680 billion in 1974 to $14 trillion in 2008. It doubled in just the last seven years. The average household now has thirteen credit cards and owes $120,000 on a mortgage. By some standards, however, households were the pinnacles of thrift. Politicians at the state and local level, eager to give their constituents new basketball stadiums and twelve-lane highways without raising taxes, started to borrow against the future. They issued bonds to pay for pet projects, bonds that were backed by future taxes or lottery earnings. But even those politicians were put to shame by the true king of borrowers: the federal government. In 1990, the national debt stood at $3 trillion. By the end of 2008, it had climbed into the eleven-digit realm, surpassing $10 trillion. (At the time of this writing, it was at $10.9 trillion.) The famous National Debt Clock in New York City ran out of space to display all the figures. Its owners plan to install a new and expanded clock this year.

The United States became a nation of debtors, in other words. There's nothing wrong with debt—loans and leverage, used prudently, are the heartbeats of a modern economy— but taken to such extremes, it's a killer. And both sides of the equation must balance—the United States never could have arrived at such a position had there not been nations willing to lend it the money. That's where the economic and political empowerment of the developing world—the "rise of the rest," as I call it—comes in, and it's best symbolized by the rise of China.

Despite heady years of growth, Chinese households and corporations have tended to be cautious. They bank about half their earnings, always preparing for the metaphorical rainy day. Such extreme thriftiness in combination with high growth led to China's accumulation of vast new pools of capital. But this was not simply a Confucian cultural trait. The Chinese government had discouraged spending and encouraged savings, in part as a way to ensure that inflation stayed low and their currency stayed undervalued—which made Chinese goods cheap and attractive to the Western consumer. In addition, countries like China were soured by the Asian crisis of 1996, when Asia's economies fell and Western bankers came to the rescue but demanded onerous terms. After they recovered, Asian governments—and others outside Asia as well—decided to accumulate their own reserves, so that the next time around, they wouldn't have to rely on the kindness of strangers.

So, instead of reinvesting their ever-growing savings in their domestic economy, Chinese authorities stashed it away. But how should a government hoard its money? By buying what was then—and still is now—considered the safest investment in the world: U.S. treasury bills. Through their accumulation of massive quantities of American debt, the Chinese ended up subsidizing the behavior that caused it—American consumption. They financed our spending binge and built up a vast hoard of dollar IOUs. The Chinese oversaved, the Americans overconsumed. The system seemed to balance out.

And it wasn't just China. Eight other emerging-market countries have accumulated war chests of $100 billion or more, mostly in dollars. But China alone sits on foreign-currency reserves of over $2 trillion, again most of it in dollars. Last September, China became America's largest foreign creditor, surpassing Japan, which no longer buys large amounts of U.S. Treasuries. (With 10 percent of all currently outstanding T-bills in its possession, China is likely America's largest creditor, period, but the U.S. Treasury doesn't track domestic lenders.) China now holds the world's largest IOU slip, and it carries the signature of Uncle Sam.

Oversaving at a global level has proved to be as much of a

problem as overconsuming. The Harvard economist Dani Rodrik has estimated that sending so much money abroad instead of investing it productively costs the Chinese roughly one percentage point of GDP a year, or more than $40 billion annually. China's lending was also essentially a massive stimulus program for the United States. It kept interest rates low, which encouraged homeowners to refinance, hedge fund managers to ramp up leverage, and investment banks to goose their balance sheets. China's lending created cheap money, says *Financial Times* columnist Martin Wolf, and "cheap money encouraged an orgy of financial innovation, borrowing and spending."

"There can be no return to business as usual," Wolf has written. But in the short term, we seem destined for more of the status quo. Not long before taking office, President Barack Obama warned of the prospect of "trillion-dollar deficits for years to come," as his administration boosts spending on everything from green technology to health care to reinflate our sagging economy. Most of that money will have to be borrowed from China. The Chinese also have their own economic problems to sort through, and they are spending $600 billion—a whopping 15 percent of their GDP—to combat them. We are, in effect, asking China to simultaneously finance the two largest fiscal expansions in human history: ours and its own. And the country has every incentive to continue its T-bill shopping spree. Without it, China's exports will suffer, and its lofty growth rates will fall to earth.

The Chinese do, however, have options. Joseph Stiglitz, the Nobel Prize–winning economist, explains that "they will certainly try to keep American consumption going, but if it becomes clear that it isn't working, they do have a Plan B."

Plan B would be to focus on boosting China's own consumption through government spending and increasing credit to its people. As the historian Niall Ferguson writes, "the big question today is whether Chimerica [China plus America] stays together or comes apart because of this crisis. If it stays together, you can see a path out of the woods. If it splits up, say goodbye to globalization."

The best scenario would be for China and the United States to work together to slowly unwind their mutual suicide pact. China would benefit by having more money to reinvest in its domestic economy. The United States would benefit from being forced to make some hard decisions that will ultimately make it better off. Since at least the 1980s, America has recognized that it could spend with abandon, forever delaying the date of repayment. This has not been good for its foreign or domestic policy. It's made Washington arrogant, lazy, and careless. But the free ride is coming to an end.

Hurtling Toward the Post-American World

Although the scale of this financial crisis is far beyond anything in recent memory, it is not unprecedented. The history of capitalism is filled with bubbles, panics, financial meltdowns, and recessions. The Dutch lost their minds over tulips in the 1600s; railway mania struck the British in the 1840s. Even in the last few decades, there have been financial calamities in Mexico, Argentina, Brazil, and nearly every other Latin American country. Russia and its former satellites went bankrupt in the 1990s, and contagion struck Asia at the end of that decade. The 1998 collapse of Long-Term Capital Management, one of the world's largest hedge funds, was so worrisome that the Federal Reserve organized a bailout to keep the financial system from collapsing.

The crisis of 2008 is different precisely because it did not originate in some developing-world backwater; it emerged from the heart of global capitalism, the United States, and coursed its way through the arteries of international finance. It does not, despite the opinions of some pundits, signal the end of capitalism. But it might well mean the end of a certain kind of global dominance for the United States. The current economic upheaval will only hasten the move to a post-American world. If the Iraq War and George W. Bush's foreign policy had the effect of delegitimizing America's military–political power in the eyes of the world, the financial crisis has had the effect of delegitimizing America's economic power.

Whatever people thought of American foreign policy, they all agreed that the United States was the most modern, sophisticated, and productive economy in the world—with the most advanced capital markets. As a result, it held hegemony not just in military power and diplomacy but in the realm of ideas. Central bankers and treasury ministers around the world studied the basics of their profession at American schools. Politicians developed their economies by following the advice prescribed by the Washington consensus. The innovations of Silicon Valley were the envy of the world. New York's deep, lucrative capital markets were admired and imitated on every continent except Antarctica.

As Brad Setser, a Fellow at the Council on Foreign Relations, has noted, globalization after World War II was almost synonymous with Americanization. "Foreign borrowers looking to raise funds tended to issue bonds denominated in dollars, made use of New York law, and met the Securities and Exchange Commission's standards for disclosure," he writes. American ideas and institutions were made all the more attractive by the country's economic success.

The collapse of Wall Street will significantly erode the legacy of that success. The American economy will shrink or stagnate in 2009, and it will potentially grow slowly for years after that, burdened by debt. Most of Europe will be in the same boat. Naturally, economic activity everywhere has been affected by this collapse of the first world. And finance being totally globalized, stock markets everywhere have collapsed. But the underlying economies in the big emerging markets— China, India, and Brazil—are now large enough that they have significant economic activity of their own (domestic demand) that does not rely on exports to the West. As a result, the International Monetary Fund estimates that 100 percent of global growth in 2009 will come from emerging markets. While the financial markets of these countries are coupled with that of the United States, their actual economies are, for the first time in history, beginning to gain some independence from it.

Global power is, above all, dominance over ideas, agendas, and models. The revelation that much of the financial innovation that occurred in the last decade created little more than a house of cards erodes American power. Selling American ideas to the rest of the world will require more effort from here on out. Developing countries will pick and choose the economic policies that best suit them, and with growing confidence. "The U.S. financial system was regarded as a model, and we tried our best to copy whatever we could," said Yu Yongding, a former adviser to China's central bank, in late

September 2008. "Suddenly we find our teacher is not that excellent, so the next time when we're designing our financial system we will use our own mind more."

The rise of the rest is at heart an economic phenomenon, but the transition we are witnessing is not just a matter of dollars and cents. It has political, military, and cultural consequences. As countries become stronger and richer, and as the United States struggles to earn back the world's faith, we're likely to see more challenges and greater assertiveness from rising nations. In one month this past summer, India was willing to frontally defy the United States at the Doha trade talks, Russia attacked and occupied parts of Georgia, and China hosted the most spectacular and expensive Olympic Games in history (which cost more than $40 billion). Ten years ago, not one of the three would have been powerful or confident enough to act as it did. Even if their growth rates decline, which they surely will, these countries will not quietly relinquish their new roles in the global system.

Consider just a few examples. Over the last decade, the United States has expanded its influence into what was for centuries the Russian sphere of influence. In the post–Cold War era of American dominance, Moscow acquiesced. It needed Washington for cash and support. But by 2008 Russia was a revived power. In mid-February 2009 the Kyrgyz Republic finalized its decision to close Manas Air Base, a U.S. base providing essential air support for operations in Afghanistan, which was particularly important after the 2005 closure of another air base in Uzbekistan. The motivation was money. The United States had been paying $55 million a year to lease the base and had indicated a willingness to pay $100 million a year. The Russian government, inimically opposed to the idea of a semipermanent U.S. military presence in its backyard, offered a $2.3 billion aid package that dwarfed the American financial support and included $180 million in debt cancellation, $150 million in aid, and a $2 billion loan to complete the construction of a hydroelectric power station. The power plant will be a joint venture and will boost the Kyrgyz Republic's power output by 40 percent, possibly bringing the country's power export to its full potential. Even with oil prices down to $40 a barrel, Russia will still be in a position to adopt a more independent foreign policy.

Even a new American ally like India maintains its independence from the United States. New Delhi is grateful to Washington for its support in legitimizing India as a normal nuclear power, but it still pushed back on core security issues. Despite much American pressure, India simply does not see Iran as the threat that the United States does. India agreed to vote once with the United States at the International Atomic Energy Agency but continues to have extensive contact with Iran, including the conducting of joint naval exercises. India sees Iran as a commercial partner and refuses to isolate it in any way. In April 2008, President Mahmoud Ahmadinejad's pilots requested a refueling stop in New Delhi as the Iranian leader was returning home from a visit to Sri Lanka. The Indian government immediately issued a formal invitation and turned the six-hour stop into a state visit.

The current state of the IMF and World Bank also provides a useful lesson. These institutions, dominated by U.S. ideas and money, have long been seen as vehicles for American influence. And today, Setser writes, "emerging economies like China, Russia, India, Saudi Arabia, Korea, and even Brazil not only do not need the IMF; they increasingly are in a position to compete with it. Saudi Arabia already backstops Lebanon. Venezuela helped Argentina repay the IMF. Chinese development financing provides an alternative to World Bank lending."

For an even better example of just how profound the changes associated with the rise of the rest will be, reread the coverage of the November 2008 G20 summit in Washington, DC. Every prior financial crisis had been handled by the IMF, the World Bank, or the G7 (and, later, the G8). In past crises, the West played the part of the stern schoolteacher rebuking a wayward classroom. The lessons they imparted now seem discredited. Recall that during the Asian financial crisis the United States and other Western countries demanded that the Asians take three steps—let bad banks fail, keep spending under control, and keep interest rates high. In its own crisis, the West has done exactly the opposite on all three fronts.

In any event, this crisis was one that the West couldn't tackle by itself. For an effective response in a highly connected global economy, all of the world's major players—including the top emerging economies—needed to participate. To supply cash, countries like China and Saudi Arabia were crucial. As for legitimacy, the old Western clubs were archaic, relics of a bygone world, and could no longer sell a global solution on their own. As the crisis has made clear, even the United States can no longer act independently. So for the first time a meeting of the heads of government of the G20—the G8 plus the major emerging nations—was convened.

Of course, not everything has changed. The G20 meeting was still held in Washington, and President George W. Bush got to play the major role in setting the agenda. It's a new world, but not necessarily one from which America has been ousted. Indeed, America is still the single most important country on the globe, able to exercise influence in every realm and on every continent in a way that no other major power can. It remains, in the words of the German writer Josef Joffe, "the default superpower." But we now live in a world in which common action is not just desirable, but vital.

All Hang Together

International cooperation is a tricky animal. Even where there's a will, there is often no clear way. Afghanistan is the model for a successful multilateral operation—at least in theory. The initial invasion had the support of the United Nations and the global community. The military effort, now more than seven years old, includes troops from Britain, Canada, Poland—even France. The World Bank, USAID, and national governments have given billions to rebuild the country's infrastructure. Yet the war is still close to failure. Hamid Karzai's government controls less than a third of the country. Outside Kabul, warlords are the ultimate source of authority. The Taliban, although weakened, remains worryingly resilient. Opium has become the country's chief export. And most countries—from bordering states like Pakistan to European partners like Germany—are anxious to get out of their commitments rather than see them through. Narrow nationalism trumps enlightened internationalism all too often.

The lesson of Afghanistan suggests that multilateralism is neither easy nor always effective. But the Afghanistan effort suffered from lack of attention—the Bush administration was too busy selling and then waging a war in Iraq—and can still be salvaged. Besides, today's problems demand a multilateral solution even when one is extraordinarily difficult to achieve. Consider almost any serious problem we face today; chances are it implicates more than one country. Terrorism, financial contagion, infectious disease, energy, security—all these challenges require coordinated responses, and in some cases institutions that can implement them.

Take a simple example like infectious disease. An outbreak today is almost guaranteed to spread far and wide. That means we all have an incentive to determine the nature of the pathogen as quickly as possible, isolate the victims, and work toward a cure. Ideally, the World Health Organization would be able to step in, require samples of the virus to be sent to it, make a definitive diagnosis, and set protocols to be followed. Unfortunately, it is underfunded and undermanned, and lacks the authority to make rules that everyone must follow. China hid an outbreak of avian influenza within its borders for weeks before the world caught on. Indonesia, at one point, refused to turn over flu samples because it worried that they would be used to create expensive vaccines the country couldn't afford.

This is the world that confronts President Barack Obama: a messy and contentious one, with few easy answers. But for all its problems, it is still a remarkably peaceful one. War between the great powers is unthinkable. By some measures, like civilian casualties, we're living through the most peaceful times ever. And Al Qaeda, the first great threat of the twenty-first century, has become rootless and defensive as Muslims around the world have been repulsed by its glorification of violence and willingness to kill civilians, even when those civilians are Muslim. The election of Barack Obama, a globe-trotting, multiethnic American with a Muslim father and the middle name of Hussein, has left the terrorist group flabbergasted. In a recent video, its leaders resorted to making feckless personal attacks against the new president, calling him a "house Negro." Their worries are understandable: Obama's election is a symbol of hope to the world and a threat to Al Qaeda's hateful ideology.

There is, of course, the age-old worry that in times of transition, peace will be overturned. Ever since Thucydides observed that the shift in power from Sparta to Athens was the fundamental cause of the Peloponnesian War, scholars have watched such moments with apprehension. But this time, if properly managed, the rise of the rest need not be destabilizing. America is not sinking fast, about to be replaced by a single country. Everyone is, in a deep sense, in this crisis together. Other countries can play major stabilizing roles. And not just in economics. During the Russia–Georgia conflict, it was French president Nicolas Sarkozy who went to Moscow, not Bush. When Israel and Syria entered into talks last summer, it was Turkey that played peace broker, not Washington. And when Lebanese factions once again fell on each other with guns and violence last May, the only person able to bring them to the negotiating table was the Sheikh of Qatar. None of these cases featured the United States. Ten years ago this was unthinkable. Today it is commonplace. Although a more assertive world means more antagonists and demagogues, it also means more negotiators and regional leaders with a stake in keeping the peace. If that impulse can be organized and encouraged, the world will be a better place for it.

Most major powers share some basic interests and ideals with the United States. Those shared incentives should keep the world moving in a direction toward greater stability and increased prosperity. The real danger remains that Washington will underplay its hand, producing chaos and instability, or overplay its hand, leading other countries to resent it and go their own way. The management of U.S. political and military power remains the single most important task for global stability. The United States must provide rules, institutions, and services that help solve the world's major problems, while giving other countries—crucially the emerging powers—a stake in the system.

In recent decades, the United States has not provided this leadership. But neither has Paris, London, Moscow, Beijing, or New Delhi. Europe has been reluctant to cede power to the IMF and other forums, and many emerging-market countries guard their sovereignty as jealously as does the United States, often even more so. Whoever is to blame, unless we find ways to expand and enhance the rules and institutions of global cooperation—around economics, energy, climate change, disease, drugs, migration, and a host of other issues, the world will experience more crises and government responses will be hasty and ad hoc—too little, too late. We cannot come out of the present crisis with real strength unless the major countries of the world work together on a massive and sustained scale.

If, on the other hand, we come together and work on the common problems of humanity, imagine the opportunities it could create for everyone. Imagine if we created new rules of the road that allowed this extraordinary process of globalization and growth to persist and spread to every section of society, raising standards of living and health for the poorest of the poor, allowing more and more people to develop their potential.

If we do work together and put this crisis behind us, the opportunities remain endless. The world economy provides the promise of a decent life for people everywhere. Communications allow us all to know each other and learn from each other as never before. Political cooperation can tame the fires of great power rivalries. People are doing amazing things every day in every place on earth. Now it's time for their governments to match this human ingenuity with their own innovation and create new forms of cooperation. The great challenge for Barack Obama and this generation of leaders is to create a new system of international relations, one that produces genuine and effective global cooperation on the great common issues that plague us all. This is the great project of the twenty-first century: a new architecture that ensures peace, growth, and freedom for the world.

1

The Rise of the Rest

This is a book not about the decline of America but rather about the rise of everyone else. It is about the great transformation taking place around the world, a transformation that, though often discussed, remains poorly understood. This is natural. Changes, even sea changes, take place gradually. Though we talk about a new era, the world seems to be one with which we are familiar. But in fact, it is very different.

There have been three tectonic power shifts over the last five hundred years, fundamental changes in the distribution of power that have reshaped international life—its politics, economics, and culture. The first was the rise of the Western world, a process that began in the fifteenth century and accelerated dramatically in the late eighteenth century. It produced modernity as we know it: science and technology, commerce and capitalism, the agricultural and industrial revolutions. It also produced the prolonged political dominance of the nations of the West.

The second shift, which took place in the closing years of the nineteenth century, was the rise of the United States. Soon after it industrialized, the United States became the most powerful nation since imperial Rome, and the only one that was stronger than any likely combination of other nations. For most of the last century, the United States has dominated global economics, politics, science, and culture. For the last twenty years, that dominance has been unrivaled, a phenomenon unprecedented in modern history.

We are now living through the third great power shift of the modern era. It could be called "the rise of the rest." Over the past few decades, countries all over the world have been experiencing rates of economic growth that were once unthinkable. While they have had booms and busts, the overall trend has been unambiguously upward. This growth has been most visible in Asia but is no longer confined to it. That is why to call this shift "the rise of Asia" does not describe it accurately. In 2006 and 2007, 124 countries grew at a rate of 4 percent or more. That includes more than 30 countries in Africa, two-thirds of the continent. Antoine van Agtmael, the fund manager who coined the term "emerging markets," has identified the 25 companies most likely to be the world's next great multinationals. His list includes four companies each from Brazil, Mexico, South Korea, and Taiwan; three from India; two from China; and one each from Argentina, Chile, Malaysia, and South Africa.

Look around. The tallest building in the world is now in Taipei, and it will soon be overtaken by one being built in Dubai. The world's richest man is Mexican, and its largest publicly traded corporation is Chinese. The world's biggest plane is built in Russia and Ukraine, its leading refinery is under construction in India, and its largest factories are all in China. By many measures, London is becoming the leading financial center, and the United Arab Emirates is home to the most richly endowed investment fund. Once quintessentially American icons have been appropriated by foreigners. The world's largest Ferris wheel is in Singapore. Its number one casino is not in Las Vegas but in Macao, which has also overtaken Vegas in annual gambling revenues. The biggest movie industry, in terms of both movies made and tickets sold, is Bollywood, not Hollywood. Even shopping, America's greatest sporting activity, has gone global. Of the top ten malls in the world, only one is in the United States; the world's biggest is in Beijing. Such lists are arbitrary, but it is striking that only ten years ago, America was at the top in many, if not most, of these categories.

It might seem strange to focus on growing prosperity when there are still hundreds of millions of people living in desperate poverty. But in fact, the share of people living on a dollar a day or less plummeted from 40 percent in 1981 to 18 percent in 2004, and is estimated to fall to 12 percent by 2015. China's growth alone has lifted more than 400 million people out of poverty. Poverty is falling in countries housing 80 percent of the world's population. The 50 countries where the earth's poorest people live are basket cases that need urgent attention. In the other 142—which include China, India, Brazil, Russia, Indonesia, Turkey, Kenya, and South Africa—the poor are slowly being absorbed into productive and growing economies. For the first time ever, we are witnessing genuinely global growth. This is creating an international system in which countries in all parts of the world are no longer objects or observers but players in their own right. It is the birth of a truly global order.

A related aspect of this new era is the diffusion of power from states to other actors. The "rest" that is rising includes many nonstate actors. Groups and individuals have been empowered, and hierarchy, centralization, and control are being undermined. Functions that were once controlled by governments are now shared with international bodies like the World Trade Organization and the European Union. Nongovernmental groups are mushrooming every day on every issue in every country. Corporations and capital are moving from place to place, finding the best location in which to do business, rewarding some governments while punishing others. Terrorists like Al Qaeda, drug cartels, insurgents, and militias of all kinds are finding space to operate within the nooks and crannies of the international system. Power is shifting away from nation-states, up, down, and sideways. In such an atmosphere, the traditional applications of national power, both economic and military, have become less effective.

The emerging international system is likely to be quite different from those that have preceded it. One hundred years ago, there was a multipolar order run by a collection of European governments, with constantly shifting alliances, rivalries, miscalculations, and wars. Then came the bipolar duopoly of the Cold War, more stable in many ways, but with the superpowers reacting and overreacting to each other's every move. Since 1991, we have lived under an American imperium, a unique, unipolar world in which the open global economy has expanded and accelerated dramatically. This expansion is now driving the next change in the nature of the international order.

At the politico-military level, we remain in a single-superpower world. But in every other dimension—industrial, financial, educational, social, cultural—the distribution of power is shifting, moving away from American dominance. That does not mean we are entering an anti-American world. But we are moving into a *post-American world*, one defined and directed from many places and by many people.

What kinds of opportunities and challenges do these changes present? What do they portend for the United States and its dominant position? What will this new era look like in terms of war and peace, economics and business, ideas and culture?

In short, what will it mean to live in a post-American world?

2

The Cup Runneth Over

Imagine that it is January 2000, and you ask a fortune-teller to predict the course of the global economy over the next several years. Let's say that you give him some clues, to help him gaze into his crystal ball. The United States will be hit by the worst terrorist attack in history, you explain, and will respond by launching two wars, one of which will go badly awry and keep Iraq—the country with the world's third-largest oil reserves—in chaos for years. Iran will gain strength in the Middle East and move to acquire a nuclear capability. North Korea will go further, becoming the world's eighth declared nuclear power. Russia will turn hostile and imperious in its dealings with its neighbors and the West. In Latin America, Hugo Chávez of Venezuela will launch the most spirited anti-Western campaign in a generation, winning many allies and fans. Israel and Hezbollah will fight a war in southern Lebanon, destabilizing Beirut's fragile government, drawing in Iran and Syria, and rattling the Israelis. Gaza will become a failed state ruled by Hamas, and peace talks between Israel and the Palestinians will go nowhere. "Given these events," you say to the sage, "how will the global economy fare over the next six years?"

This is not really a hypothetical. We have the forecasts of experts from those years. They were all wrong. The correct prediction would have been that, between 2000 and 2007, the world economy would grow at its fastest pace in nearly four decades. Income per person across the globe would rise at a faster rate (3.2 percent) than in any other period in history.

In the two decades since the end of the Cold War, we have lived through a paradox, one we experience every morning when reading the newspapers. The world's politics seems deeply troubled, with daily reports of bombings, terror plots, rogue states, and civil strife. And yet the global economy forges ahead, not without significant interruptions and crises, but still vigorously upward on the whole. Markets do panic but over economic not political news. The front page of the newspaper seems unconnected to the business section.

I remember speaking to a senior member of the Israeli government a few days after the war with Hezbollah in July 2006. He was genuinely worried about his country's physical security. Hezbollah's rockets had reached farther into Israel than people had believed possible, and the Israeli military response had not inspired confidence. Then I asked him about the economy—his area of competence. "That's puzzled all of us," he said. "The stock market was higher on the last day of the war than on its first! The same with the shekel [Israel's currency]." The government might have been spooked, but the market wasn't.

Or consider the Iraq War, which has produced deep, lasting chaos in the country and over two million refugees crowded into its neighbors. That kind of political crisis seems certain to spill over. But to travel in the Middle East these past years is to be struck by how *little* Iraq's troubles have destabilized the region. Everywhere you go, people angrily denounce American foreign policy. But where is the actual evidence of regional instability? Most Middle Eastern countries—Jordan, Saudi Arabia, and Egypt, for example—are booming. Turkey, which shares a border with Iraq, has averaged better than 7 percent annual growth since the war began. Abu Dhabi and Dubai, one hour from Baghdad by plane, continue to build eye-catching, iconic skyscrapers as if they were on another planet. The countries that have involved themselves in Iraq—Syria and Iran—operate largely outside the global economy and thus have less to lose by making trouble.

What explains this mismatch between a politics that spirals downward and an economy that stays robust? First, it's worth looking more carefully at the cascade of bad news. It seems that we are living in crazily violent times. But don't believe everything you see on television. Our anecdotal impression turns out to be wrong. War and organized violence have declined dramatically over the last two decades. Ted Robert Gurr and a team of scholars at the University of Maryland's Center for International Development and Conflict Management tracked the data carefully and came to the following conclusion: "the general magnitude of global warfare has decreased by over sixty percent [since the mid-1980s], falling by the end of 2004 to its lowest level since the late 1950s."[1] Violence increased steadily throughout the Cold War—increasing sixfold between the 1950s and early 1990s—but the trend peaked just before the collapse of the Soviet Union in 1991 and "the extent of warfare among and within states lessened by nearly half in the first decade after the Cold War." Harvard's polymath professor Steven Pinker argues "that today we are probably living in the most peaceful time in our species' existence."[2]

One reason for the mismatch between reality and our sense of it might be that, over these same decades, we have experienced a revolution in information technology that now brings us news from around the world instantly, vividly, and continuously. The immediacy of the images and the intensity of the twenty-four-hour news cycle combine to produce constant hyperbole. Every weather disturbance is "the storm of the century." Every bomb that explodes is BREAKING NEWS. It is difficult to put this all in context because the information revolution is so new. We didn't get daily footage on the roughly two million who died in the killing fields of Cambodia in the 1970s or the million who perished in the sands of the Iran-Iraq war in the 1980s. We have not even seen much footage from the war in Congo in the 1990s, where millions died. But now, we see almost daily, live broadcasts of the effects of IEDs or car bombs or rockets—tragic events, to be sure, but often with death tolls under ten. The randomness of terrorist violence, the targeting of civilians, and the ease with which modern societies can be penetrated add to our disquiet. "That could have been me," people say after a terrorist attack.

It *feels* like a very dangerous world. But it isn't. Your chances of dying as a consequence of organized violence of any kind are low and getting lower. The data reveal a broad trend away from wars among major countries, the kind of conflict that produces massive casualties.

I don't believe that war has become obsolete or any such foolishness. Human nature remains what it is and international politics what it is. History has witnessed periods of calm that have been followed by extraordinary bloodshed. And numbers are not the only measure of evil. The nature of the killings in the former Yugoslavia in the early 1990s—premeditated, religiously motivated, systematic—makes that war, which had 200,000 casualties, a moral obscenity that should register very high on any scale. Al Qaeda's barbarism—cold-blooded beheadings, the deliberate targeting of innocents—is gruesome despite its relatively low number of casualties.

Still, if we are to understand the times we are living in, we must first accurately describe them. And they are, for now, in historical context, unusually calm.

The Islamic Threat

Islamic terror, which makes the headlines daily, is a large and persistent problem, but one involving small numbers of fanatics. It feeds on the dysfunctions of the Muslim world, the sense (real and imagined) of humiliation at the hands of the West, and easy access to technologies of violence. And yet, does it rank as a threat on the order of Germany's drive for world domination in the first half of the twentieth century? Or Soviet expansionism in the second half? Or Mao's efforts to foment war and revolution across the Third World in the 1950s and 1960s? These were all challenges backed by the power and purpose of major countries, often with serious allies, and by an ideology that was seen as a plausible alternative to liberal democracy. By comparison, consider the jihadist threat. Before 9/11, when groups like Al Qaeda operated under the radar, governments treated them as minor annoyances, and they roamed freely, built some strength, and hit symbolic, often military targets, killing Americans and other foreigners. Even so, the damage was fairly limited. Since 2001, governments everywhere have been aggressive in busting terrorists' networks, following their money, and tracking their recruits—with almost immediate results. In Indonesia, the largest Muslim nation in the world, the government captured both the chief and the military leader of Jemaah Islamiah, the country's deadliest jihadist group and the one that carried out the Bali bombings in 2002. With American help, the Filipino army battered the Qaeda-style terrorist outfit Abu Sayyaf. The group's leader was killed by Filipino troops in January 2007, and its membership has declined from as many as two thousand guerrillas six years ago to a few hundred today. In Egypt and Saudi Arabia—Al Qaeda's original bases and targets of attack—terrorist cells have been rounded up, and those still at large have been unable to launch any new attacks in three years. Finance ministries—especially the U.S. Department of the Treasury—have made life far more difficult for terrorists. Global organizations cannot thrive without being able to move money around, and so the more terrorists' funds are tracked and targeted, the more they have to resort to small-scale and hastily improvised operations. This struggle, between governments and terrorists, will persist, but it is the former who have the upper hand.

In Iraq, where terrorist attacks have declined, a complication that is revealing has weakened Al Qaeda. In its original fatwas and other statements, Al Qaeda made no mention of Shiites, condemning only the "Crusaders" and "Jews." But Iraq changed things. Searching for ways to attract Sunni support, Al Qaeda morphed into an anti-Shiite group, espousing a purist Sunni worldview. The late Abu Mussab al-Zarqawi, the head of Al Qaeda in Mesopotamia, bore a fierce hatred for Shiites derived from his Wahhabi-style puritanism. In a February 2004 letter to Osama bin Laden, he claimed, "The danger from the Shia . . . is greater . . . than the Americans . . . . [T]he only solution is for us to strike the religious, military, and other cadres among the Shia with blow after blow until they bend to the Sunnis." If there ever was a debate between him and bin Laden, Zarqawi won. As a result, a movement that had hoped to rally the entire Muslim world to jihad against the West was dragged into a dirty internal war within Islam.

The split between Sunnis and Shiites is only one of the divisions within the Islamic world. Within that universe are Shiites and Sunnis, Persians and Arabs, Southeast Asians and Middle Easterners, and, importantly, moderates and radicals. Just as the diversity within the communist world ultimately made it less threatening, so do the many varieties of Islam undermine its ability to coalesce into a single, monolithic foe. Some Western leaders speak of a single worldwide Islamist movement—absurdly lumping together Chechen separatists in Russia, Pakistani-backed militants in India, Shiite warlords in Lebanon, and Sunni jihadists in Egypt. In fact, a shrewd strategist would emphasize that all these groups are distinct, with differing agendas, enemies, and friends. That would rob them of their claim to represent Islam. It would also describe them as they often really are: small local gangs of misfits hoping to attract attention through nihilism and barbarism.

Conflicts involving radical Islamic groups persist, but these typically have more to do with specific local conditions than with global aspirations. Although North Africa has seen continued terror, particularly in Algeria, the main group there, the

Salafist Group for Call and Combat (known by its French abbreviation, GSPC), is part of a long war between the Algerian government and Islamic opposition forces and cannot be seen solely through the prism of Al Qaeda or anti-American jihad. The same is true of the main area where there has been a large and extremely dangerous increase in the strength of Al Qaeda, the Afghanistan-Pakistan borderlands. It is here that Al Qaeda Central, if there is such an entity, is housed. But the group has been able to sustain itself despite the best efforts of NATO troops because it had dug deep roots in the area during the years of the anti-Soviet campaign. Its allies, the Taliban, are a local movement that has long been supported by a section of the Pashtuns, an influential ethnic group in Afghanistan and Pakistan.

Here is the bottom line. In the six years since 9/11, Al Qaeda Central—the group led by Osama bin Laden and Ayman Zawahiri—has been unable to launch a major attack anywhere. It was a terrorist organization; it has become a communications company, producing the occasional videotape rather than actual terrorism.* Jihad continues, but the jihadists have had to scatter, make do with smaller targets, and operate on a local level—usually through groups with almost no connection to Al Qaeda Central. And this improvised strategy has a crippling weakness: it kills locals, thus alienating ordinary Muslims—a process that is well underway in countries as diverse as Indonesia, Iraq, and Saudi Arabia. Over the last six years, support for bin Laden and his goals has fallen steadily throughout the Muslim world.

---

* Even if an attack were to take place tomorrow, the fact that, for six years, Al Qaeda Central has been unable to organize one explosion anywhere is surely worth noting.

Between 2002 and 2007, approval of suicide bombing as a tactic—a figure that was always low—has dropped by over 50 percent in most Muslim countries that have been tracked. There have been more denunciations of violence and fatwas against bin Laden than ever before, including from prominent clerics in Saudi Arabia. Much more must happen to modernize the Muslim world, but the modernizers are no longer so scared. They have finally realized that, for all the rhetoric of the madrassas and mosques, few people want to live under the writ of Al Qaeda. Those who have, whether in Afghanistan or Iraq, have become its most dedicated opponents. In contrast to Soviet socialism or even fascism in the 1930s, no society looks with admiration and envy on the fundamentalist Islamic model. On an ideological level, it presents no competition to the Western-originated model of modernity that countries across the world are embracing.

A cottage industry of scaremongering has flourished in the West—especially in the United States—since 9/11. Experts extrapolate every trend they don't like, forgoing any serious study of the data. Many conservative commentators have written about the impending Islamization of Europe (Eurabia, they call it, to make you even more uncomfortable). Except that the best estimates, from U.S. intelligence agencies, indicate that Muslims constitute around 3 percent of Europe's population now and will rise to between 5 and 8 percent by 2025, after which they will probably plateau. The watchdogs note the musings of every crackpot Imam, search the archives for each reference to the end of days, and record and distribute the late-night TV musings of every nutcase who glorifies martyrdom. They erupt in fury when a Somali taxi driver somewhere refuses to load a case of liquor into his car, seeing it as the beginning of sharia in the West. But these episodes do not reflect the basic direction of the Muslim world. That world is also modernizing, though more slowly than the rest, and there are those who try to become leaders in rebellion against it. The reactionaries in the world of Islam are more numerous and extreme than those in other cultures—that world does have its dysfunctions. But they remain a tiny minority of the world's billion-plus Muslims. And neglecting the complicated context in which some of these pseudoreligious statements are made—such as an internal Iranian power struggle among clerics and nonclerics—leads to hair-raising but absurd predictions, like Bernard Lewis's confident claim that Iran's President Mahmoud Ahmadinejad planned to mark an auspicious date on the Islamic calendar (August 22, 2006) *by ending the world*. (Yes, he actually wrote that.)

The ideological watchdogs have spent so much time with the documents of jihad that they have lost sight of actual Muslim societies. Were they to step back, they would see a frustration with the fundamentalists, a desire for modernity (with some dignity and cultural pride for sure), and a search for practical solutions—not a mass quest for immortality through death. When Muslims travel, they flock by the millions to see the razzle-dazzle of Dubai, not the seminaries of Iran. The minority that wants jihad is real, but it operates within societies where such activities are increasingly unpopular and irrelevant.

In the West, the effects of terrorism have diminished with each additional attack. After September 11, global financial markets collapsed and did not return to September 10 levels for two months. After the Madrid bombings in 2004, the Spanish market took a month to recover. After the London

bombings in July 2005, British stocks were back to prebomb-
ing levels in twenty-four hours. The broader economic picture
is similar. After 9/11, the United States lost hundreds of billions of dollars in economic activity. The next large attack, the
Bali nightclub bombing in 2002, had a similarly dramatic
effect on the Indonesian economy, with tourism vanishing and
trade and investment drying up for months. A year later, after
another Indonesian bombing, this time at the Marriott hotel
in Jakarta, the market dropped only briefly, and the Indonesian economy suffered little damage. Bombings in Morocco
and Turkey in 2003 had similarly small effects. The 2004
bombings in Spain and 2005 bombings in Britain did nothing
to undermine growth.

Of course, things would be different if a major terrorist
organization were to acquire significant weapons of mass
destruction. A nuclear attack could result in mass panic and a
broader breakdown. But such weapons are harder to get than
many think, and a more sustained effort from Washington
could make it nearly impossible to acquire them in any quantity. Biological terror may seem most worrying because of the
ease of acquiring biological agents, but dispersing them effectively is difficult and may lack the dramatic results terrorists
crave. And none of this is to suggest that anti-terror activities
are unnecessary, but rather that careful, calibrated, intelligent
policies are likely to be quite successful.

In some unspoken way, people have recognized that the best
counterterrorism policy is resilience. Terrorism is unusual in
that it is a military tactic defined by the response of the
onlooker. If we are not terrorized, then it doesn't work. And,
from New York and London to Mumbai and Jakarta, people are
learning this fact through experience and getting on with life

even amid the uncertainty. The most likely scenario—a series of backpack or truck bombings in the United States—would be a shock, but in a couple of weeks its effects would fade and the long-term consequences would likely be minimal. In vast, vigorous, and complex societies—the American economy is now $13 trillion—problems in a few places do not easily spill over. Modern civilization may be stronger than we suspect.

The challenges from rogue states are also real, but we should consider them in context. The GDP of Iran is 1/68 that of the United States, its military spending 1/110 that of the Pentagon.* If this is 1938, as many conservatives argue, then Iran is Romania, not Germany. North Korea is even more bankrupt and dysfunctional. Its chief threat—the one that keeps the Chinese government awake at night—is that it will implode, flooding the region with refugees. That's power? These countries can cause trouble in their neighborhood and must be checked and contained, but we need to keep in mind the larger world of which they are a relatively small part. Look at Latin America. Venezuela is a troublemaker, but what has that meant on the ground? The broad trend in the region—

---

* A note on terminology: For such a straightforward idea, gross domestic product (GDP) is a surprisingly complicated measurement. Although tradable items like iPods or Nikes cost roughly the same from one country to the next, goods that can't flow across borders—such as haircuts in Beijing—cost less in developing economies. So the same income goes much further in India than in Britain. To account for this, many economists use a measure of GDP called purchasing power parity (PPP), which substantially inflates the incomes of developing countries. Proponents say this better reflects quality of life. Still, when it comes to the stuff of raw national power, measuring GDP at market exchange rates makes more sense. You can't buy an aircraft carrier, fund a UN peacekeeping mission, announce corporate earnings, or give foreign aid with dollars measured in PPP. This is why, in general, throughout this book I will calculate GDP using market exchange rates. Where PPP is more appropriate, or when the only numbers one can find are in that form, I will make a note of it.

exemplified by the policies of the major countries like Brazil, Mexico, and Chile—has been toward open markets, trade, democratic governance, and an outward orientation. And that trend, not Hugo Chávez's insane rants, represents the direction of history.

The Great Expansion

Today's relative calm has a deep structural basis. Across the world, economics is trumping politics. What Wall Street analysts call "political risk" has been almost nonexistent. Wars, coups, and terrorism have lost much of their ability to derail markets more than temporarily. Again, this may not last (it has not historically), but it has been the world we have lived in for at least a decade.

This is not the first time that political tumult and economic growth have come together. Two earlier periods seem much like ours: the turn-of-the-century boom of the 1890s and 1900s, and the postwar boom of the 1950s and early 1960s. In both, politics was turbulent and yet growth was robust. These two periods had one feature in common: large countries were entering the world economy, increasing its size and changing its shape. The expansion of the pie was so big that it overwhelmed day-to-day dislocations.

In the late nineteenth and early twentieth centuries, fears of war between European great powers were frequent, often triggered by crises in the Balkans, North Africa, and other hot spots. But the world economy boomed despite flash points and arms races. This was the era of the first great movements of capital, from Europe to the New World. As Germany and

the United States industrialized quickly, they became two of
the three largest economies in the world.

The 1950s and early 1960s are sometimes remembered as
placid, but they were in fact tension-filled times—defined by
the early years of the Cold War, fears of conflict with the
Soviet Union and China, and a real war in Korea. There were
periodic crises—the Taiwan Strait, the Congo, the Suez
Canal, the Bay of Pigs, Vietnam—that often mushroomed into
war. And yet the industrial economies sailed along strongly.
This was the second great age of capital movement, with
money from the United States pouring into Europe and East
Asia. As a consequence, Western Europe rebuilt itself from
the ashes of World War II, and Japan, the first non-Western
nation to successfully industrialize, grew over 9 percent a year
for twenty-three years.

In both periods, these "positive supply shocks"—an economists' term for a long-run spike in production—caused long,
sustained booms, with falling prices, low interest rates, and
rising productivity in the emerging markets of the day (Germany, the United States, Japan). At the turn of the twentieth
century, despite robust growth in demand, wheat prices
declined by 20 to 35 percent in Europe, thanks to American
granaries.[3] (Similarly, the price of manufactured goods is
falling today because of lowered costs in Asia, even as
demand for them soars.) In both periods, the new players
grew through exports, but imports expanded as well. Between
1860 and 1914, America's imports increased fivefold, while
its exports increased sevenfold.[4]

We are living through the third such expansion of the
global economy, and by far the largest. Over the last two
decades, about two billion people have entered the world of

markets and trade—a world that was, until recently, the province of a small club of Western countries.* The expansion was spurred by the movement of Western capital to Asia and across the globe. As a result, between 1990 and 2007, the global economy grew from $22.8 trillion to $53.3 trillion, and global trade increased 133 percent. The so-called emerging markets have accounted for over half of this global growth, and they now account for over 40 percent of the world economy measured at purchasing power parity (or over 30 percent at market exchange rates). Increasingly, the growth of newcomers is being powered by their own markets, not simply by exports to the West—which means that this is not an ephemeral phenomenon.

Some people dismiss such trends by pointing to the rise of Japan in the 1980s, when Westerners were scared that the Japanese would come to dominate the world economy. That turned out to be a phantom fear: Japan in fact went into a fifteen-year slump. But the analogy is misleading. In 1985, Japan was already the second-largest economy in the world. Many experts believed it was on track to unseat the United States as the largest, but because Japan's economy, institutions, and politics were still not fully modernized, the country could not make that final leap. China, by contrast, is still a poor country. It has a per capita GDP of $2,500. It will certainly face many problems as and when it becomes a first-world country. But, for the foreseeable future, it will surely manage to double the size of its economy just by continuing to

* I say two billion because the rural poor in South Asia, China, and Africa are not, in any significant sense, participating in the global economy. But millions of them move to the cities every year.

make toys and shirts and cell phones. India, starting at an even lower base income, will also be able to grow for several decades before hitting the kinds of challenges that derailed Japan. Even if India and China never get past middle-income status, they are likely to be the second- and third-largest economies in the world for much of the twenty-first century.

It is an accident of history that, for the last several centuries, the richest countries in the world have all happened to have small populations. The United States was the biggest of the bunch by far, which is why it has been the dominant player. But such dominance was possible only in a world in which the truly large countries were mired in poverty, unable or unwilling to adopt policies that made them grow. Now the giants are on the move, and, naturally, given their size, they will have a large footprint on the map. Even if the average person in these countries still seems poor by Western standards, their total wealth will be massive. Or to put it in mathematical terms: any number, however small, becomes a large number when multiplied by 2.5 billion (the approximate population of China plus India). It is these two factors—a low starting point and a large population—that guarantee the magnitude and long-term nature of the global power shift.

The Three Forces: Politics, Economics, and Technology

How did all this come to be? To answer that question, we have to go back a few decades, to the 1970s, and recall the way most countries ran their economies at the time. I remember the atmosphere vividly because I was growing up in India, a country that really didn't think it was playing on the same field as the United States. In the minds of India's policy and intellectual elites, there was a U.S.-led capitalist model on one end of the spectrum and a Soviet-led socialist model on the other. New Delhi was trying to carve a middle way between them. In this respect, India was not unusual. Brazil, Egypt, and Indonesia—and in fact, the majority of the world—were on this middle path. But it turned out to be a road to nowhere, and this was becoming apparent to many people in these countries by the late 1970s. As they stagnated, Japan and a few other East Asian economies that had charted a quasi-capitalist course succeeded conspicuously, and the lesson started to sink in.

But the earthquake that shook everything was the collapse of the Soviet Union in the late 1980s. With central planning totally discredited and one end of the political spectrum in ruins, the entire debate shifted. Suddenly, there was only one basic approach to organizing a country's economy. This is why Alan Greenspan has described the fall of the Soviet Union as the seminal *economic* event of our time. Since then, despite all the unease about various liberalization and market-ization plans, the general direction has not changed. As Margaret Thatcher famously put it in the years when she was reviving the British economy, "There is no alternative."

The ideological shift in economics had been building over the 1970s and 1980s even before the fall of the Berlin Wall. Conventional economic wisdom, embodied in organizations such as the International Monetary Fund and the World Bank, had become far more critical of the quasi-socialist path of countries like India. Academic experts like Jeffrey Sachs traveled around the world advising governments to liberalize, liberalize, liberalize. Graduates of Western economics programs, such as Chile's "Chicago Boys," went home and implemented market-friendly policies. Some developing countries worried about becoming rapacious capitalists, and Sachs recalls explaining to them that they should debate long and hard whether they wanted to end up more like Sweden, France, or the United States. But, he would add, they didn't have to worry about that decision for a while: most of them were still much closer to the Soviet Union.

The financial force that has powered the new era is the free movement of capital. This, too, is a relatively recent phenomenon. The post–World War II period was one of fixed exchange rates. Most Western countries, including France and Italy, had capital controls restricting the movement of currency in and out of their borders. The dollar was pegged to gold. But as global trade grew, fixed rates created frictions and inefficiencies and prevented capital from being put to its best use. Most Western countries removed controls during the 1970s and 1980s. The result: a vast and ever-growing supply of capital that could move freely from one place to the next. Today, when people think about globalization, they still think of it mostly in terms of the huge amount of cash—currency traders swap about $2 trillion *a day*—that sloshes around the globe, rewarding some countries and punishing others. It is globalization's celestial mechanism for discipline.

Along with freely floating money came another policy revolution: the spread of independent central banks and the taming of inflation. Hyperinflation is the worst economic malady that can befall a nation. It wipes out the value of money, savings, assets, and thus work. It is worse even than a deep recession. Hyperinflation robs you of what you have now (savings), whereas a recession robs you of what you might have had (higher standards of living if the economy had grown). That's why hyperinflation has so often toppled governments and produced revolution. It was not the Great Depression that brought the Nazis to power in Germany but rather hyperinflation, which destroyed the middle class by making its savings worthless.

It is rare that one can look back at a war that was so decisively won. In the late 1980s, dozens of large, important countries were beset by hyperinflation. In Argentina it was at 3,500 percent, in Brazil 1,200 percent, and in Peru 2,500 percent. In the 1990s, one after the other of these developing countries moved soberly toward monetary and fiscal discipline. Some accepted the need to float their currencies; others linked their currencies to the euro or the dollar. As a result, there are today only twelve countries worldwide where inflation is over 15 percent, and most of them are failed states like Haiti, Burma, and Zimbabwe. This broad atmosphere of low inflation has been crucial to the political stability and good economic fortunes of the emerging nations.

Along with these political and economic factors moving countries toward a new consensus came a series of technological innovations that pushed in the same direction. It is difficult today to remember life back in the dark days of the 1970s, when news was not conveyed instantly. But by the 1990s, events happening anywhere—East Berlin, Kuwait, Tiananmen Square—were transmitted in real time everywhere. We tend to think of news mainly as political. But prices are also a kind of news, and the ability to convey prices instantly and transparently across the globe has triggered another revolution of efficiency. Today, it is routine to compare prices for products in a few minutes on the Internet. Twenty years ago, there was a huge business in arbitrage because such instant price comparison was so difficult.

The expansion of communications meant that the world got more deeply connected and became "flat," in Thomas Friedman's famous formulation. Cheap phone calls and broadband made it possible for people to do jobs for one country in another country—marking the next stage in the ongoing story of capitalism. With the arrival of big ships in the fifteenth century, goods became mobile. With modern banking in the seventeenth century, capital became mobile. In the 1990s, labor became mobile. People could not necessarily go to where the jobs were, but jobs could go to where people were. And they went to programmers in India, telephone operators in the Philippines, and radiologists in Thailand. The cost of transporting goods and services has been falling for centuries. With the advent of broadband, it has dropped to zero for many services. Not all jobs can be outsourced—not by a long shot—but the effect of outsourcing can be felt everywhere.

In a sense, this is how trade has always worked—textile factories shifted from Great Britain to Japan in the early twentieth century, for example. But instant and constant communications means that this process has accelerated sharply. A clothing factory in Thailand can be managed almost as if it were in the United States. Companies now use dozens of countries as parts of a chain that buys, manufactures, assembles, markets, and sells goods.

Since the 1980s, these three forces—politics, economics, and technology—have pushed in the same direction to produce a more open, connected, exacting international environment. But they have also given countries everywhere fresh opportunities to start moving up the ladder of growth and prosperity.

Consider the sea change in two representative (non-Asian) countries. Twenty years ago, Brazil and Turkey would have been considered typical "developing" countries, with sluggish growth, rampant inflation, spiraling debt, an anemic private sector, and a fragile political system. Today, both are well managed and boast historically low inflation, vigorous growth rates, falling debt levels, a thriving private sector, and increasingly stable democratic institutions. Brazil's inflation rate is now, for the first time in history, roughly the same as that of the United States. Brazil and Turkey still have problems—what country doesn't?—but they are serious nations on the rise.

Markets have already shifted their perceptions of these countries. Their debt is no longer regarded as any more risky than first-world debt. In fact, many emerging markets are piling up large surpluses, so much so that they now hold 75 percent of the world's foreign-exchange reserves. China alone has over $1.5 trillion dollars in its accounts. Goldman Sachs has predicted that, by 2040, five emerging-market countries—China, India, Brazil, Russia, and Mexico—will together have a larger economic output than the G-7 countries, the seven Western nations that have dominated global affairs for centuries.

The Problems of Plenty

For the last two decades, we have spent much time, energy, and attention worrying about crises and breakdown in the global economy and terrorism, nuclear blackmail, and war in geopolitics. This is natural—preparing for the worst can help avert it. And we have indeed had bad news—from wars in the Balkans and Africa, to terrorism around the world, to economic crises in East Asia, Russia, and—most dangerously—the United States. But focusing on the gloom has also left us unprepared for many of the largest problems we face: *which are the product not of failure but of success.* The fact that we are living in a world of synchronous global growth is good news, for the most part, but it is also raising a series of complex and potentially lethal dilemmas.

Global growth is the big story of our times. It explains the rise of liquidity—the ever-growing piles of money moving around the world—that has kept credit cheap and assets (including real estate, stocks, and bonds) expensive. At the same time, the boom in low-wage countries has prevented inflation from rising too much. One way to think about India and China is as two great global deflation machines, pumping out goods (China) and services (India) for a fraction of what they would cost to produce in the West.[5] This is one of the chief reasons that central banks haven't had to worry much about inflation and have been able to maintain low interests for almost two decades, an unusually long stretch of time. Of course, low interest rates and cheap credit also cause people to act foolishly or greedily, inflating bubbles in technology stocks, housing, subprime mortgages, or emerging market equities— bubbles that eventually pop. As the world gets more interconnected, and financial instruments more exotic, many observers worry that the virtuous cycle of growth and confidence could turn into a vicious one of panic and depression. But, so far, even as the unwinding of crises is extremely painful, the diverse new sources of growth and massive quantities of new capital have given the global economic system as a whole greater resilience.

Consider rising oil prices. The oil shock of the naughts (how else to describe the decade 2000 to 2010?) has been different from previous ones. In the past, prices rose because oil producers—OPEC—artificially restricted supply and thus forced up the cost of gasoline. In recent years, by contrast, prices have risen because of *demand* from China, India, and other emerging markets, as well as the continuing, massive demand in the developed world. If prices are rising because economies are growing, it means that economies have the vigor and flexibility to handle increased costs by improving productivity (and, to a lesser extent, by passing them on to consumers). As a result, the price hikes of the naughts have been more easily digested. Had we asked our fortune-teller in 2001 to assess the effect of a quadrupling in oil prices, he would have surely predicted a massive global recession.

It's not just oil that has become more expensive. Commodity prices are at a 200-year high. Raw materials of all kinds are increasingly dear. Agricultural produce is now so expensive that developing countries face a growing political problem of how to respond to food inflation. The cost of construction has exploded from New York to Dubai to Shanghai. Even the humble gas, helium, which is used not merely in party balloons but also in MRI machines and microchip factories, is in short supply globally—and it's the second-most-abundant element in the universe. These pressures will surely at some point end the era of low inflation that has undergirded global prosperity.

Meanwhile, robust growth has also produced a number of anomalies. Within an increasingly globalized and disciplined world, certain countries—those endowed with natural resources, especially petroleum and natural gas—are getting free rides. They are surfing the wave of global growth, getting rich without having to play by most of the rules that govern the global

economy. This phenomenon is the strange but inevitable outgrowth of the success of everyone else. These countries are the
nonmarket parasites on a market world.

Consider the principal political challenges to the United
States and to Western ideas of international order. In the Middle East they come from Iran, in Latin America from Venezuela,
and in Eurasia from Russia. All have newfound strength built on
oil. Sudan's ability to defy the world over Darfur is difficult to
imagine absent its oil reserves. Petroleum brings in eye-popping
amounts of cash. Iran's take from oil in 2006 amounted to $50
billion—enough to dispense patronage to interest groups, bribe
the army, and stay in power while still having piles left over to
foment trouble abroad. This situation is unlikely to change.
Resource-rich countries will thrive as long as the others are
growing. It's the yin and yang of today's globalization.

Not all resource-rich countries are rogues, and the climate
of good economic management has led some to use their
riches more wisely than before. Canada is becoming a major
power, and yet acting extremely responsibly. The Persian
Gulf, where so much of the oil revenue flows, is investing
more of its profits in infrastructure and industry, rather than
in Swiss bank accounts and Monte Carlo casinos (though
there is certainly much of that as well). Dubai has become an
efficiently run, business-friendly entrepôt, a Middle Eastern
Singapore. Other Gulf states are now trying to emulate its success. Saudi Arabia, which for decades has mismanaged its vast
fortune, plans to invest $70 billion in new petrochemical proj-
ects, aiming to become a leading petrochemical producer by
2015. The Gulf states have made $1 trillion in capital invest-
ments over the last five years, and McKinsey and Company
estimates that they could invest another $2 trillion over the

next decade. This is a state-directed form of capitalism, which is likely to result in narrow development and unlikely to produce self-sustaining growth (although there are strong state-directed elements in European and East Asian capitalism as well). But it is much closer to the global capitalist norm than the economic systems in these countries—from Russia to Saudi Arabia—a generation ago.

The most acute problem of plenty is the impact of global growth on natural resources and the environment. It is not an exaggeration to say that the world is running out of clean air, potable water, agricultural produce, and many vital commodities. Some of these problems can be fixed—by improving efficiency and developing new sources of supply—but progress has been far too slow. Agricultural productivity, for example, is rising. But feeding a global population of eight billion, which we will get to by 2025, will require crop yields to reach four tons per hectare from only three tons today. Similarly, our ability to manage and conserve water is not growing nearly as fast as our consumption of it. World population tripled in the twentieth century, but water consumption increased sixfold. Americans use more than four hundred liters of water a day to drink, cook, and clean themselves. People in poorer countries today are lucky to get forty, but as they get richer, their rising demands will cause greater stress.[6] Violent clashes over water have already broken out in Africa and the Middle East. Historically, populations have moved to find water; if water sources dry up in the future, tens of millions of people will be forced to start moving.

Over the last decade, many predictions about the effects of climate change have proven to be underestimates because global growth has exceeded all projections. The most recent assessment of the Intergovernmental Panel on Climate Change was released in mid-2007. By the year's end, scientists had shown that the polar ice caps are melting twice as fast as the report expected.[7] There is greater demand for electricity, more cars, and more planes than anyone imagined fifteen years ago. And it keeps growing. The McKinsey Global Institute projects that, from 2003 to 2020, the number of vehicles in China will rise from 26 million to 120 million. And then there's India, Russia, the Middle East—the rest.

Demand for electricity is projected to rise over 4 percent a year for decades. And that electricity will come mostly from the dirtiest fuel available—coal. Coal is cheap and plentiful, so the world relies on it to produce most of its electricity. To understand the impact on global warming, consider this fact. Between 2006 and 2012, China and India will build eight hundred new coal-fired power plants—with combined CO_2 emissions five times the total savings of the Kyoto accords.

The Rise of Nationalism

In a globalized world, almost all problems spill over borders. Whether it's terrorism, nuclear proliferation, disease, environmental degradation, economic crisis, or water scarcity, no issue can be addressed without significant coordination and cooperation among many countries. But while economics, information, and even culture might have become globalized, formal political power remains firmly tethered to the nation-state, even as the nation-state has become less able to solve most of these problems unilaterally. And increasingly, nation-states are becoming less willing to come together to solve common problems. As the number of players—governmental and nongovernmental—increases and each one's power and confidence grows, the prospects for agreement and common action diminish. This is the central challenge of the rise of the rest—to stop the forces of global growth from turning into the forces of global disorder and disintegration.

The rise of pride and confidence among other nations, particularly the largest and most successful ones, is readily apparent. For me, it was vividly illustrated a few years ago in an Internet café in Shanghai, where I was chatting with a young Chinese executive. He was describing the extraordinary growth that was taking place in his country and a future in which China would be modern and prosperous. He was thoroughly Westernized in dress and demeanor, spoke excellent English, and could comfortably discuss the latest business trends or gossip about American pop culture. He seemed the consummate product of globalization, the person who bridges cultures and makes the world a smaller, more cosmopolitan place. But when we began talking about Taiwan, Japan, and the United States, his responses were filled with bile. He explained in furious tones that were Taiwan to dare to declare independence, China should instantly invade it. He said that Japan was an aggressor nation that could never be trusted. He was sure that the United States deliberately bombed the Chinese embassy during the Kosovo war in 1999, to terrify the Chinese people with its military might. And so on. I felt as if I were in Berlin in 1910, speaking to a young German professional, who in those days would have also been both thoroughly modern and thoroughly nationalist.

As economic fortunes rise, so does nationalism. This is understandable. Imagine that you lived in a country that had been poor and unstable for centuries. And then, finally, things turn and your nation is on the rise. You would be proud and anxious to be seen. This desire for recognition and respect is surging throughout the world. It may seem paradoxical that globalization and economic modernization are breeding political nationalism, but that is so only if we view nationalism as a backward ideology, certain to be erased by the onward march of progress.

Nationalism has always perplexed Americans. When the United States involves itself abroad, it always believes that it is genuinely trying to help other countries better themselves. From the Philippines and Haiti to Vietnam and Iraq, the natives' reaction to U.S. efforts has taken Americans by surprise. Americans take justified pride in their own country—we call it patriotism—and yet are genuinely startled when other people are proud and possessive of theirs.

In the waning days of Britain's rule in India, its last viceroy, Lord Louis Mountbatten, turned to the great Indian leader Mahatma Gandhi and said in exasperation, "If we just leave, there will be chaos." Gandhi replied, "Yes, but it will be *our* chaos." That sense of being governed by one's "own," without interference, is a powerful feeling in emerging countries, especially those that were once colonies or quasi-colonies of the West.

Zbigniew Brzezinski recently called attention to what he terms a "global political awakening." He pointed to rising mass passions, fueled by various forces—economic success, national pride, higher levels of education, greater information and transparency, and memories of the past. Brzezinski noted the disruptive aspects of this new force. "The population of much of the developing world is politically stirring and in many places seething with unrest," he wrote. "It is acutely conscious of social injustice to an unprecedented degree . . . [and this] is creating a community of shared perceptions and envy that can be galvanized and channeled by demagogic political or religious passions. These energies transcend sovereign borders and pose a challenge both to existing states as well as to the existing global hierarchy, on top of which America still perches."[8]

In many countries outside the Western world, there is pent-up frustration with having had to accept an entirely Western or American narrative of world history—one in which they either are miscast or remain bit players. Russians have long chafed at the standard narrative about World War II, in which Britain and the United States heroically defeat the forces of fascist Germany and Japan. Given mainstream U.S. historical accounts, from Stephen Ambrose to Ken Burns, Americans could be forgiven for believing that Russia played a minor part in the decisive battles against Hitler and Tojo. In fact, the eastern front was the central arena of World War II. It involved more land combat than all other theaters of the war put together and resulted in thirty million deaths. It was where three-quarters of all German forces fought and where Germany incurred 70 percent of its casualties. The European front was in many ways a sideshow, but in the West it is treated as the main event. As the writer Benjamin Schwarz has pointed out, Stephen Ambrose "lavishes [attention] on the U.S.-British invasion of Sicily, which drove 60,000 Germans from the island, but completely ignores Kursk—the largest battle in history, in which at least 1.5 million Soviets and Germans fought, and which occurred at exactly the same time. . . . [M]uch as it may make us squirm, we must admit that the struggle against Nazi Germany . . . was primarily, as the great military historian John Erickson called it, 'Stalin's war.'"[9]

Or consider the perspective on the same war from another spot on the map. An Indian friend explained to me, "For Britain and America, World War II is a heroic struggle in which freedom triumphs over evil. For us, it was a battle to which Britain committed India and its armed forces without bothering to consult us. London told us to die for an idea of freedom that it was at that very moment brutally denying to us."

Such divergent national perspectives have always existed, but today, thanks to greater education, information, and confidence, they are widely disseminated on new news networks, cable channels, and Internet sites of the emerging world. Many of the "rest" are dissecting the narratives, arguments, and assumptions of the West and countering them with a different view of the world. "When you tell us that we support a dictatorship in Sudan to have access to its oil," a young Chinese official told me in 2006, "what I want to say is, 'And how is that different from your support for a medieval monarchy in Saudi Arabia?' We see the hypocrisy, we just don't say anything, yet."

After the Cold War ended, there was a general hope and expectation that China and Russia would move inexorably into the post–World War II Western political and economic system. When George H. W. Bush spoke of "a new world order," he meant simply that the old Western one would be extended worldwide. Perhaps this view stemmed from the postwar experience with Japan and Germany, both of which rose to the heights of economic power and yet were accommodating, cooperative, and largely silent members of the existing order. But perhaps those were special circumstances. The two countries had unique histories, having waged aggressive wars and become pariahs as a consequence, and they faced a new threat from Soviet communism and relied on American military power for their protection. The next round of rising powers might not be so eager to "fit in."

We still think of a world in which a rising power must choose between two stark options: integrate into the Western order, or reject it, becoming a rogue nation and facing the penalties of excommunication. In fact, rising powers appear to be following a third way: entering the Western order but doing so on their own terms—thus reshaping the system itself. As the political scientists Naazneen Barma, Ely Ratner, and Steven Weber point out, in a world where everyone feels empowered, countries can choose to bypass this Western "center" entirely and forge their own ties with one another.[10] In a post-American world, there may be no center to integrate into. U.S. Secretary of State James Baker suggested in 1991 that the world was moving toward a hub-and-spoke system, with every country going through the United States to get to its destination. The twenty-first-century world might be better described as one of point-to-point routes, with new flight patterns being mapped every day. (This is true even in a physical sense: in just ten years, the number of Russian visitors to China increased more than fourfold, from 489,000 in 1995 to 2.2 million in 2005.) The focus has shifted. Countries are increasingly interested in themselves—the story of their rise—and pay less attention to the West and the United States. As a result, the urgent discussions on the presidential campaign trail throughout 2007 about the need to lessen anti-Americanism are somewhat off-point. The world is moving from anger to indifference, from anti-Americanism to post-Americanism.

The fact that new powers are more strongly asserting their interests is the reality of the post-American world. It also raises the political conundrum of how to achieve international objectives in a world of many actors, state and nonstate. According to the old model of getting things done, the United States and a few Western allies directed the show while the Third World either played along or stayed outside the box and remained irrelevant as a result. Nongovernmental players were too few and too weak to worry about. Now, look at something like trade negotiations, and you see the developing world acting with greater and greater force. Where they might once have taken any deal offered by the West or ignored the process altogether, countries like Brazil and India play hardball until they get the deal of their choice. They have heard Western CEOs explain where the future lies. They have read the Goldman Sachs BRIC report. They know that the balance of power has shifted.

The Kyoto accord (now treated as sacred because of President Bush's cavalier rejection of them) is in fact a treaty marked by its adherence to the old worldview. Kyoto assumed that if the West came together and settled on a plan, the Third World would adopt the new framework and the problem would be solved. That may be the way things have been done in international affairs for decades, but it makes little sense today. China, India, Brazil, and other emerging powers will not follow along with a Western-led process in which they have not participated. What's more, governments on their own can do only so much to tackle a problem like climate change. A real solution requires creating a much broader coalition that includes the private sector, nongovernmental groups, cities and localities, and the media. In a globalized, democratized, and decentralized world, we need to get to individuals to alter their behavior.

Taxes, tariffs, and wars are the old ways to do this, but states now have less room to maneuver on these fronts. They need more subtle and sophisticated ways to effect change.

The traditional mechanisms of international cooperation are relics of another era. The United Nations system represents an outdated configuration of power. The permanent members of the UN Security Council are the victors of a war that ended sixty years ago. The body does not include Japan or Germany, the world's second- and third-largest economies (at market exchange rates), or India, the world's largest democracy, or any Latin American or African country. The Security Council exemplifies the antique structure of global governance more broadly. The G-8 does not include China, already the world's fourth-largest economy, or India and South Korea, the twelfth and thirteenth. By tradition, the IMF is always headed by a European and the World Bank by an American. This "tradition," like the customs of an old segregated country club, may be charming and amusing to insiders, but to outsiders it is bigoted and outrageous.

A further complication: when I write of the rise of nationalism, I am describing a broader phenomenon—the assertion of identity. The nation-state is a relatively new invention, often no more than a hundred years old. Much older are the religious, ethnic, and linguistic groups that live within nation-states. And these bonds have stayed strong, in fact grown, as economic interdependence has deepened. In Europe, the Flemish and French in Belgium remain as distinct as ever. In Britain, the Scots have elected a ruling party that proposes ending the three-hundred-year-old Acts of Union that created the United Kingdom of England, Scotland, and Wales. In India, national parties are losing ground to regional ones. In

Kenya, tribal distinctions are becoming more important. In much of the world, these core identities—deeper than the nation-state—remain the defining features of life. It is why people vote, and what they die for. In an open world economy, these groups know that they need the central government less and less. And in a democratic age, they gain greater and greater power if they stay together as a group. This twin ascendancy of identity means that, when relating to the United States or the United Nations or the world at large, Chinese and Indian nationalism grows. But within their own countries, sub-nationalism is also growing. What is happening on the global stage—the rise of identity in the midst of economic growth—is also happening on the local stage. The bottom line: it makes purposeful national action far more difficult.

As power becomes diversified and diffuse, legitimacy becomes even more important—because it is the only way to appeal to all the disparate actors on the world stage. Today, no solution, no matter how sensible, is sustainable if it is seen as illegitimate. Imposing it will not work if it is seen as the product of one country's power and preferences, no matter how powerful that country. The massacres in Darfur, for example, are horrific, and yet military intervention there—the most effective way of stopping it—would succeed only if sanctioned by the major powers as well as Sudan's African neighbors. If the United States acted alone or with a small coalition—invading its third Muslim country in five years—the attempt would almost certainly backfire, providing the Sudanese government with a fiery rallying cry against "U.S. imperialism." The Bush administration's foreign policy record offers a perfect illustration of the practical necessity of legitimacy. And yet, beyond Bush's failures, the dilemma remains: if many countries need to cooperate to get things done, how to make this happen in a world with more players, many of them more powerful?

The Last Superpower

Many observers and commentators have looked at the vitality of this emerging world and concluded that the United States has had its day. Andy Grove, the founder of Intel, puts it bluntly. "America is in danger of following Europe down the tubes," he says, "and the worst part is that nobody knows it. They're all in denial, patting themselves on the back as the *Titanic* heads straight for the iceberg full speed ahead." Thomas Friedman describes watching waves of young Indian professionals get to work for the night shift at Infosys in Bangalore. "Oh, my God, there are so many of them, and they just keep coming, wave after wave. How in the world can it possibly be good for my daughters and millions of other Americans that these Indians can do the same jobs as they can for a fraction of the wages?"[11] "Globalization is striking back," writes Gabor Steingart, an editor at Germany's leading news magazine, *Der Spiegel*, in a bestselling book. As its rivals have prospered, he argues, the United States has lost key industries, its people have stopped saving money, and its government has become increasingly indebted to Asian central banks.[12]

What's puzzling, however, is that these trends have been around for a while—and they have actually helped America's bottom line. Over the past twenty years, as globalization and outsourcing have accelerated dramatically, America's growth rate has averaged just over 3 percent, a full percentage point higher than that of Germany and France. (Japan averaged 2.3

percent over the same period.) Productivity growth, the elixir of modern economics, has been over 2.5 percent for a decade now, again a full percentage point higher than the European average. Even American exports held up, despite a decade-long spike in the value of the dollar that ended recently. In 1980, U.S. exports represented 10 percent of the world total; in 2007, that figure was still almost 9 percent. According to the World Economic Forum, the United States remains the most competitive economy in the world and ranks first in innovation, ninth in technological readiness, second in company spending for research and technology, and second in the quality of its research institutions. China does not come within thirty countries of the United States in any of these, and India breaks the top ten on only one count: market size. In virtually every sector that advanced industrial countries participate in, U.S. firms lead the world in productivity and profits.

The United States' share of the global economy has been remarkably steady through wars, depressions, and a slew of other powers rising. With 5 percent of the world's population, the United States has generated between 20 and 30 percent of world output for 125 years. There will surely be some slippage of America's position over the next few decades. This is not a political statement but a mathematical one. As other countries grow faster, America's relative economic weight will fall. But the decline need not be large-scale, rapid, or consequential, as long as the United States can adapt to new challenges as well as it adapted to those it confronted over the last century. In the next few decades, the rise of the emerging nations is likely to come mostly at the expense of Western Europe and Japan, which are locked in a slow, demographically determined decline.

America will face the most intense economic competition it has ever faced. The American economic and social system knows how to respond and adjust to such pressures. The reforms needed are obvious but because they mean some pain now for long-term gain, the political system cannot make them. The more difficult challenge that the United States faces is international. It will confront a global order quite different from the one it is used to operating in. For now, the United States remains the most powerful player. But every year the balance shifts.

For the roughly two decades since 1989, the power of the United States has defined the international order. All roads have led to Washington, and American ideas about politics, economics, and foreign policy have been the starting points for global action. Washington has been the most powerful outside actor on every continent in the world, dominating the Western Hemisphere, remaining the crucial outside balancer in Europe and East Asia, expanding its role in the Middle East and Central and South Asia, and everywhere remaining the only country that can provide the muscle for any serious global military operation. For every country—from Russia and China to South Africa and India—its most important relationship in the world has been the relationship with the United States.

That influence reached its apogee with Iraq. Despite the reluctance, opposition, or active hostility of much of the world, the United States was able to launch an unprovoked attack on a sovereign country and to enlist dozens of countries and international agencies to assist it during and after the invasion. It is not just the complications of Iraq that have unwound this order. Even had Iraq been a glorious success, the method of its execution would have made utterly clear the unchallenged power of the United States—and it is this exercise of unipolar-

ity that has provoked a reaction around the world. The unipolar order of the last two decades is waning not because of Iraq
but because of the broader diffusion of power across the world.

On some matters, unipolarity seems already to have ended.
The European Union now represents the largest trade bloc on
the globe, creating bipolarity, and as China and then other
emerging giants gain size, the bipolar realm of trade might
become tripolar and then multipolar. In every realm except military, similar shifts are underway. In general, however, the notion
of a multipolar world, with four or five players of roughly equal
weight, does not describe reality today or in the near future.
Europe cannot act militarily or even politically as one. Japan and
Germany are hamstrung by their past. China and India are still
developing. Instead, the international system is more accurately
described by Samuel Huntington's term "uni-multipolarity," or
what Chinese geopoliticians call "many powers and one superpower." The messy language reflects the messy reality. The
United States remains by far the most powerful country but in a
world with several other important great powers and with
greater assertiveness and activity from all actors. This hybrid
international system—more democratic, more dynamic, more
open, more connected—is one we are likely to live with for several decades. It is easier to define what it is not than what it is,
easier to describe the era it is moving away from than the era it
is moving toward—hence *the post-American world*.

The United States occupies the top spot in the emerging
system, but it is also the country that is most challenged by the
new order. Most other great powers will see their role in the
world expand. That process is already underway. China and
India are becoming bigger players in their neighborhoods and
beyond. Russia has ended its post-Soviet accommodation
and is becoming more forceful, even aggressive. Japan, though

not a rising power, is now more willing to voice its views and positions to its neighbors. Europe acts on matters of trade and economics with immense strength and purpose. Brazil and Mexico are becoming more vocal on Latin American issues. South Africa has positioned itself as a leader of the African continent. All these countries are taking up more space in the international arena than they did before.

For the United States, the arrow is pointing in the opposite direction. Economics is not a zero-sum game—the rise of other players expands the pie, which is good for all—but geopolitics is a struggle for influence and control. As other countries become more active, America's enormous space for action will inevitably diminish. Can the United States accommodate itself to the rise of other powers, of various political stripes, on several continents? This does not mean becoming resigned to chaos or aggression; far from it. But the only way for the United States to deter rogue actions will be to create a broad, durable coalition against them. And that will be possible only if Washington can show that it is willing to allow other countries to become stakeholders in the new order. In today's international order, progress means compromise. No country will get its way entirely. These are easy words to write or say but difficult to implement. They mean accepting the growth in power and influence of other countries, the prominence of interests and concerns. This balance—between accommodation and deterrence—is the chief challenge for American foreign policy in the next few decades.

I began this chapter by arguing that the new order did not herald American decline, because I believe that America has enormous strengths and that the new world will not throw up a new superpower but rather a diversity of forces that Washington can navigate and even help direct. But still, as the rest of the world rises, in purely economic terms, America will experience relative decline. As others grow faster, its share of the pie will be smaller (though the shift will likely be small for many years). In addition, the new nongovernmental forces that are increasingly active will constrain Washington substantially.

This is a challenge for Washington but also for everyone else. For almost three centuries, the world has been undergirded by the presence of a large liberal hegemon—first Britain, then the United States. These two superpowers helped create and maintain an open world economy, protecting trade routes and sea lanes, acting as lenders of last resort, holding the reserve currency, investing abroad, and keeping their own markets open. They also tipped the military balance against the great aggressors of their ages, from Napoleon's France, to Germany, to the Soviet Union. For all its abuses of power, the United States has been the creator and sustainer of the current order of open trade and democratic government—an order that has been benign and beneficial for the vast majority of humankind. As things change, and as America's role changes, that order could begin to fracture. The collapse of the dollar—to the point where there was no global reserve currency—would be a problem for the world just as much as for America. And solving common problems in an era of diffusion and decentralization could turn out to be far more difficult without a superpower.

Some Americans have become acutely conscious of the changing world. American business is increasingly aware of the shifts taking place around the world and is responding to them rapidly and unsentimentally. Large U.S.-based multinationals almost uniformly report that their growth now relies on penetrating new foreign markets. With annual revenue growth of 2–3 percent a year in the United States and 10–15 percent a year abroad, they know they have to adapt to a post-American world—or else lose out in it. A similar awareness is visible in America's universities, where more and more students study and travel abroad and interact with foreign students. Younger Americans live comfortably with the knowledge that the latest trends—in finance, architecture, art, technology—might originate in London, Shanghai, Seoul, Tallinn, or Mumbai.

But this outward orientation is not yet common in American society more broadly. The American economy remains internally focused, though this is changing, with trade making up 28 percent of GDP (compared with 38 percent for Germany). Insularity has been one of nature's blessings to America, bordered as it is by two vast oceans and two benign neighbors. America has not been sullied by the machinations and weariness of the Old World and has always been able to imagine a new and different order—whether in Germany, Japan, or even Iraq. But at the same time, this isolation has left Americans quite unaware of the world beyond their borders. Americans speak few languages, know little about foreign cultures, and remain unconvinced that they need to rectify this. Americans rarely benchmark to global standards because they are sure that their way must be the best and most advanced. The result is that they are increasingly suspicious of this emerging global era. There is a growing gap between America's worldly business elite and cosmopolitan class, on the one hand, and the majority of the American people, on the other. Without real efforts to bridge it, this divide could destroy America's competitive edge and its political future.

Popular suspicions are fed and encouraged by an irresponsible national political culture. In Washington, new thinking about a new world is sorely lacking. It is easy enough to criticize the Bush administration for its arrogance and unilateralism, which have handicapped America abroad. But the problem is not confined to Bush, Cheney, Rumsfeld, or the Republicans, even though they have become the party of chest-thumping machismo, proud to be despised abroad. Listen to some Democrats in Washington, and you hear a weaker unilateralism—on trade, labor standards, and various pet human rights issues. On terrorism, both parties continue to speak in language entirely designed for a domestic audience with no concern for the poisonous effect it has everywhere else. American politicians constantly and promiscuously demand, label, sanction, and condemn whole countries for myriad failings. Over the last fifteen years, the United States has placed sanctions on half the world's population. We are the only counry in the world to issue annual report cards on every other country's behavior. Washington, D.C., has become a bubble, smug and out of touch with the world outside.

The 2007 Pew Global Attitudes Survey showed a remarkable increase worldwide in positive views about free trade, markets, and democracy. Large majorities in countries from China and Germany to Bangladesh and Nigeria said that growing trade ties between countries were good. Of the forty-seven countries polled, however, the one that came in dead last in terms of support for free trade was the United States. In the five years the survey has been done, no country has seen as great a drop-off as the United States.

Or take a look at the attitudes toward foreign companies. When asked whether they had a positive impact, a surprisingly large number of people in countries like Brazil, Nigeria, India, and Bangladesh said yes. Those countries have typically been suspicious of Western multinationals. (South Asia's unease has some basis; after all, it was initially colonized by a multinational corporation, the British East India Company.) And yet, 73 percent in India, 75 percent in Bangladesh, 70 percent in Brazil, and 82 percent in Nigeria now have positive views of these companies. The figure for America, in contrast, is 45 percent, which places us in the bottom five. We want the world to accept American companies with open arms, but when they come here—that's a different matter. Attitudes on immigration represent an even larger reversal. On an issue where the United States has been the model for the world, the country has regressed toward an angry defensive crouch. Where we once wanted to pioneer every new technology, we now look at innovation fearfully, wondering how it will change things.

The irony is that the rise of the rest is a consequence of American ideas and actions. For sixty years, American politicians and diplomats have traveled around the world pushing countries to open their markets, free up their politics, and embrace trade and technology. We have urged peoples in distant lands to take up the challenge of competing in the global economy, freeing up their currencies, and developing new industries. We counseled them to be unafraid of change and learn the secrets of our success. And it worked: the natives have gotten good at capitalism. But now we are becoming suspicious of the very things we have long celebrated—free markets, trade, immigration, and technological change. And all this is happening when the tide is going our way. Just as the world is opening up, America is closing down.

Generations from now, when historians write about these times, they might note that, in the early decades of the twenty-first century, the United States succeeded in its great and historic mission—it globalized the world. But along the way, they might write, it forgot to globalize itself.

HA HA HA

3

A Non-Western World?

In 1492, as everybody knows, Christopher Columbus set sail on one of the most ambitious expeditions in human history. What is less well known is that eighty-seven years earlier a Chinese admiral named Zheng He began the first of seven equally ambitious expeditions. Zheng's ships were much bigger and better constructed than those of Columbus, or Vasco da Gama, or any of Europe's other great fifteenth- and sixteenth-century seafarers. On his first trip, in 1405, he took 317 vessels and 28,000 men, compared with Columbus' 4 boats and 150 sailors. The largest vessels in the Chinese fleet, the "treasure ships," were over four hundred feet—more than four times the length of Columbus' flagship, *Santa Maria*—and had nine masts. Each required so much wood that three hundred acres of forest were felled to build a single one. There were ships designed to carry horses, supplies, food, water, and, of course, troops. The smallest vessel in Zheng's flotilla, a highly maneuverable five-masted warship, was still twice as large as the legendary Spanish galleon.

The Chinese ships were constructed with special woods, intricate joints, sophisticated waterproofing techniques, and an adjustable centerboard keel. The treasure ships had large, luxurious cabins, silk sails, and windowed halls. All were constructed on dry docks in Nanjing, the world's largest and most advanced shipbuilding port. In the three years after 1405, 1,681 ships were built or refitted at Nanjing. Nothing remotely comparable could have happened in Europe at the time.[1]

Size mattered. These massive fleets were meant to "shock and awe" the inhabitants of the surrounding area, making clear the power and reach of the Ming dynasty. On his seven voyages between 1405 and 1433, Zheng traveled widely through the waters of the Indian Ocean and around Southeast Asia. He gave gifts to the natives and accepted tributes. When encountering opposition, he did not hesitate to use military might. On one voyage, he brought back a captured Sumatran pirate; on another, a rebellious chief from Ceylon. He returned from all of them with flowers, fruits, precious stones, and exotic animals, including giraffes and zebras for the imperial zoo.

But Zheng's story ends oddly. By the 1430s, a new emperor had come to power. He abruptly ended the imperial expeditions and turned his back on trade and exploration. Some officials tried to keep the tradition going, but to no avail. In 1500, the court decreed that anyone who built a ship with more than two masts (the size required to go any distance at sea) would be executed. In 1525, coastal authorities were ordered to destroy any oceangoing vessels they encountered and throw the owners in prison. In 1551, it became a crime to go to sea on a multimast ship for any purpose. When the Qing dynasty came to power in 1644, it continued this basic policy, but it had less faith in decrees: instead, it simply scorched a 700-

mile-long strip of China's southern coast, rendering it unin-habitable. These measures had the desired effect: China's shipping industry collapsed. In the decades after Zheng's last voyage, dozens of Western explorers traveled to the waters around India and China. But it took three hundred years for a Chinese vessel to make its way to Europe—on a visit to Lon-don for the Great Exhibition of 1851.

What explains this remarkable turnaround? The Chinese elite was divided over the country's outward approach, and Bei-jing's new rulers considered the naval expeditions failures. They were extremely expensive, forced higher taxes on an already strained population, and provided very little return. Trade had flourished as a result of some of these contacts, but most of it had benefited only traders and pirates. In addition, by the mid-fifteenth century, Mongols and other raiders were threatening the empire's frontiers, demanding attention and consuming resources. Seafaring seemed like a costly distraction.

It was a fateful decision. Just as China chose to turn away from the outside world, Europe was venturing abroad, and it was Europe's naval expeditions that allowed it to energize itself and spread its power and influence across the globe. If China had kept its navy afloat, would the course of modern history have been different? Probably not. China's decision to turn inward was not simply one bad strategic call. It was an expres-sion of a civilization's stagnation. Behind the decision to end the expeditions lay the whole complex of reasons why China* and most of the non-Western world lagged behind the Western

---

* In this chapter, I use many examples involving China and India as a proxy for the non-Western world because they were among the most advanced Asian civilizations of the preindustrial era. Everything that is true about their slipping behind the West in the fifteenth and sixteenth centuries applies to most of the non-Western world.

world for so many centuries. And lag they did. For hundreds of years after the fifteenth century, while Europe and the United States industrialized, urbanized, and modernized, the rest of the world remained poor and agricultural.

If we are to understand what the "rise of the rest" means, we must understand just how long the rest has been dormant. It turns out that the intellectual and material dominance of the West is neither a recent nor an ephemeral phenomenon. We have lived in a Western world for over half a millennium. Despite the rise of other nations and continents, the shadows of the West will be long and its legacies deep for decades to come, perhaps longer.

It has become commonplace to say that actually China and India were as rich as the West right up until the 1800s. The dominance of the West, according to this perspective, has been a 200-year blip, and we are now returning to a more normal balance. This statement also implies that the West's advantages may be largely accidental—the result of "coal and colonies,"[2] that is, the discovery of a cheap energy source and the domination of the rich lands of Asia, Africa, and the Americas. This view, which embraces a multicultural sensibility that denies any special status to the West, has its political advantages. But while it may be politically correct, it is historically incorrect.

One reason for this misinterpretation is that analysts often focus solely on the total size of the Chinese and Indian economies. Historically, this has been a misleading statistic. Until the modern age, a country's economy could not be mobilized, extracted, or put to use in any meaningful sense. The fact that in, say, the seventeenth century, millions of peasants in remote and unconnected corners of China were working the land in grinding poverty did not really contribute to the nation's usable wealth or power, even though their output added up to a large number. Population was the main ingredient of GDP, and production was largely agricultural. Since China and India had four times the population of Western Europe in 1600, their GDP was, of course, larger. Even in 1913, when Britain was the world's leading power, with cutting-edge technology and industrial production and trade many times larger than all of Asia's, China could claim a greater total GDP.

In studying the preindustrial age, before big government, communications, transport, and broad-based taxation, aggregate GDP alone tells us little about national power or a country's level of advancement. It doesn't say anything about the dynamism of the society or its ability to make new discoveries and inventions. And it was mastery in these areas that gave a country new ways to create wealth and its government power.

We get a much clearer picture of the real standing of countries if we consider *economic growth* and *GDP per capita*. Western European GDP per capita was higher than that of both China and India by 1500; by 1600, it was 50 percent higher than China's. From there, the gap kept growing. Between 1350 and 1950—*six hundred years*—GDP per capita remained roughly constant in China and India (hovering around $600 for China and $550 for India). In the same period, Western European GDP per capita went from $662 to $4,594, a *594 percent increase*.*

European travelers in the seventeenth century routinely

---

* Throughout this chapter and others, GDP estimates from before 1950 come from Angus Maddison, whose book *The World Economy: A Millennial Perspective* is an important source for income, population, and other figures from the deep past. All of Maddison's numbers are in PPP dollars. For long-run comparisons, this is appropriate.

pointed out that Chinese and Indian living conditions were well below those in northwestern Europe. The economist Gregory Clark calculates that in the eighteenth century the average daily wage of a laborer in Amsterdam could buy him 21 pounds of wheat, in London 16 pounds, and in Paris 10. In China, a day's wages would buy about 6.6 pounds of wheat (or its equivalent). Clark has also examined records to determine differences in the number of famines, which points in the same direction. The West, in short, was more prosperous than the East long before the eighteenth century.

Still, it was not always thus. For the first centuries of the second millennium, the East was ahead of the West by almost every measure. As Europe foundered in the depths of the Middle Ages, both the Middle East and Asia prospered, with lively traditions of scholarship, invention, and trade. The Middle East was at the forefront of civilization, preserving and building on Greek and Roman knowledge and producing pathbreaking work in fields as diverse as mathematics, physics, medicine, anthropology, and psychology. Arabic numerals, of course, were invented there, as was the concept of zero. The word "algebra" comes from the title of a book, *Al-Jabr wa-al-Muqabilah*, by an Arab scholar. The word "algorithm" derives from the scholar's name, al-Khwarizmi. Militarily, the Ottomans were the envy of their rivals and continued to expand their empire, battling Western states in Central Asia and Europe until the seventeenth century. India, during its most vibrant eras, boasted scientific prowess, artistic genius, and architectural splendor. Even in the early sixteenth century, under Krishnadevaraya, the southern Indian city of Vijayanagar was described by many foreign visitors as one of the great cities of the world, comparable to Rome. A few centuries earlier, China was probably richer and more technologically sophisticated than any other country, using various technologies—gunpowder, movable type, the stirrup—that the West would stumble upon only centuries later. Even Africa had a higher average income than Europe during this period.

The tide began to turn in the fifteenth century—and by the sixteenth century, Europe had moved ahead. With the revolution in thought that is termed the Renaissance, men like Copernicus, Vesalius, and Galileo gave birth to modern science. Indeed, the hundred years between 1450 and 1550 marked the most significant break in human history—between faith, ritual, and dogma, on the one hand, and observation, experimentation, and critical thought, on the other. And it happened in Europe, pushing that civilization forward for centuries. By 1593, when an English ship equipped with eighty-seven guns traveled 3,700 miles to arrive in Istanbul, an Ottoman historian would call it "a wonder of the age the like of which has not been seen or recorded."[3] By the seventeenth century, almost every kind of technology, product, and complex organization (like a corporation or an army) was more advanced in Western Europe than anywhere else in the world.

To believe that Asian societies were, in any material sense, on par with the West in 1700 or 1800 is to believe that the scientific and technological advances that revolutionized the Western world over the preceding three hundred years had no effect on its material condition, which is absurd.* Scientific

---

* Archaeological records provide one more interesting piece of evidence. Skeletal remains from the eighteenth century show that Asians were much shorter than Europeans at the time, indicating poorer nutrition (and, by implication, lower income).

advances were not merely about creating new machines. They reshaped the mental outlook of Western societies. Take the mechanical clock, which was invented in Europe in the thirteenth century. The historian Daniel Boorstin calls it "the mother of machines." "The clock," he notes, "broke down the walls between kinds of knowledge, ingenuity, and skill, and clockmakers were the first consciously to apply the theories of mechanics and physics to the making of machines."[4] Its broader effects were even more revolutionary. The clock freed man from dependence on the sun and moon. It made it possible to order the day, define the night, organize work, and—perhaps most important—measure the cost of labor, by tracking the number of hours that went into a project. Before the clock, time had no measurable value.

By the sixteenth century, when the Portuguese brought them to China, Europe's mechanical clocks were much more sophisticated than the clumsy water clocks made in Beijing. The Chinese, however, saw little value in these machines, viewing them as toys, and they never bothered to learn how to run them. Having acquired some, they needed Europeans to stay behind to work their inventions. Similarly, when the Portuguese brought cannons to Beijing a hundred years later, they had to supply operators for the machines. China could consume modern technology, but it could not produce it. And by the eighteenth century, Beijing no longer even wanted to see foreign gadgets. In a famous letter to George III, the Qienlong emperor, who ruled from 1736 to 1795, rejected Britain's request for trade, explaining, "We have never set much store on strange and ingenious objects, nor do we need any more of your country's manufactures." The Chinese had closed their minds to the world.[5]

Without new technologies and techniques, Asia fell prey to the classic Malthusian problem. Thomas Malthus' famous 1798 treatise, *An Essay on the Principle of Population*, is remembered today for its erroneous pessimism, but, in fact, many of Malthus' insights were highly intelligent. He observed that food production in England rose at an arithmetic rate (1, 2, 3, 4, . . .) but population grew at a geometric rate (1, 2, 4, 8, 16, . . .). This mismatch, unless altered, would ensure that the country would be hungry and impoverished, and that only catastrophes like famine and disease could raise living standards (by shrinking the population).* Malthus' dilemma was quite real, but he failed to appreciate the power of technology. He did not recognize that these very pressures would generate a human response in Europe—the agricultural revolution, which vastly expanded the production of food. (The continent also eased population pressures by exporting tens of millions of people to various colonies, mostly in the Americas.) So Malthus was wrong about Europe. His analysis, however, well described Asia and Africa.

Strength Is Weakness

And yet, how to make sense of those extraordinary Chinese voyages? Zheng He's dazzling fleet is just one part of a larger picture of remarkable achievements in China and India—

---

* Disasters raised living standards by killing off large numbers of people, leaving fewer people to share the fixed pool of income. Growing wealth, on the other hand, caused people to have more babies and live longer, so incomes fell, as, over time, did population. This is called the "Malthusian trap." You can see why he's considered a pessimist.

palaces, courts, cities—at the very time that the West was moving ahead of them. The Taj Mahal was built in 1631 to honor the Mogul emperor Shah Jahan's beloved wife, Mumtaz Mahal. A British traveler, William Hodges, was one of many to point out that there was nothing like it in Europe. "The fine materials, the beautiful forms, and the symmetry of the whole," he wrote, "far surpasses anything I ever beheld." Building the Taj took enormous talent and skill, as well as astonishing feats of engineering. How could a society produce such wonders of the world and yet not move ahead more broadly? If China could put together such spectacular and sophisticated naval expeditions, why could it not make clocks?

Part of the answer lies in the way the Moguls built the Taj Mahal. Twenty thousand laborers worked night and day on the site for twenty years. They built a ramp ten miles long just to move materials up to the 187-foot-high dome. The budget was unlimited, and no value was placed on the man-hours put into the project. If you had to ask, you couldn't afford the Taj. Zheng He's flotilla was produced by a similar command system, as was Beijing's Forbidden City. Begun in 1406, the city required the labor of a million men—and another million soldiers to watch over them. If all of a large society's energies and resources are directed at a few projects, those projects often become successes—but isolated successes. The Soviet Union boasted an extraordinary space program well into the 1970s, even though by then it was technologically the most backward of all the industrial nations.

But throwing more manpower at a problem is not the path to innovation. The historian Philip Huang makes a fascinating comparison between the farmers of the Yangtze Delta and those of England, the richest regions of China and Europe respectively in 1800.[6] He points out that, by some measures, the two areas might seem to have been at equivalent economic levels. But in fact, Britain was far ahead in the key measure of growth—labor productivity. The Chinese were able to make their land highly productive, but they did so by putting more and more people to work on a given acre—what Huang calls "output without development." The English, on the other hand, kept searching for ways to make labor more productive, so that each farmer was producing more crops. They discovered new labor-saving devices, using animals and inventing machines. When the multi-spindle wheel, which required one trained operator, was developed, for example, it was widely adapted in England. But in China, the inferior but cheaper single spindle persisted, because it could be used by many untrained operators. (Since labor had little value, why spend money on labor-saving machines?) Ultimately, the result was that a small number of Britons were able to farm huge swaths of land. By the eighteenth century, the average farm size in southern England was 150 acres; in the Yangtze delta, it was about 1 acre.

The naval expeditions also illustrate the difference in the Eastern and Western approaches. The European missions were less grand but more productive. They were often entirely private or public-private partnerships and used new methods to pay for the trips. The Dutch pioneered innovations in finance and taxation; their herring traders were using futures contracts widely by the 1580s. And these financial mechanisms marked a crucial advance, because they ensured funding for an ever-increasing number of expeditions. Each trip was intended to turn a profit, make new discoveries, and find new products. The project moved forward by trial and error, with every expedition building on past ones. Over time, a chain reaction of entrepreneurship, exploration, science, and learning developed.

In China, by contrast, the voyages depended on the interests and power of one monarch. When he was gone, they stopped. In one case, a new emperor even ordered the destruction of ship schematics, so the capacity to build them was lost. The Chinese used cannons effectively in the thirteenth century. Three hundred years later, they couldn't operate one without a European to show them how. The Harvard economic historian David Landes concludes that China failed to "generate a continuous, self-sustaining process of scientific and technological advance."[7] Its achievements ended up being episodic and ephemeral. This was the tragedy of Asia: even when there was knowledge, there was no learning.

Is Culture Destiny?

Why did non-Western countries stand still while the West moved forward? These questions have been debated for centuries, and there is no neat answer. Private property rights, good institutions of governance, and a strong civil society (that is, one not dominated by the state) were clearly crucial for growth in Europe and, later, the United States. In contrast, the Russian czar theoretically owned his entire country. In China, the Ming court was run by mandarins who disdained commerce. Almost everywhere in the non-Western world, civil society was weak and dependent on the government. Local businessmen in India were always captive to the whims of the court. In China, rich merchants would abandon their businesses to master Confucian classics so that they could become favorites of the court.

The Moguls and the Ottomans were warriors and aristocrats who thought of trade as unglamorous and unimportant (even though the Middle East had a long merchant tradition). In India, this bias was reinforced by the low position of businessmen in the Hindu caste hierarchy. Historians have taken particular note of Hindu beliefs and practices as barriers to development. Paul Kennedy argues, "The sheer rigidity of Hindu religious taboos militated against modernization: rodents and insects could not be killed, so vast amounts of foodstuffs were lost; social mores about handling refuse and excreta led to permanently insanitary conditions, a breeding ground for bubonic plagues; the caste system throttled initiative, instilled ritual, and restricted the market; and the influence wielded over Indian local rulers by the Brahman priests meant that this obscurantism was effective at the highest level."[8] J. M. Roberts makes a broader point about the Hindu worldview, observing that it was "a vision of endless cycles of creation and reabsorbtion into the divine [which led] to passivity and skepticism about the value of practical action."[9]

But if culture is everything, how to account for China and India now? Today, their remarkable growth is often explained with paeans to their distinctive cultures. Confucianism was once bad for growth; now it is good. The Hindu mind-set, once an impediment, is now seen to embody a kind of practical worldliness that undergirds entrepreneurial capitalism. The success of the Chinese and Hindu diaspora seemingly provides daily confirmation of such theories.

The late Daniel Patrick Moynihan, America's leading scholar-senator, once said, "The central conservative truth is that it is culture, not politics, that determines the success of a society. The central liberal truth is that politics can change a culture and save it from itself." That gets it just about right. Culture is important, terribly important. But it can change. Cultures are complex. At any given moment, certain attributes are prominent and seem immutable. And then politics and economics shift, and those attributes wane in importance, making space for others. The Arab world was once the center of science and trade. In recent decades, its chief exports have been oil and Islamic fundamentalism. Any cultural argument must be able to explain both periods of success and periods of failure.

Why was Asian commercialism—so prominent now—buried for centuries? A large part of the explanation must lie in the structure of their states. Most countries in Asia had powerful and centralized predatory states that extracted taxes from their subjects without providing much in return. From the fifteenth century through the nineteenth, Asian rulers largely fit the stereotype of the Oriental tyrant. After the Moguls swept into India from the north in the fifteenth century, their rapacious rule consisted of demanding taxes and tributes and building palaces and forts while neglecting infrastructure, communications, trade, and discovery. (The reign of Akbar, 1556–1605, was a brief exception.) Hindu princes in southern India were not much better. Businessmen had to keep interest rates high in anticipation of frequent and arbitrary taxation by their rulers. No one had much of an incentive to build wealth, since it was likely to be confiscated.

In the Middle East, centralization came much later. When the region was ruled in a relatively lax and decentralized manner under the Ottoman Empire, trade, commerce, and innovation flourished. Goods, ideas, and people from everywhere mingled freely. But in the twentieth century, an effort to create "modern" and powerful nation-states resulted in dictatorships that brought economic and political stagnation. Civic organizations were marginalized. With strong states and weak societies, the Arab world fell behind the rest of the world by almost every measure of progress.

Why was this type of centralized state being limited and constrained in Europe, even as it flourished in much of the non-Western world? Partly because of the Christian church, which was the first major institution that could contest the power of kings. Partly because of Europe's landed elite, which had an independent base in the countryside and acted as a check on royal absolutism. (The Magna Carta, the first great "bill of rights" of the Western world, was actually a charter of baronial privileges, forced on the king by his nobles.) Partly—and, some would say, ultimately—because of geography.

Europe is broken up by wide rivers, tall mountains, and large valleys. This topography produced many natural borders and encouraged political communities of varying sizes—city-states, duchies, republics, nations, and empires. In 1500, Europe had more than five hundred states, city-states, and principalities. This diversity meant there was constant competition of ideas, people, art, money, and weapons. People who were mistreated or shunned in one place could escape to another and thrive. States that succeeded were copied. Those that failed, died. Over time, this competition helped Europe become highly skilled at both making wealth and making war.[10]

Asia, by contrast, consists of vast flatlands—the steppes in Russia, the plains in China. Armies can move through these areas quickly and with little opposition. (The Chinese had to build the Great Wall because they could not rely on any natural barrier to protect their territory.) This geography helped sustain large, centralized land empires that were able to maintain their grip on power for centuries. Consider, for instance, the episode with which we began this chapter, the Ming dynasty's decision to end sea exploration after Zheng He's voyages. Perhaps the most notable fact about the ban on sea expeditions was that *it worked*. Such a policy could not have been implemented in Europe. No king was powerful enough to enforce such a decree, and even if one had been, the people and their expertise would have simply moved to a neighboring nation, city-state, or principality. In China, the emperor could turn back time.

Europe's waterways were also a blessing. Its rivers flowed gently into sheltered, navigable bays. The Rhine is a wide, slow-moving river that can be used as a highway for goods and people. The Mediterranean is calm, almost a lake, with many big ports. Compare this to Africa. Despite being the second-largest continent, Africa has the shortest coastline, much of which is too shallow to build major ports. Most of its big rivers—fast-moving, dramatic, vertiginous—are not navigable. Add to that the tropical heat and propensity for disease and food spoilage, and you have a compelling geographic explanation for African underdevelopment—surely not the only factor, but a significant one.

These grand explanations may make it seem as if things could not have turned out any other way, but in fact, such structural factors tell you only a society's predispositions, what the odds favor. Sometimes, the odds can be beaten. Despite its geographic diversity, Europe was once conquered by a great land empire, Rome, which tried—with diminishing success—to keep the empire centralized. The Middle East did well at one point under a vast empire. China prospered for centuries despite its flat geography, and India also had its periods of effervescence. European advantages, so clear in retrospect, were initially small and related mostly to the weapons and techniques of war. Over time, however, the advantages multiplied and reinforced each other, and the West moved further and further ahead of the rest.

The Spoils of Victory

Contact with the rest of the world stimulated Europe. The discovery of new seaways, rich civilizations, and strange peoples stirred the energy and imagination of the West. Everywhere Europeans went they found goods, markets, and opportunities. By the seventeenth century, Western nations were increasing their influence over every region and culture with which they came into contact. No part of the world would remain untouched, from the lands across the Atlantic to the far reaches of Africa and Asia. By the end of the eighteenth century, even Australia and the small islands of the South Pacific had been marked for use by Europeans. The Far East—China and Japan—at first remained insulated from this influence, but by the mid-nineteenth century they, too, fell prey to Western advances. The rise of the West led to the beginnings of a global civilization—one that was defined, shaped, and dominated by the nations of Western Europe.

Initially, Europeans were focused on finding products that people might want back home. This sometimes took the form of plunder; at other times, trade. They brought back furs from the Americas, spices from Asia, and gold and diamonds from Brazil. Soon, however, their involvement became more permanent. Their interests varied, depending on the climate. In temperate regions, starting with North and South America, Europeans settled, re-creating Western-style societies in far-off places. That was the beginning of what they called the New World. In lands they found uninhabitable, often tropical climes like Southeast Asia and Africa, they created a system of agriculture to produce crops that would be of interest in domestic markets. The Dutch set up vast farms in the East Indies, as did the Portuguese in Brazil. These were soon eclipsed by the French and English plantations in the Caribbean, which used Africans as slaves for labor.

Within a hundred years of initial European contact, one trend was unmistakable and irreversible: these encounters changed or destroyed the existing political, social, and economic arrangements in non-Western societies. The old order collapsed or was destroyed, or often a combination of the two. This was true no matter the country's size, from tiny Burma, where the traditional structure crumbled under British rule, to the large tribes of Africa, where European nations drew new borders, created new divisions, and put favored groups into power. In many cases, this external influence introduced modernity, even if sometimes accompanied by great brutality. In other cases, European influence was regressive, destroying old ways but creating little to replace them. In any event, America, Asia, and Africa were forever and irreversibly altered by their discovery by the West.

The direction of European expansion was determined by the balance of power. For several centuries, despite their mastery of the oceans, European nations did not have any military advantage over Turks and Arabs. So they traded with—but did not try to dominate—the lands of the Middle East and North Africa until the early nineteenth century. In Asia, the Europeans saw few easy pathways into the continent and instead set up trading posts and offices and contented themselves with the scraps ignored by the Chinese. In sub-Saharan Africa and the Americas, by contrast, they were clearly stronger than the natives and knew it. Portuguese expansion started in Africa, with moves into the Congo and the Zambezi in the early sixteenth century. But the climate there was inhospitable for settlement, so they turned to the Western Hemisphere.

America was a mistake—Columbus was searching for a path to the Indies and bumped up against a large obstacle—but it turned out to be a happy accident. The Americas became Europe's great escape valve for four hundred years. Europeans left for the New World for a variety of reasons—overcrowding, poverty, and religious persecution at home or simply the desire for adventure—and when they landed, they found civilizations that were sophisticated in some ways but militarily primitive. Tiny bands of European adventurers—Cortés, Pizarro—could defeat much larger native armies. This, coupled with European diseases that the natives could not withstand, led to the wholesale destruction of tribes and cultures.

Colonization was often done not by countries but by corporations. The Dutch and British East India companies were licensed monopolies, created to end competition among the businessmen of each country. The French equivalent, the Compagne des Indes, was an independently run state corporation. Initially, these commercial enterprises were uninterested in territory and concerned only with profits, but once invested in new areas, they wanted more stability and control. The European powers, meanwhile, wanted to keep rival countries out. Thus began the land grabs and construction of formal empires, of which Britain's grew to become the largest.

With formal empire came grand ambitions. Westerners began looking beyond money alone to power, influence, and culture. They became, depending on your view, ideological or idealistic. European institutions, practices, and ideas were introduced and imposed, though always maintaining racial preferences—the British court system was brought to India, for example, but Indian magistrates could not try whites. Over time, the European impact on its colonies was huge. And it then spread well beyond the colonies. Niall Ferguson has argued that the British empire is responsible for the worldwide spread of the English language, banking, the common law, Protestantism, team sports, the limited state, representative government, and the idea of liberty.[11] Such an argument might gloss over the hypocrisy and brutality of imperial control—economic looting, mass executions, imprisonments, torture. Some—the Dutch and the French, for example— might quibble with the exclusively English provenance of such ideas. But in any case, it is undeniable that, as a consequence of empire, European ideas and practices blanketed the globe.

Even in the Far East, where the West never made formal annexations, European impact was massive. When the weak and dysfunctional Qing court tried to ban the opium trade in the early nineteenth century, Britain—whose treasury had become addicted to revenues from opium—launched a naval attack. The Anglo-Chinese wars, often called the Opium Wars, highlighted the power gap between the two countries. At their conclusion in 1842, Beijing was forced to agree to a series of concessions over and above the resumption of the opium trade: it ceded Hong Kong, opened five ports for British residents, granted all Britons exemption from Chinese laws, and paid a large indemnity. In 1853, Western ships—this time American —entered Japanese waters and put an end to Japan's policy of "seclusion" from the world. Japan subsequently signed a series of trade treaties that gave Western countries and their citizens special privileges. Formal empire continued to grow as well, extending into the lands of the sickly Ottoman Empire as well as Africa. This process of domination culminated in the early twentieth century, at which point a handful of Western capitals ruled 85 percent of the world's land.

Westernization

In 1823, the East India Company decided to set up a school in Calcutta to train locals. It seemed wise and straightforward enough. But the policy sparked a fiery letter to Britain's prime minister, William Pitt, from a leading Indian citizen of Calcutta, Raja Ram Mohan Roy. The letter is worth quoting at length.

> When this seminary of learning was proposed . . . we were filled with sanguine hopes that this sum would be laid out in employing European gentlemen of talents and education to instruct the natives of India in Mathematics, Natural Philosophy, Chemistry, Anatomy, and other useful sciences, which the Nations of Europe have carried to a degree of perfection that has raised them above the inhabitants of other parts of the world.
>
> We now find that the Government are establishing a San-

skrit school under Hindoo Pundits to impart such knowledge as is already current in India. This seminary . . . can only be expected to load the minds of the youth with grammatical niceties and metaphysical distinctions of little or no value to the possessors or to society. . . .

The Sanskrit language, so difficult that almost a life time is necessary for its perfect acquisition, is well-known to have been for ages a lamentable check on the diffusion of knowledge. . . . Neither can much improvement arise from such speculations as the following; which are the themes suggested by the Vedant? In what manner is the soul absorbed into the deity? What relation does it bear to the divine essence? . . . I beg leave to state, with due deference to your Lordship's exalted status, that if the plan now adopted be followed, it will completely defeat the object proposed.[12]

Whenever you hear the argument that Westernization was purely a matter of arms and force, think of this letter—and hundreds of letters, memos, and orders like it. There was coercion behind the spread of Western ideas, but there were also many non-Westerners eager to learn the ways of the West. The reason for this was simple. They wanted to succeed, and people always tend to copy those who have succeeded.

The West's prowess at amassing wealth and waging war was obvious to its neighbors by the seventeenth century. One of them, Peter the Great of Russia, spent months traveling through Europe, dazzled by its industries and its militaries. Determined to learn from them, he returned home and decreed a series of radical reforms: reorganizing the army along European lines, modernizing the bureaucracy, moving the capital from Asiatic Moscow to a new, European-style city on the western edge of the Russian empire, which he named St. Petersburg. He reformed the tax code and even tinkered with the structure of the Orthodox Church to make it more Western. Men were ordered to shave their beards and wear European-style clothing. If a man persisted in the old ways, he had to pay a beard tax of one hundred rubles a year.

Since Peter the Great, there has been a long, distinguished list of non-Westerners who have sought to bring the ideas of the West to their countries. Some have been as radical as Peter. Perhaps the most famous of them was Kemal Atatürk, who took over the collapsing Ottoman state in 1922 and declared that Turkey had to abandon its past and embrace European culture to "catch up" with the West. He created a secular republic, romanized the Turkish script, abolished the veil and the fez, and dismantled all the religious underpinnings of the Ottoman caliphate. Earlier, in Japan in 1885, the great theorist of the Meiji Reformation, Yukichi Fukuzawa, wrote a famous essay, "Leaving Asia," in which he argued that Japan needed to turn its back on Asia, particularly China and Korea, and "cast its lot with the civilized countries of the West." Many Chinese reformers made similar arguments. Sun Yat-sen bluntly acknowledged Europe's superior status and the need to copy it to get ahead.

Jawaharlal Nehru, independent India's first prime minister, believed that ending his country's "backwardness" required borrowing politically and economically from the West. Having been educated at Harrow and Cambridge, he had the outlook of a Western liberal: he once privately described himself as "the last Englishman to rule India." Nehru's contemporaries around the world were similarly steeped in Western thought. Postcolonial leaders tried to free themselves from the West politically but still wanted the Western path to modernity. Even the fiercely anti-Western Gamal Abdul Nasser of Egypt wore tailored suits and read voraciously in European history. His sources for policy ideas were invariably British, French, and American scholars and writers. His favorite movie was Frank Capra's *It's a Wonderful Life*.

We sometimes recall these leaders' fiery anti-Western rhetoric and Marxist orientation and think of them as having rejected the West. In fact, they were simply borrowing from the radical traditions of the West. Marx, Engels, Rosa Luxemburg, and Lenin were all Western intellectuals. Even today, when people in Asia or Africa criticize the West, they are often using arguments that were developed in London, Paris, or New York. Osama bin Laden's critique of America in a September 2007 video tape—which included references to Noam Chomsky, inequality, the mortgage crisis, and global warming —could have been penned by a left-wing academic at Berkeley. In Joseph Conrad's *Youth*, the narrator recalls his first encounter with "the East": "And then, before I could open my lips, the East spoke to me, but it was in a Western voice. . . . The voice swore and cursed violently; it riddled the solemn peace of the bay by a volley of abuse. It began by calling me Pig, and from that went crescendo into unmentionable adjectives—in English."

Non-Western leaders who admired the West have been most impressed by its superiority at producing wealth and winning wars. After its defeat at the hand of European forces in Vienna in 1683, the Ottoman Empire decided that it had to learn from the ways of its adversaries. It bought weapons from Europe and, after realizing that it needed more than machines, started importing organizational skills, techniques, and modes of thought and behavior. By the nineteenth century, Middle Eastern commanders were organizing their troops into Western-style armies, with the same platoons and battalions, the same colonels and generals.[13] Militaries around the world converged to a single Western model. Today, whether in China, Indonesia, or Nigeria, a country's armed forces are largely standardized around a nineteenth-century Western template.

Men like Roy, Fukuzawa, and Nehru were not making an argument about intrinsic cultural superiority. They were not Uncle Toms. In Roy's letter, he repeatedly compared Indian science in his day to European science before Francis Bacon. It was history, not genetics, that mattered. Sun Yat-sen was intimately familiar with the glories of China's past and with the richness of its tradition of learning. Fukuzawa was a scholar of Japanese history. Nehru spent his years in British jails writing passionate nationalist histories of India. They all believed in the glory of their own cultures. But they also believed that at that moment in history, in order to succeed economically, politically, and militarily, they had to borrow from the West.

Modernization

The issue that non-Western reformers were struggling with in the twentieth century has returned as a central question for the future: Can you be modern without being Western? How different are the two? Will international life be substantially different in a world in which the non-Western powers have enormous weight? Will these new powers have different values? Or does the process of becoming rich make us all the same? These are not idle thoughts. In the next few decades, three of the world's four biggest economies will be non-Western (Japan, China, and India). And the fourth, the United States, will be increasingly shaped by its growing non-European population.

Some contemporary scholars, most famously Samuel P. Huntington, have argued that modernization and Westernization are wholly distinct. The West, Huntington argues, was Western before it was modern. It acquired its distinctive character around the eighth or ninth century but became "modern" only around the eighteenth century. Becoming a modern society is about industrialization, urbanization, and rising levels of literacy, education, and wealth. The qualities that make a society Western, in contrast, are special: the classical legacy, Christianity, the separation of church and state, the rule of law, civil society. "Western civilization," Huntington writes, "is precious not because it is universal but because it is unique."[14]

Add to this intellectual case the visceral strangeness of non-Western lands—the fact that they look, feel, and sound so different. The Japanese offer the most common illustration of this point. Japan is a highly modern nation. In terms of technology —high-speed trains, cell phones, robotics—it is more cutting-edge than most Western countries. But to outsiders, particularly Western visitors, it remains strange and foreign. If wealth did not Westernize Japan, the argument goes, it will not Westernize the rest. A world in which Indians, Chinese, Brazilians, and Russians are all richer and more confident will be a world of enormous cultural diversity and exoticism.

Still, the West has been around for so long and has spread so far that it isn't clear what the break between modernization and Westernization will mean. So much of what we think of as

modern is, at least outwardly, Western. Today's forms of government, business, leisure, sports, vacations, and holidays all
have their origins in European customs and practices. Christmas is celebrated in more places today than ever before—even
if it means no more than champagne, lights, and gifts (champagne itself, of course, is a Western invention). Valentine's
Day, named in honor of a Christian saint and commercialized
by Western greeting card companies, is becoming a thriving
tradition in India. Blue jeans were created as the perfect fit for
rugged California gold miners, but now are as ubiquitous in
Ghana and Indonesia as in San Francisco. It's difficult to
imagine what the modern world would look like without the
impact of the West.

Kishore Mahbubani, a thoughtful Singaporean diplomat
and intellectual, recently predicted that, in the emerging world
order, non-Western powers would retain their distinctive ways
even as they got richer. In India, he argued in a speech in
2006, the number of women wearing saris (the traditional
Indian dress) would actually grow.[15] But in fact, while Mahbubani was proclaiming the sari's rise, the Indian press was
reporting precisely the opposite phenomenon. Over the last
decade, Indian women have been casting aside the sari for
more functional attire. The elaborate sari industry, with its different materials, weaves, and styles, is declining even in the
midst of India's heady boom. (Why? Well, ask a young Indian
professional to explain whether wrapping herself in six to nine
yards of fabric, often starched, then carefully pleating and
folding it, is something of a bother.) Increasingly, Indian
women are following a kind of fusion fashion that combines
indigenous and international styles. The Indian *salwar kurta* (a
loose-fitting pant-tunic combination), for example, has gained

widespread use. Saris are being relegated to special and cere-
monial occasions, just like the kimono in Japan.

This might seem superficial, but it isn't. Women's clothing is
a powerful indicator of a society's comfort with modernity.
Not surprisingly, the Muslim world has the biggest problems
with its women wearing Western-style clothes. It is also the
region where women remain the farthest behind by any objective yardstick—literacy, education, participation in the workforce. The veil and chador might be perfectly acceptable
choices of dress, but they coincide with an outlook that rejects
the modern world in other ways as well.

For men, Western clothing is ubiquitous. Ever since armies
began dressing in Western-style uniforms, men around the
world have adopted Western-style work clothes. The business
suit, a descendant of a European army officer's outfit, is now
standard for men from Japan to South Africa to Peru—with
the laggard (or rebel) once again being the Arab world. The
Japanese, for all their cultural distinctiveness, go one step further and on special occasions (such as the swearing in of their
government) wear morning coats and striped pants, the style
for Edwardian diplomats in England a hundred years ago. In
India, wearing traditional clothes was long associated with
patriotism; Gandhi insisted on it, as a revolt against British
tariffs and British textiles. Now the Western business suit has
become the standard attire for Indian businessmen and even
many young government officials, which speaks of a new postcolonial phase in India.* In the United States, of course, many

---

* Not entirely. The gender difference persists. While successful Indian men in government and business now routinely wear Western dress, many fewer prominent Indian
women do the same.

businessmen in new industries dispense with formal dress altogether, adopting a casual jeans-and-T-shirt style. This, too, has caught on in some other countries, especially with younger people in technology-based industries. The pattern remains the same. Western styles have become the standard mode of work dress for men, signifying modernity.

The Death of the Old Order

Westernization is not merely about appearances. Executives all over the world manage their companies by means of what we could call "standard" business practices. The truth is that these standards, from double-entry bookkeeping to dividends, are all Western in origin. And it's not just true of business. Over the last two centuries, and especially the last two decades, government institutions everywhere have also become more alike, encompassing parliaments, regulatory agencies, and central banks. Surveying several countries in Europe and Latin America, two scholars found that the number of independent regulatory agencies (American-style bodies) rose sevenfold between 1986 and 2002.[16] Even politics has an increasingly familiar feel across the globe. American consultants are routinely paid princely fees to tell Asian and Latin American politicians how best to appeal to their own countrymen.

Books, movies, and television showcase distinctly local tastes, but the structure of these industries (as well as many aspects of the content) is becoming more standardized. Bollywood, for instance, is moving away from its tradition of cheap budgets and lengthy run times, toward shorter, more commercial films with Hollywood investors and export potential.[17] Walk down a street anywhere in the industrialized world today, and you see variations on the same themes—bank machines, coffeehouses, clothing stores with their seasonal sales, immigrant communities, popular culture and music.

What is vanishing in developing countries is an old high culture and traditional order. It is being eroded by the rise of a mass public, empowered by capitalism and democracy. This is often associated with Westernization because what replaces the old—the new dominant culture—looks Western, and specifically American. McDonald's, blue jeans, and rock music have become universal, crowding out older, more distinctive forms of eating, dressing, and singing. But the story here is about catering to a much larger public than the small elite who used to define a country's mores. It all looks American because America, the country that invented mass capitalism and consumerism, got there first. The impact of mass capitalism is now universal. The French have been decrying the loss of their culture for centuries, when, in fact, all that has happened is the decline of a certain old and hierarchical order. Did the majority of French people, most of whom were poor peasants, eat at authentic bistros—or anywhere outside their homes—in the nineteenth century? Chinese opera is said to be dying. But is that because of Westernization or because of the rise of China's mass culture? How many Chinese peasants listened to opera in their villages decades ago? The new mass culture has become the most important culture because, in a democratic age, quantity trumps quality. How many listen matters more than *who* listens.

Consider the changes in one of the most traditional places in the world. In 2004, Christian Caryl, a *Newsweek* foreign correspondent, moved to Tokyo, having spent the preceding decade in Moscow and Berlin. He expected to find the exotic and deeply insular country he had read about. "What I have found, instead," he wrote in an essay, "is another prosperous and modern Western country with some interesting quirks—an Asian nation that would not feel out of place if it were suddenly dropped inside the borders of Europe."[18] "We moved into our new house," he recalled, "and soon found ourselves preparing for our first bizarre Japanese holiday: Halloween." He quoted the American scholar Donald Richie, who has lived and taught in Japan for fifty years, explaining that young Japanese students today cannot understand the world of their parents, with its formalism, manners, and etiquette. "They don't know anything about the family system because the family system doesn't exist anymore," says Richie. "So I have to reconstruct it for them." The traditional, intricately polite version of Japanese used in the movies sounds alien to them, as if it came from a "vanished" world.

What sounds young and modern today is English. No language has ever spread so broadly and deeply across the world. The closest comparison is with Latin during the Middle Ages, and it is a poor one. Latin was used by a narrow elite in a time of widespread illiteracy, and most non-Western countries were not even part of the Christian world. Today, almost one-fourth of the planet's population, 1.5 billion people, can speak some English. And the rate of English's spread is increasing almost everywhere, from Europe to Asia to Latin America. Globalization, which brings ever more contact and commerce, creates an incentive for an easy means of communication. The larger the number of players, the greater the need for a common standard. Some 80 percent of the electronically stored information in the world is in English. When diplomats from the twenty-five governments of the European Union gather to discuss business in Brussels, they have hundreds of interpreters. But mostly they all speak English.

Does a common language make people think in similar ways? We will never know for sure. Over the last century, however, English has become the language of modernity. The word for tank in Russian is "tank." When Indians speaking in Hindi want to say nuclear, they usually say "nuclear." In French, weekend is "le weekend." In Spanish, Internet is "Internet." And increasingly, the English that people speak is Americanized, with certain distinctive features. It is colloquial, irreverent, and casual. Perhaps that irreverence will spill over into other realms.

Of course, that possibility worries the elders. Most newly modernizing societies want to combine their new wealth with elements of the old order. "We have left the past behind," Lee Kuan Yew said to me about his part of the world, "and there is an underlying unease that there will be nothing left of us which is part of the old." But even this anxiety is familiar from the Western experience. When Asian leaders today speak of the need to preserve their distinctive Asian values, they sound just like Western conservatives who have sought to preserve similar moral values for centuries. "Wealth accumulates and men decay," wrote the poet Oliver Goldsmith in 1770 as England industrialized. Perhaps China and India will go through their own Victorian era, a time when energetic capitalism went alongside social conservatism. And perhaps that combination will endure. After all, the appeal of tradition and family values remains strong in some very modern countries—the United States, Japan, South Korea. But in general, and over time, growing wealth and individual opportunity does produce a social transformation. Modernization brings about some form of women's liberation. It overturns the hierarchy of age, religion, tradition, and feudal order. And all of this makes societies look more and more like those in Europe and North America.

The Mixed-up Future

When thinking about what the world will look like as the rest rise and the West wanes, I am always reminded of a brilliant Indian movie, *Shakespeare Wallah*, made in 1965. It features a troupe of traveling Shakespearean actors in postcolonial India who are coming to grips with a strange, sad fact. The many schools, clubs, and theaters that had clamored for their services are quickly losing interest. The English sahibs are gone, and there is no one left to impress with an interest in the Bard. The passion for Shakespeare, it turned out, was directly related to British rule in India. Culture follows power.

What is replacing these merry bands of minstrels? The movies. In other words, part of the story in *Shakespeare Wallah* is the rise of mass culture. Bollywood—India's indigenous mass culture—is a cultural mongrel. Because it is part of mass culture, it borrows from the world's leader in (and perhaps originator of) mass culture—the United States. Many Bollywood films are thinly disguised remakes of American classics, with six to ten songs thrown in. But they also retain core Indian elements. The stories are often full of sacrificing mothers, family squabbles, fateful separation, and superstition. The West and East are all mixed up.

The world we're entering will look like Bollywood. It will be thoroughly modern—and thus powerfully shaped by the West—

but it will also retain important elements of local culture. Chinese rock music sounds vaguely like its Western counterpart, with similar instruments and beats, but its themes, lyrics, and vocals are very Chinese. Brazilian dances combine African, Latin, and generically modern (that is, Western) moves.

Today, people around the world are becoming more comfortable putting their own indigenous imprint on modernity. When I was growing up in India, modernity was in the West. We all knew that the cutting edge of everything, from science to design, was being done there. That is no longer true. An established Japanese architect explained to me that, when he was growing up, he knew that the best and most advanced buildings were built only in Europe and America. Now, the young architects in his office see great buildings being built every month in China, Japan, the Middle East, and Latin America. Today's younger generation can stay at home and create and access their own version of modernity—as advanced as anything in the West, but more familiar.

Local and modern is growing side by side with global and Western. Chinese rock vastly outsells Western rock. Samba is booming in Latin America. Domestic movie industries everywhere, from Latin America to East Asia to the Middle East, are thriving—and even taking domestic market share from Hollywood imports. Japanese television, which used to buy vast quantities of American shows, now leans on the United States for just 5 percent of its programming.[19] France and South Korea, long dominated by American movies, now have large film industries of their own. Local modern art, often a strange mixture of abstract Western styles and traditional folk motifs, is flourishing almost everywhere in the world. You can easily be fooled by looking at the Starbucks and Coca-Cola signs around the world. The real effect of globalization has been an efflorescence of the local and modern.

Look more closely at the hegemony of English. While many more people are speaking English, the greatest growth on television, radio, and the Internet is in local languages. In India, people thought that opening up the airwaves would lead to a boom in private, all-news channels in English, the language most of the experts speak. But the bigger boom—growing at three to four times the pace—has been in programs in local languages. Hindi, Tamil, Telugu, Gujarati, and Marathi are all doing well in this globalized world. Mandarin is proliferating mightily on the web. Spanish is gaining ground in many countries, including the United States. In the first stage of globalization, everyone watched CNN. In the second stage, it was joined by the BBC and Sky News. Now every country is producing its own version of CNN—from Al Jazeera and Al Arabia to New Delhi's NDTV and Aaj Tak.

These news channels are part of a powerful trend—the growth of new narratives. When I was growing up in India, current affairs, particularly global current affairs, were defined through a Western lens. You saw the world through the eyes of the BBC and Voice of America. You understood it through *Time*, *Newsweek*, the *International Herald Tribune*, and (in the old days) the *Times* of London. Today, there are many more channels of news that, more crucially, represent many quite different perspectives on the world. If you watch Al Jazeera, you will, of course, get a view of the Arab-Israeli conflict unlike any in the West. But it is not just Al Jazeera. If you watch an Indian network, you will get a very different view of Iran's nuclear quest. Where you sit affects how you see the world.

Will these differences make "the rest" behave differently in business, government, or foreign policy? That's a complicated matter. In the world of business, the bottom line is the bottom line. But how people get there varies enormously, even within the West. The structure of economic activity in Italy is quite different from that in Britain. The American economy looks very distinct from the French economy. Japanese business practices differ from Chinese or Indian business practices. And these differences will multiply.

The same is in some ways true of foreign policy. There are some underlying realities. Basic issues of security and influencing the immediate neighborhood are crucial components of a national security policy. But beyond that, there can be real divergence, though these may or may not relate to culture. Take human rights, an issue on which non-Western countries in general and China and India in particular are likely to have very different outlooks from those of the United States. There are a couple of basic reasons for this. First, they see themselves as developing countries and, therefore, too poor to be concerned with issues of global order, particularly those that involve enforcing standards and rights abroad. Second, they are not Protestant, proselytizing powers and thus will be less eager to spread universal values across the globe. Neither Hinduism nor Confucianism believes in universal commandments or the need to spread the faith. So for both practical and cultural reasons, both countries are unlikely to view human rights issues as central to their foreign policy.

Of course, no civilization develops in a hermetic box. Even when it comes to religion and a basic worldview, countries have mixed-up backgrounds, with local elements overlaid with outside influences. India, for example, is a Hindu country that was ruled for four hundred years by Muslim dynasties, and then by a Protestant power. China did not experience direct outside rule, but its Confucian background was brutally cast aside and overlaid by Communist ideology for forty years. Japan has chosen to adopt many American styles and mind-sets over the last century. Africa has its own long-standing traditions, but it is also home to the largest and fastest-growing Christian population on earth. In Latin America, churches remain vital to the country's life in a way that is unimaginable in Europe. We hear a great deal about Protestant evangelicalism in the United States, but it is in Brazil and South Korea that it is growing fastest. If Christian values lie at the heart of the Western tradition, then how should one characterize a country like South Africa, which has more than seven thousand Christian denominations? Or Nigeria, which has more Anglicans than England?

The West and the rest have been interacting for millennia. Legend has it that Christianity came to Africa with Saint Mark in A.D. 60. Some of the earliest Christian communities in the world were settled in northern Africa. The Middle East preserved and advanced Western science for centuries. Russia has been struggling with its Western and non-Western identities for at least four hundred years. In much of the world, the West has been around so long that it is in some sense part of the fabric of that civilization. That is why it seems perfectly natural that the largest casino in the world has been built in Macao, China—and it is an imitation of St. Mark's Square in Venice, which is itself strongly influenced by Moorish (Islamic) design. Is it Chinese, Western, Moorish, or modern? Probably all of the above.

Modernity has come with the rise of the West, and so it has taken a Western face. But as the modern world expands and embraces more of the globe, modernity becomes a melting pot. Trade, travel, imperialism, immigration, and missionary work have all mixed things up. Every culture has its distinct elements, and some of them survive modernization. Others don't, and as capitalism marches on, the older feudal, formal, family-based, and hierarchical customs die—as they did in the West. The impact of modern, Western values continues to be strong. China and India might be less inclined to act on human rights, but they have to respond to the reality that this issue is on the global agenda. In the case of India, being a democracy with a liberal intellectual elite, there is a vocal constituency within the country whose outlook, on this topic, is largely shaped by Western values.

The question "Will the future be modern or Western?" is more complicated than it might seem. The only simple answer is yes. The only complex one is to look at specific countries—to understand their past and present, their culture and folkways, the manner in which they have adapted to the Western world and modernized. I will try to do that next with the two most important rising powers—India and China. This is also the best way to understand the new geopolitics. After all, the real challenge we will face in the future is not a vague one of differing attitudes but a concrete one of differing geography, history, interests, and capabilities. To speak of the "rise of Asia" misses the point. There is no such thing as Asia, which is really a Western construct. There are many very different countries that are part of that construct—China, Japan, India, Indonesia—and they harbor differences and suspicions about one another. The world looks different to China and India not simply because of who they are but also because of where they sit. The great shift taking place in the world might prove to be less about culture and more about *power*.

4

The Challenger

Americans may admire beauty, but they are truly dazzled by bigness. Think of the Grand Canyon, the California redwoods, Grand Central Terminal, Disney World, SUVs, the American armed forces, General Electric, the Double Quarter Pounder (with Cheese), and the Venti Latte. Europeans prefer complexity, the Japanese revere minimalism. But Americans like size, preferably supersize.

That's why China hits the American mind so hard. It is a country whose scale dwarfs the United States. With 1.3 billion people, it has four times America's population. For more than a hundred years, American missionaries and businessmen dreamed of the possibilities—1 billion souls to save, 2 billion armpits to deodorize—but never went beyond dreams. China was very big, but very poor. Pearl Buck's bestselling book (and play and movie), *The Good Earth*, introduced a lasting portrait of China: an agrarian society with struggling peasants, greedy landowners, famines and floods, plagues, and poverty.

Napoleon famously, and probably apocryphally, said, "Let

‿ ιina sleep, for when China wakes, she will shake the world."
And for almost two hundred years, China seemed to follow his
instruction, staying dormant and serving as little more than an
arena in which the other great powers acted out their ambitions. In the twentieth century, Japan, once China's imitator,
bested it in war and peace. During World War II, the United
States allied with it and gave it aid and, in 1945, a seat on the
UN Security Council. When Washington and Beijing became
foes after the Communist takeover of 1949, China slipped further behind. Mao Zedong dragged the country through a
series of catastrophic convulsions that destroyed its economic,
technological, and intellectual capital. Then, in 1979, things
began shaking.

China's awakening is reshaping the economic and political
landscape, but it is also being shaped by the world into which
it is rising. Beijing is negotiating the same two forces that are
defining the post-American world more broadly—globalization
and nationalism. On the one hand, economic and technological pressures are pushing Beijing toward a cooperative integration into the world. But these same forces produce disruption
and social upheaval in the country, and the regime seeks new
ways to unify an increasingly diverse society. Meanwhile,
growth also means that China becomes more assertive, casting
a larger shadow on the region and the world. The stability and
peace of the post-American world will depend, in large measure, on the balance that China strikes between these forces of
integration and disintegration.

When historians look back at the last decades of the twentieth century, they might well point to 1979 as a watershed.
That year, the Soviet Union invaded Afghanistan, digging its
grave as a superpower. And that year, China launched its eco-

nomic reforms. The signal for the latter event came in December 1978 at an unlikely gathering: the Third Plenum of the Eleventh Central Committee of the Communist Party of China, typically an occasion for empty rhetoric and stale ideology. Before the formal meeting, at a working-group session, the newly empowered party boss, Deng Xiaoping, gave a speech that turned out to be the most important in modern Chinese history. He urged that the regime focus on economic development and let facts—not ideology—guide its path. "It doesn't matter if it is a black cat or a white cat," Deng said. "As long as it can catch mice, it's a good cat." Since then, China has done just that, pursuing a path of modernization that is ruthlessly pragmatic.

The results have been astonishing. China has grown over 9 percent a year for almost thirty years, the fastest rate for a major economy in recorded history. In that same period, it has moved around 400 million people out of poverty, the largest reduction that has taken place anywhere, anytime. The average Chinese person's income has increased nearly sevenfold. China, despite drawbacks and downsides, has achieved, on a massive scale, the dream of every Third World country—a decisive break with poverty. The economist Jeffrey Sachs puts it simply: "China is the most successful development story in world history."

The magnitude of change in China is almost unimaginable. The size of the economy has *doubled* every eight years for three decades. In 1978, the country made 200 air conditioners a year; in 2005, it made 48 million. China today exports in a single day more than it exported in all of 1978. For anyone who has been visiting the country during this period, there are more examples and images of change than one can recount.

Fifteen years ago, when I first went to Shanghai, Pudong, in the east of the city, was undeveloped countryside. Today, it is the city's financial district, densely studded with towers of glass and steel and lit like a Christmas tree every night. It is eight times the size of London's new financial district, Canary Wharf, and only slightly smaller than the entire city of Chicago. The city of Chongqing, meanwhile, actually patterns itself after Chicago, which was the world's fastest-growing city a hundred years ago. Chongqing, which is expanding every year by 300,000 people, would probably get that designation today. And Chongqing is just the head of a pack; the twenty fastest-growing cities in the world are all in China.

Despite Shanghai's appeal to Westerners, Beijing remains the seat of Chinese politics, culture, and art, and even its economy. The city is being remade to an extent unprecedented in history. (The closest comparison is Haussmann's makeover of Paris in the nineteenth century.) Largely in preparation for the 2008 Olympics, Beijing is building six new subway lines, a 43-kilometer light-rail system, a new airport terminal (the world's largest, of course), 25 million square meters of new property, a 125-kilometer "green belt," and a 12-square-kilometer Olympic Park. When looking at the models of a new Beijing, one inevitably thinks of Albert Speer's grandiose plans for postwar Berlin, drawn up in the 1940s; in fact, Albert Speer Jr., the son, also an architect, designed the 8-kilometer boulevard that will run from the Forbidden Palace to the Olympic Park. He sees no real comparison between the transformation of Beijing and his father's designs for Hitler. This is "bigger," he says. "Much bigger."[1]

Every businessman these days has a dazzling statistic about China, meant to stun the listener into silence. And they are impressive numbers—most of which will be obsolete by the time you read them. China is the world's largest producer of coal, steel, and cement. It is the largest cell phone market in the world. It had 28 billion square feet of space under construction in 2005, more than five times as much as in America. Its exports to the United States have grown by 1,600 percent over the past fifteen years. At the height of the industrial revolution, Britain was called "the workshop of the world." That title belongs to China today. It manufactures two-thirds of the world's photocopiers, microwave ovens, DVD players, and shoes.

To get a sense of how completely China dominates low-cost manufacturing, take a look at Wal-Mart. Wal-Mart is one of the world's largest corporations. Its revenues are eight times those of Microsoft and account for 2 percent of America's GDP. It employs 1.4 million people, more than GM, Ford, GE, and IBM put together. It is legendary for its efficient— some would say ruthless—efforts to get the lowest price possible for its customers. To that end, it has adeptly used technology, managerial innovation, and, perhaps most significantly, low-cost manufacturers. Wal-Mart imports about $18 billion worth of goods from China each year. The vast majority of its foreign suppliers are there. Wal-Mart's global supply chain is really a China supply chain.

China has also pursued a distinctly open trade and investment policy. For this among many reasons, it is not the new Japan. Beijing has not adopted the Japanese (or South Korean) path of development, which was an export-led strategy that kept the domestic market and society closed. Instead, China opened itself up to the world. (It did this partly because it had no choice, since it lacked the domestic savings of Japan

or South Korea.) Now China's trade-to-GDP ratio is 70 percent, which makes it one of the most open economies in the
world. Over the last fifteen years, imports from the United
States have increased more than sevenfold. Procter & Gamble
now earns $2.5 billion a year in China, and familiar products
like Head & Shoulders shampoo and Pampers diapers are
extraordinarily popular with consumers there. Starbucks predicts that by 2010 it will have more cafés in China than in the
United States. China is also very open to international brand
names, whether of goods or people. Foreign architects have
built most of the gleaming towers and grand developments
that define the new China. And when looking for the man to
direct China's debut on the world stage, the Olympic opening
festivities, Beijing chose an American, Steven Spielberg. It is
inconceivable that Japan or India would have given a foreigner
such a role.

China is also the world's largest holder of money. Its
foreign-exchange reserves are $1.5 trillion, 50 percent more
than those of the next country (Japan) and three times the
holdings of the entire European Union. Holding such massive
reserves may or may not be a wise policy, but it is certainly an
indication of China's formidable resilience in the face of any
shocks or crises. At the end of the day, it is this combination of
factors that makes China unique. It is the world's largest country, fastest-growing major economy, largest manufacturer,
second-largest consumer, largest saver, and (almost certainly)
second-largest military spender.* China will not replace the

---

* China's official military budget would put it third in the world, after the United
States and the United Kingdom. But most analysts agree that many large expenditures
are not placed on the official budget, and that, properly accounted for, China's military
spending is second—though a *very* distant second—to that of the United States.

United States as the world's superpower. It is unlikely to sur-
pass it on any dimension—military, political, or economic—for
decades, let alone have dominance in all areas. But on issue
after issue, it has become the second-most-important country
in the world, adding a wholly new element to the international
system.

Central Planning That Works?

There are those who doubt China's economic record. Some
journalists and scholars argue that the numbers are fudged,
corruption is rampant, banks are teetering on the edge,
regional tensions are mounting, inequality is rising dangerously
—and the situation is coming to a head. It's only fair to point
out that many of them have been saying this for two decades
now, and so far, at least, their central prediction—regime
collapse—has not taken place. China has many problems, but
it still has one thing that every developing country would kill
for—robust growth. An expanding pie makes every other problem, however grave, somewhat more manageable. One of the
regime's most intelligent critics, the scholar Minxin Pei, readily acknowledges that "compared with other developing countries, the Chinese story is far more successful than any we can
think of."

For a regime that is ostensibly Communist, Beijing is astonishingly frank in its acceptance of capitalism. I asked a Chinese official once what the best solution to rural poverty was.
His answer: "We have to let markets work. They draw people
off the land and into industry, out of farms and into cities. Historically that has been the only answer to rural poverty. We

have to keep industrializing." When I have put the same question to Indian or Latin American officials, they launch into
complicated explanations of the need for rural welfare, subsidies for poor farmers, and other such programs, all designed to
slow down market forces and retard the historical—and often
painful—process of market-driven industrialization.

But Beijing's approach has also been different from that
advocated by many free-market economists—a program of
simultaneous reforms on all fronts that is sometimes called the
"Washington consensus." Most significantly, it is different
from Russia's shock therapy approach under Boris Yeltsin,
which Chinese leaders studied carefully and often cite as a
negative example, probably agreeing with Strobe Talbot's
pithy description when he served in the Clinton administration: "Too much shock, too little therapy." Rather than a big
bang, Beijing chose an incremental approach, one that I
would call a grow-the-denominator strategy. Instead of immediately shutting down all inefficient enterprises, ending bad
loans, and enacting large-scale privatization, it adopted policies that grew the economy around these loss-making areas, so
that over time bad areas become a smaller and smaller part of
the overall economy (the denominator). By doing this, Beijing
bought time to solve its problems gradually. Only now is it
starting to clean up its banks and financial sector, ten years
after most experts urged it to, and it is doing so at a far slower
pace than experts recommended. Today, it can implement
such reforms in the context of an economy that has doubled in
size and diversified considerably. It's capitalism with Chinese
characteristics.

Central planning was not supposed to work. And in some
sense it doesn't, even in China. Beijing has much less knowl-

edge and control of the rest of China than it would like and than outsiders recognize. One figure tells the story. The Chinese central government's share of tax receipts is around 50 percent;[2] the number for the U.S. federal government (a weak government by international standards) is nearly 70 percent. In other words, decentralized development is now the defining reality of economic and, increasingly, political life in China. To an extent, this loss of control is planned. The government has encouraged the blossoming of a real free market in many areas, opened the economy to foreign investment and trade, and used its membership in the World Trade Organization to force through reforms in its economy and society. Many of its successes (rising entrepreneurship) and its failures (declining health care) are the result of the *lack* of coordination between the center and the regions. This problem, of spiraling decentralization, will be China's greatest challenge, and one to which we'll return.

It is awkward to point out, but unavoidable: not having to respond to the public has often helped Beijing carry out its strategy. Other governments enviously looking on have taken note of this fact. Indian officials like to observe that their Chinese counterparts don't have to worry about voters. "We have to do many things that are politically popular but are foolish," said a senior member of the Indian government. "They depress our long-term economic potential. But politicians need votes in the short term. China can take the long view. And while it doesn't do everything right, it makes many decisions that are smart and far-sighted." This is evident in China's current push in higher education. Recognizing that the country needs a better-trained workforce in order to move up the economic value chain, the central government has committed itself to boosting scholarships and other types of aid in 2008 to $2.7 billion, up from $240 million in 2006. Officials have plans to expand overall government spending on education, which was a measly 2.8 percent of GDP in 2006, to 4 percent by 2010, a large portion of which will be devoted to a small number of globally competitive elite institutions. Such a focus would be impossible in democratic India, for example, where vast resources are spent on short-term subsidies to satisfy voters. (India's elite educational institutions, by contrast, are under pressure to limit merit-based admissions and accept half their students on the basis of quotas and affirmative action.)

It is unusual for a nondemocratic government to have managed growth effectively for so long. Most autocratic governments quickly become insular, corrupt, and stupid—and preside over economic plunder and stagnation. The record of Marcos, Mobutu, and Mugabe is far more typical. (And lest one veers into cultural explanations, keep in mind that the record of the Chinese government under Mao was atrocious.) But in China today, the government, for all its faults, maintains a strong element of basic pragmatism and competence. "I've dealt with governments all over the world," says a senior investment banker, "and the Chinese are probably the most impressive." This view is broadly representative of business leaders who travel to China. "People have to . . . make their own value judgments against what they deem to be the greater good all the time," Bill Gates told *Fortune* magazine in 2007. "I personally have found the Chinese leaders to be fairly thoughtful about these things."

This is not, however, a complete picture. While China is growing fast and opportunities abound on every level, the state—thanks to the incremental reform approach—still commands many heights in the economy. Even today, state-owned enterprises make up about half of GDP. Of the thirty-five largest companies on the Shanghai stock market, thirty-four are either partly or wholly owned by the government. And state control is often at odds with openness, honesty, and efficiency. China's banks, which remain mostly government entities, disperse tens of billions of dollars a year to shore up ailing companies and funnel money to regions, groups, and people for noneconomic reasons. Corruption appears to be rising, and the share of corruption cases involving high-level officials is up dramatically, from 1.7 percent in 1990 to 6.1 percent in 2002.[3] Regional differences are widening, and inequality is skyrocketing, causing social tensions. A much cited statistic— from the government itself—tells of an important trend. In 2004, there were 74,000 protests of some kind or the other in China; ten years earlier, there were just 10,000.

These two pictures can be reconciled. China's problems are in many ways a consequence of its success. Unprecedented economic growth has produced unprecedented social change. China has compressed the West's two hundred years of industrialization into thirty. Every day, tens of thousands of people are moving from villages to cities, from farms to factories, from west to east, at a pace never before seen in history. They are not just moving geographically; they are leaving behind family, class, and history. It is hardly a surprise that the Chinese state is struggling to keep up with this social upheaval. In describing the declining capacity of the Chinese state, Minxin Pei points out that the authorities cannot manage something as simple as road safety anymore: the fatality rate is 26 per 10,000 vehicles (compared with 20 in India and 8 in Indonesia).[4] But it is, at the same time, crucial to note that the number of cars on China's roads has been growing by 26 percent a year, compared with 17 percent for India and 6 percent for Indonesia. When India overtakes China in growth, as it is set to do, I would wager that it will also see a marked rise in its accident rate, democratic government or not.

Consider the environmental consequences of China's growth—not to the planet as a whole but to China itself. Some 26 percent of the water in China's largest river systems is so polluted that they have "lost the capacity for basic ecological function."[5] There are nine thousand chemical plants along the banks of the Yangtze River alone. Beijing is already the world's capital according to one measure—air pollution. Of China's 560 million urban residents, only 1 percent breathe air considered safe by European Union standards.[6] But it is also worth pointing out that almost all these figures and assessments come from the Chinese government. Beijing has placed environmental considerations higher on its agenda than most developing countries have. Senior officials in China talk about the need for green GDP and growth with balance, and environmental considerations figure prominently in President Hu Jintao's plan for a "harmonious society." One Western consulting firm has examined China's new laws regarding air pollution and calculated that demand for products that remove particulates from the air will increase 20 percent a year for the foreseeable future, creating a $10 billion market. Beijing is trying to manage a difficult dilemma: reducing poverty requires robust growth, but growth means more pollution and environmental degradation.

The greatest problem China faces going forward is not that its government is incurably evil; it is the risk that its government will lose the ability to hold things together—a problem that encompasses but goes well beyond spiraling decentralization. China's pace of change is exposing the weaknesses of its Communist Party and state bureaucracy. For several years, the government's monopoly on power allowed it to make massive reforms quickly. It could direct people and resources where needed. But one product of its decisions is economic, social, and political turmoil, and the insular and hierarchical structure of the party makes it less competent to navigate these waters. The Communist Party of China—the party of workers and peasants—is actually one of the most elite organizations in the world. It is composed of 3 million largely urban educated men and women, a group that is thoroughly unrepresentative of the vast peasant society that it leads. Few of its high officials have real retail political skills. Those promoted tend to be good technocrats who are also skilled at the art of intraparty maneuvering and patronage. It remains to be seen whether these leaders have the charisma or ability to engage in mass politics—the skills they will need to govern a population of 1.3 billion people that is becoming increasingly assertive.

In places like Taiwan and South Korea in the 1970s and 1980s, economic growth was accompanied by gradual legal, social, and political reforms. Those regimes were authoritarian, not totalitarian—an important distinction—and thus did not seek all-encompassing control over society, which made loosening the grip easier. They were also pushed to open up their systems by the United States, their greatest benefactor. Beijing faces no such pressures. As China changes, the totalitarian structure has cracked, or become irrelevant, in places. People have many more choices and freedoms than before. They can work, move, own property, start businesses, and, to a limited extent, worship whomever they want. But political control remains tight and shows little signs of easing in certain core areas. For example, Beijing has developed an elaborate system to monitor use of the Internet that has been surprisingly effective.

The Communist Party spends an enormous amount of time and energy worrying about social stability and popular unrest. This is surely a sign that it faces a problem of uncertain dimensions and with no clear solution. Compare that with China's democratic neighbor to the south. India's politicians worry about many things—mostly losing elections—but rarely about social revolution or the survival of the regime itself. They don't panic at the thought of protests or strikes, instead viewing them as part of the normal back-and-forth between ruler and ruled. Governments that are confident about their systemic legitimacy don't get paranoid about an organization like the Falun Gong, whose members gather together for breathing exercises.

Many American writers have rushed to claim that China disproves the notion that economic reforms lead to political reform—that capitalism leads to democracy. China might yet prove to be an exception, but it is too soon to tell. The rule has held everywhere from Spain and Greece to South Korea, Taiwan, and Mexico: countries that marketize and modernize begin changing politically around the time that they achieve middle-income status (a rough categorization, that lies somewhere between $5,000 and $10,000).* Since China's income

---

* This is a tough statistic to get exactly right because researchers have used different yardsticks (PPP, 1985 dollars, etc.). But the basic point that China is below the threshold for democratic transition is accurate.

level is still below that range, it cannot be argued that the country has defied this trend. And as Chinese standards of living rise, political reform is becoming an increasingly urgent issue. The regime will almost certainly face significant challenges over the next fifteen years, even if this does not mean that China will turn into a Western-style liberal democracy overnight. It is more likely to evolve first into a "mixed" regime, much like many Western countries in the nineteenth century or East Asian countries in the 1970s and 1980s, which combined popular participation with some elements of hierarchy and elite control. Keep in mind that Japan is the most mature democracy in East Asia, and it has a ruling party that has never lost power in sixty years.

In late 2006, in a meeting with a visiting American delegation, Chinese Premier Wen Jiabao was asked what Chinese leaders meant by the word "democracy" when they spoke about China's movement toward it. Wen explained that for them it contained three key components: "elections, judicial independence, and supervision based on checks and balances." John Thornton, the Goldman Sachs executive turned China scholar who was leading the delegation, researched those three areas thoroughly and found that there had been some (small) movement toward provincial elections, more anticorruption measures, and even more movement toward a better system of law. In 1980, Chinese courts accepted 800,000 cases; in 2006, they accepted ten times that number. In a balanced essay in *Foreign Affairs*, Thornton paints a picture of a regime hesitantly and incrementally moving toward greater accountability and openness.[7]

Incremental steps may not be enough. China's ruling Communists should read, or reread, their Marx. Karl Marx was a lousy economist and ideologist, but he was a gifted social scientist. One of his central insights was that, when a society changes its economic foundation, the political system that rests on it inevitably changes as well. As societies become more market-oriented, Marx argued, they tend to turn toward democracy. The historical record confirms this connection between market economics and democracy, though naturally with some time lags. Excluding countries whose wealth comes from oil, in the entire world today there is only one country that has reached a Western level of economic development and is still not a fully functioning democracy—Singapore. But Singapore, a small city-state with an abnormally competent ruling elite, remains an unusual exception. Many leaders have tried to replicate Lee Kuan Yew's balancing act, creating wealth and modernity while maintaining political dominance. None has succeeded for long. And even Singapore is changing rapidly, becoming a more open society—even, on some issues (especially cultural and social issues like homosexuality), more open than other East Asian societies. Looking at dozens of countries over decades of development, from South Korea to Argentina to Turkey, one finds that the pattern is strong—a market-based economy that achieves middle-income status tends, over the long run, toward liberal democracy. It may be, as many scholars have noted, the single most important and well-documented generalization in political science.

Many in China's younger generation of leaders understand the dilemma their country faces and talk privately about the need to loosen up their political system. "The brightest people in the party are not studying economic reform," a young Chinese journalist well connected to the leadership in Beijing told me. "They are studying political reform." Ministers in Singapore confirm that Chinese officials are spending a great deal of time studying the system Lee Kuan Yew built, and the Communist Party has also sent delegations to Japan and Sweden to try to understand how those countries have created a democratic polity dominated by a single party. They look at the political system, the electoral rules, the party's formal and informal advantages, and the hurdles outsiders have to cross. Whether these are sham exercises or efforts to find new ways to maintain control, they suggest that the party knows it needs to change. But the challenge for China is not technocratic; it is political. It is a matter not of reconfiguring power but of relinquishing power—breaking down vested interests, dismantling patronage networks, and forsaking institutionalized privileges. None of this would mean giving up control of the government, at least not yet, but it would mean narrowing its scope and role and authority. And with all its new management training, is China's Communist Party ready to take that great leap forward?

Most autocratic regimes that have modernized their economies—Taiwan, South Korea, Spain, Portugal—have weathered the political changes that followed and emerged with greater stability and legitimacy. Beijing has faced challenges before and adapted. And even if the regime mismanages this transition, political upheaval and turmoil will not necessarily stop China from growing. Whatever the future of its politics, it is unlikely that China's emergence onto the world stage will be reversed. The forces fueling its rise will not disappear even if the current regime collapses—or, more likely, splits into factions. After its revolution, France went through two centuries of political crisis, running through two empires, one quasi-fascist dictatorship, and four republics. Yet through the political tumult, it thrived economically, remaining one of the richest countries in the world.

China is hungry for success and this might well be a key reason for its enduring rise. In the twentieth century, after hundreds of years of poverty, the country went through imperial collapse, civil war, and revolution only to find itself in Mao's hellish version of communism. It lost 38 million people in the Great Leap Forward, a brutal experiment in collectivization. Then it burrowed itself deeper in isolation and destroyed its entire professional and academic class during the Cultural Revolution. Unlike India, which could be proud of its democracy despite slow economic growth, China by the 1970s was bereft of any reason to raise its head high. Then came Deng's reforms. Today, China's leaders, businessmen, and people in general have one desire in common: they want to keep moving ahead. They are unlikely to cast aside casually three decades of relative stability and prosperity.

Hiding Its Light

Whatever happens to China internally is likely to complicate life internationally. Its range of strengths—economic, political, military—ensure that its influence extends well beyond its borders. Countries with this capacity are not born every day. The list of current ones—the United States, Britain, France, Germany, Russia—has gone mostly unchanged for two centuries. Great powers are like divas: they enter and exit the international stage with great tumult. Think of the rise of Germany and Japan in the early twentieth century, or the decline of the Hapsburg and Ottoman empires in that same period, which produced multiple crises in the Balkans and the messy modern Middle East.

In recent years, that pattern has not quite held. Modern-day Japan and Germany have become the world's second- and third-largest economies but stayed remarkably inactive politically and militarily. And, so far, China has come into its own with little disruption. For the first decade of its development, the 1980s, China did not really have a foreign policy. Or, more accurately, its growth strategy *was* its grand strategy. Beijing saw good relations with America as key to its development, in part because it wanted access to the world's largest market and most advanced technology. In the UN Security Council, China usually voted for, or at least abstained from vetoing, American-sponsored resolutions. More broadly, it kept its head down in an effort, as Deng put it, to "hide its light under a bushel." This policy of noninterference and nonconfrontation mostly persists. With the exception of anything related to Taiwan, Beijing tends to avoid picking a fight with other governments. The focus remains on growth. In his two-and-a-half-hour address to the Seventeenth Party Congress in 2007, President Hu Jintao addressed economic, financial, industrial, social, and environmental issues in great detail—but neglected foreign policy almost entirely.

Many veteran Chinese diplomats get nervous talking about their country's rise to power. "It frightens me," said Wu Jianmin, the president of China's Foreign Affairs University and a former ambassador to the United Nations. "We are still a poor country, a developing country. I don't want people to think of us in . . . exaggerated terms." Xinghai Fang, the deputy CEO of the Shanghai Stock Exchange, spoke in the same vein: "Please remember, America's per capita GDP is twenty-five times ours. We have a long way to go." Such anxiety has manifested itself in an interesting debate within China over how Beijing should articulate its foreign policy doctrine. In 2002, Zheng Bijian, then deputy head of the Central Party School, coined the term "peaceful rise" to convey China's intention to move quietly up the global ladder. When Zheng spoke, people listened, because his former boss was President Hu Jintao. Hu and Premier Wen Jiabao both used the phrase subsequently, giving it official sanction. But then it fell out of favor.

Many Western analysts thought that the problem with the phrase was the word "peaceful," which could limit China's options on Taiwan. In fact, there wasn't much internal division on that matter. China regards Taiwan as a domestic matter and believes that it has all the authority it needs to use force, though as a last resort. As Zheng explained to me, "Lincoln fought a war to preserve the Union, but you can still say that the United States was rising peacefully." Some key Chinese leaders are instead worried about the phrase's second word, "rise." (A more accurate translation would be "thrust" or "surge.") Senior diplomats recoiled at the idea of going around the world talking up China's rise. In particular, they worried about critics in the United States who would see China's rise as a threat. Lee Kuan Yew suggested to Beijing that it speak of a "renaissance" rather than a rise, and party leaders argued about the phrase during a retreat at Beidaihe in the summer of 2003. Since then, they have talked about "peaceful development." "The concept is the same," said Zheng. "It's just a different phrase." True, but the shift reflects China's concern with not ruffling any feathers as it steams ahead.

The regime is working to make sure the Chinese people understand its strategy as well. In 2006 and 2007, Chinese television aired a twelve-part series, *The Rise of the Great Nations*, clearly designed as an act of public education.[8] Given the intensely political nature of the subject matter, one can be certain that it was carefully vetted to present views that the government wished to be broadcast. The series was thoughtful and intelligent, produced in BBC or PBS style, and it covered the rise of nine great powers, from Portugal and Spain to the Soviet Union and the United States, complete with interviews with scholars from around the world. The sections on the individual countries are mostly accurate and balanced. The rise of Japan, an emotional topic in China, is handled fairly, with little effort to whip up nationalist hysteria about Japanese attacks on China; Japan's postwar economic rise is praised repeatedly. Some points of emphasis are telling. The episodes on the United States, for example, deal extensively with Theodore and Franklin Roosevelt's programs to regulate and tame capitalism, highlighting the state's role in capitalism. And there are a few predictable, but shameful, silences, such as the complete omission of the terror, the purges, or the Gulag from an hour-long program on the Soviet Union. But there are also startling admissions, including considerable praise of the U.S. and British systems of representative government for their ability to bring freedom, legitimacy, and political stability to their countries.

The basic message of the series is that a nation's path to greatness lies in its economic prowess and that militarism, empire, and aggression lead to a dead end. That point is made repeatedly. The final episode—explicitly on the "lessons" of the series—lays out the keys to great power: national cohesiveness, economic and technological success, political stability, military strength, cultural creativity, and magnetism. The last is explained as the attractiveness of a nation's ideas, corresponding with concept of "soft power" developed by Joseph Nye, one of the scholars interviewed for the series. The episode ends with a declaration that, in the new world, a nation can sustain its competitive edge only if it has the knowledge and technological capacity to keep innovating. In short, the path to power is through markets, not empires.

God and Foreign Policy

Is China's way of thinking about the world distinctly, well, Chinese? In many senses, it is not. The lessons drawn from that history of great powers are ones many Westerners have drawn as well—indeed, many of the people interviewed were Western scholars. It reflects the same understanding that has driven the behavior of Germany and Japan in recent years. China's dealings with the world are practical, reflecting context and interests and its self-perception as a developing country. Despite the enormous shadow that it casts on the world, China recognizes that it is still a country with hundreds of millions of extremely poor people. Its external concerns, accordingly, have to do mostly with development. When asked about issues like human rights, some younger Chinese officials will admit that these are simply not their concerns—as if they see these as luxuries that they cannot afford. No doubt this sense is enhanced by the acute realization that human rights abroad are linked with those at home. If China were to criticize the Burmese dictatorship, what would it say to its own dissidents?

There are also, however, broader cultural elements in China's way of thinking about the world. One can easily exag-

gerate the importance of culture, using it as a façade for policies grounded in interest. But there are some real and important differences between Chinese and Western (particularly
American) worldviews that are worth exploring. They begin
with God. In the 2007 Pew survey, when asked whether one
must believe in God to be moral, a comfortable majority of
Americans (57 percent) said yes. In Japan and China, however,
much larger majorities said no—in China, a whopping 72 percent! This is a striking and unusual divergence from the norm,
even in Asia. The point is not that either country is immoral—
in fact all hard evidence suggests quite the opposite—but
rather that in neither country do people believe in God.

This might shock many in the West, but for scholars of the
subject, it is a well-known reality. East Asians do not believe
that the world has a Creator who laid down a set of abstract
moral laws that must be followed. That is an Abrahamic, or
Semitic, conception of God shared by Judaism, Christianity,
and Islam, but quite alien to Chinese civilization. People
sometimes describe China's religion as Confucianism. But
Joseph Needham, an eminent scholar of Confucianism, notes
that if you think of religion "as the theology of a transcendent
creator-deity," Confucianism is simply not a religion.[9] Confucius was a teacher, not a prophet or holy man in any sense. His
writings, or the fragments of them that survive, are strikingly
nonreligious. He explicitly warns against thinking about the
divine, instead setting out rules for acquiring knowledge,
behaving ethically, maintaining social stability, and creating a
well-ordered civilization. His work has more in common with
the writings of Enlightenment philosophers than with religious tracts.

In fact, during the Enlightenment, Confucius was hot. The

Confucian classics, Needham reports, "were read with avidity by all the great forerunners of the French Revolution, by Voltaire, Rousseau, d'Alembert, Diderot, etc."[10] Between 1600 and 1649, 30–50 China-related titles appeared in Europe every decade, and between 1700 and 1709, 599 works on China were published. This frenzy of publications on China coincided with the aftermath of the Thirty Years' War (1618–48), when religion had led to grotesque bloodshed. Many European liberals idealized Confucianism for its basis in natural, as opposed to divine, law. Voltaire put it simply in his *Philosophical Dictionary*: "No superstitions, no absurd legends, none of those dogmas which insult reason and nature." Immanuel Kant would later call Confucius "the Chinese Socrates." Leibniz, a philosopher who straddled the line between religiosity and secularism, went so far as to argue, "We need missionaries from the Chinese who might teach us the use and practice of natural religion. . . ."

Early Enlightenment thinkers celebrated Confucianism for its reliance on reason rather than on divinity as a guide to human affairs. A thesis developed: While Europe might be far ahead in scientific and technological progress, China had "a more advanced ethics," a "superior civil organization" (based on merit, not patronage), and a "practical philosophy," all of which "successfully produced a social peace and a well-organized social hierarchy." The "climax" of Enlightenment sinophilia came with Voltaire's 1759 *Essai sur les moeurs*, in which, according to the German scholar Thomas Fuchs, he "transformed China into a political utopia and the ideal state of an enlightened absolutism; he held up the mirror of China to provoke self-critical reflection among European monarchs."[11] In the following year, that most enlightened of monarchs, Frederick the Great, wrote his *Report of Phihihu*, a series of letters from a fictitious Chinese ambassador in Europe to the emperor of China. Frederick's purpose was to contrast the bigotry of the Catholic Church with Chinese rationality.

Westerners have often found it difficult to understand the difference between the place of religion in China and its place in the West. Consider the experiences of a Portuguese missionary in the Far East, Matteo Ricci, as recounted by the great Yale historian Jonathan Spence.* In his early days in China in the 1580s, Ricci, in an effort to present himself as an honored figure, shaved his head and beard and shrouded himself in the robes of a Buddhist. Only several years later did Ricci realize how misguided this was. Monks and holy men were not held in high esteem in China. He began traveling by sedan chair, or hiring servants to carry him on their shoulders, "as men of rank are accustomed to do," Ricci later wrote to Claudio Acquaviva, general of the Jesuits, in 1592. "[T]he name of foreigners and priests is considered so vile in China that we need this and other similar devices to show them that we are not priests as vile as their own." By 1595, Ricci had cast off the ascetic trappings of a monk, which had hindered his missionary work, and instead adopted the dress of a Confucian scholar. Ricci had at first scorned the Confucians for not believing in God, paradise, and the immortality of the soul. The Confucian school, Ricci wrote to a friend, was "the true temple of the literati." But he eventually saw that even though Confucianism maintained "a strictly neutral stance" toward matters of God and the afterlife, it had a strong sense of ethics, morality, and justice. Like other

---

* Matteo Ricci was the missionary who brought clocks to the Chinese emperor in the late sixteenth century.

Enlightenment figures, he came to believe that the West should learn from Confucianism.

What does God have to do with foreign policy? Historically, countries influenced by Christianity and Islam have developed an impulse to spread their views and convert people to their faith. That missionary spirit is evident in the foreign policy of countries as diverse as Britain, the United States, France, Saudi Arabia, and Iran. In the case of Britain and the United States, perhaps because they have been so powerful, the Protestant sense of purpose at the core of their foreign policies has made a deep mark on global affairs. China, in contrast, may never acquire a similar sense of destiny. Simply *being China*, and becoming a world power, in a sense fulfills its historical purpose. It doesn't need to spread anything to anyone to vindicate itself. So when Beijing seems bloodless in its stance on human rights, it is not simply that the regime is oppressive or takes a ruthlessly realpolitik view of its interests—though that certainly plays a role. The Chinese see these issues differently, not with a set of abstract rights and wrongs but with a sense of the practical that serves as a guiding philosophy.

Western businessmen have often noted that their Chinese counterparts seem to place less stock in rules, laws, and contracts. Their sense of ethics is more situational. If a Chinese businessman or official thinks the law is an ass (to quote an Englishman), he will ignore or go around it or simply suggest making up a new contract. The veneration of an abstract idea is somewhat alien to China's practical mind-set. Social relations and trust are far more important than paper commitments. Microsoft could not get Beijing to enforce its intellectual-property laws for years—until the company spent time and effort developing a relationship with the government and made clear that it wanted to help develop China's economy and educational system. Once Microsoft had convinced the Chinese government of its benign intentions, those same laws began to get enforced. Few Chinese have really internalized the notion that abstract rules, laws, and contracts are more important than a situational analysis of a case at hand, which means that Chinese political and legal development is likely to take a more circuitous and complex path than one might predict.

China's cultural traditions also affect its approach to negotiation. Boston University's Robert Weller argues, "The Chinese base their sense of cause and effect around the idea of qi energy. Qi is the stuff of fengshui, and the element in the body that is manipulated by acupuncture or Chinese herbs. It is part of a broad way of understanding the structure of the world as a set of interacting forces, complexly interrelated rather than working through a simple and linear cause and effect." "It could also have an effect on foreign policy," Weller says.[12] Such speculation can sometimes be overdone and even sound silly. But in talking to Chinese about their ways of thinking, one quickly recognizes that concepts like qi are as central to their mind-set as a moral Creator or free will is to Westerners. Foreign policy is driven by many universal forces, but there's no doubt that a basic worldview organizes the way people perceive, act, and react, particularly in crises.

Culture, however, does not exist in a vacuum. China's past and its own DNA are shaped by its modern history—the impact of the West, communism's decimation of tradition, the resulting vacuum in Chinese spiritualism, and, perhaps most of all, its recent efforts to reconcile its traditions with modernity. When you talk to Chinese economists, they don't proclaim a Confucian way to generate economic growth or curb inflation. China's Central Bank seems very modern and (in that sense) Western in its approach. That it does not jump when the United States asks it to revalue its currency may tell us more about nationalism than about culture. (After all, when was the last time that the United States changed its economic policy because a foreign government hectored it into doing so?) The Chinese have adopted Western rationalism in many areas. Some Chinese foreign policy analysts call themselves "Christian Confucians"—meaning not evangelical converts but Chinese people with a Western outlook, seeking to imbue Chinese policies with a greater sense of purpose and values. Like every non-Western country, China will make up its own cultural cocktail—some parts Eastern, some parts Western— to thrive in the twenty-first century.

Too Big to Hide

China's biggest problem has to do not with the particularities of culture but with the universalities of power. China views itself as a nation intent on rising peacefully, its behavior marked by humility, noninterference, and friendly relations with all. But many rising countries in the past have similarly believed in their own benign motives—and still ended up upsetting the system. The political scientist Robert Gilpin notes that as a nation's power increases, it "will be tempted to try to increase its control over its environment. In order to increase its own security, it will try to expand its political, economic, and territorial control, it will try to change the international system in accordance with its particular set of interests."[13] The crucial point here is that, throughout history, great powers have seen themselves as having the best intentions but being forced by necessity to act to protect their ever-expanding interests. And as the world's number two country, China will expand its interests substantially.

Ultimately, China's intentions might be irrelevant. In the messy world of international politics, intentions and outcomes are not directly linked. (No country was expecting a world war in 1914.) It's like a market in which all companies are trying to maximize profits by raising prices: the systemwide result is exactly the opposite—a fall in prices. Similarly, in international politics, another system with no single, supreme authority, the intentions of countries do not always accurately predict the outcome. Hence the Roman aphorism "If you want peace, prepare for war."

Just how peacefully China can rise will be determined by a combination of Chinese actions, other countries' reactions, and the systemic effects that this interaction produces. Given its current size, China cannot hope to slip onto the world stage unnoticed. Its search for energy and raw materials, for example, is entirely understandable. China is growing fast, consumes energy and all kinds of commodities, and needs to find steady supplies of them. Other countries buy oil, so why shouldn't Beijing do the same? The problem is size. China operates on so large a scale that it can't help changing the nature of the game.

China's perception of its interests is shifting. Men like Wu Jianmin come from an older generation of diplomats, and the younger generation is well aware of China's new power. Some China watchers worry that, in time, power will go to China's head. In a delicately phrased set of warnings delivered in

China in 2005, Lee Kuan Yew described his concerns not about China's current leadership, or even the next generation, but about the generation after that, which will have been born in a time of stability, prosperity, and rising Chinese influence. "China's youth must be made aware of the need to reassure the world that China's rise will not turn out to be a disruptive force," he said in a speech at Fudan University. Lee implied that what has kept Chinese leaders humble since Deng Xiaoping is the bitter memory of Mao's mistakes—fomenting revolutions abroad, the Great Leap Forward, and the Cultural Revolution, which together resulted in the deaths of about forty million Chinese. "It is vital," Lee went on, "that the younger generation of Chinese who have only lived through a period of peace and growth and have no experience of China's tumultuous past are made aware of the mistakes China made as a result of hubris and excesses in ideology."

For now, China's foreign policy remains entirely commercially focused, though that, too, casts its shadow. In Africa, for example, China is working to build economic ties. The continent has natural resources, particularly oil and natural gas, that China needs in order to grow. Both Beijing and African governments have welcomed new trade relations—in part because there is no colonial past or difficult history to complicate matters—and business is booming. Trade is growing around 50 percent a year, Chinese investments in Africa even faster. In many African countries, economic growth is at record highs, a fact that many attribute to their new connections with China. Some on the continent see the relationship as exploitative and resent China's new power, so Beijing is taking pains to demonstrate its good intentions. In November 2006, President Hu Jintao held a summit on Sino-African relations. All forty-eight

African countries that have diplomatic ties with China attended, most of them represented by their presidents or prime ministers. It was the largest African summit ever held outside the continent. At the meeting, China promised to double aid to Africa in two years, provide $5 billion in loans and credits, set up a $5 billion fund to encourage further Chinese investment in Africa, cancel much of the debt owed to China, provide greater access to the Chinese market, train fifteen thousand African professionals, and build new hospitals and schools across the continent. Ethiopia's prime minister, Meles Zenawi, gushed, "China is an inspiration for all of us."[14]

What could be wrong with building such ties? Nothing—except that as China moves into Africa, it is taking up economic, political, and military space that was occupied by Britain or France or the United States. This will necessarily mean friction as each great power struggles to promote its own interests and its own conception of doing the right thing in Africa. China's interpretation of its actions is that it doesn't interfere in these countries' domestic affairs—that it is, in a sense, value neutral. But is it? Moisés Naím, editor of *Foreign Policy* magazine, tells a story about the Nigerian government negotiating a $5 million loan for train systems with the World Bank in 2007. The bank had insisted that the government clean up the notoriously corrupt railway bureaucracy before it approved the loan. The deal was almost done when the Chinese government stepped in and offered the government a $9 *billion* loan to rebuild the entire train system—with no strings, no requirements, no need for any reform. The World Bank was sent home within days. Needless to say, much of that Chinese money will go into the bank accounts of key government officials rather than toward better train service for Nigerians.

Beijing has found it useful to deal directly with governments, because they almost always maintain ownership of the resources that China needs. Transactions are simpler when dealing with one centralized authority, particularly if it is an outcast and has nowhere to turn but to China. So China buys platinum and iron ore from Zimbabwe and in turn sells Robert Mugabe weapons and radio-jamming devices—despite a U.S. and European Union ban—which he uses to intimidate, arrest, and kill domestic opposition. Beijing is Mugabe's most important supporter on the UN Security Council.

In Sudan, China's involvement runs even deeper. It has invested $3 billion in the oil fields there since 1999. Chinese companies are the majority shareholders in the two largest oil conglomerates in the country, and China buys 65 percent of Sudan's oil exports. It maintains a military alliance with Sudan and, despite UN restrictions, appears to have provided arms that end up in the hands of progovernment militias in Darfur. Chinese officials often confirm that they have a close military relationship with Sudan and intend to keep it that way. Explaining his country's position, China's deputy foreign minister was frank: "Business is business. We try to separate politics from business. Secondly, I think the internal situation in Sudan is an internal affair, and we are not in a position to impose upon them."

If China were a bit player on the global stage, it wouldn't matter much what it was doing in Zimbabwe or Sudan. Cuba, for all we know, has extensive dealings with both governments, but no one cares. Beijing, on the other hand, cannot hide its light under the bushel anymore. China's dealings with these countries give them a lifeline, retard progress, and, in the long run, perpetuate the cycle of bad regimes and social tensions that plagues the African continent. This kind of relationship also ensures that while Africa's governments might view China favorably, its people will have more mixed views—as they have had of Western governments through the years.

Beijing has been slow to recognize its broader responsibility in this region, arguing that it is simply minding its own business. But in fact, it isn't even doing that. Beijing has often shown itself to be well aware of its power. One reason it has focused on Africa is that the continent has long included a number of countries that have been friendly with Taiwan. Although seven of the twenty-six governments in the world that have relations with Taiwan today are in Africa, six countries—including South Africa—have switched recognition from Taipei to Beijing over the last decade thanks to judicious offers of aid.

China has been more skillful and used better diplomacy and soft power in Asia, the region where Beijing devotes the most time, energy, and attention. Through skillful diplomacy, it has helped orchestrate a revolution in attitudes over the last two decades. In the 1980s, China did not even have relations with much of East Asia, including South Korea, Indonesia, and Singapore. By the summer of 2007, it was holding joint military exercises with the Association of Southeast Asian Nations (ASEAN). When asked in polls in 2007 whom they trusted to wield global power, respondents in countries like Thailand and Indonesia, traditional U.S. allies, chose China over the United States. Even in Australia, favorable attitudes toward China and the United States are evenly balanced.

Until recently, memories of China's revolutionary foreign policy—which in practice meant using the Chinese diaspora to foment trouble—lingered. Beijing's invasion of Vietnam, its claims in the South China Sea, and its border disputes with Russia and India had given China the image of a prickly and troublesome neighbor. By the late 1990s, however, China had adopted a very different regional policy, which became especially clear from its constructive role in the region after the East Asian crisis of 1997. Since then, Beijing has become remarkably adept at using its political and economic muscle in a patient, low-key, and highly effective manner. Its diplomacy now emphasizes a long-term perspective, a nonpreachy attitude, and strategic decision making that isn't bogged down by internal opposition or bureaucratic paralysis. It has taken a more accommodating political line, provided generous aid packages (often far outstripping those provided by the United States), and moved speedily on a free-trade deal with ASEAN. Having long avoided multilateral associations, it has more recently gotten involved in as many as possible—even creating one of its own, the East Asian Summit, which pointedly excludes the United States. China is now welcomed by the Southeast Asian nations as well. The seemingly pro-American president of the Philippines, Gloria Arroyo, publicly proclaimed, "We are happy to have China as our big brother."[15]

This change is reflected in Beijing's relations with governments throughout its neighborhood. The Vietnamese, for example, have no particular love for China. As one official there said to me, "We are clear-eyed. China has occupied Vietnam for a thousand years. It has invaded us thirteen times since then." But he also acknowledged, "it is a huge presence, our biggest exporter"—which means that their governments and peoples must approach the relationship pragmatically. Bookstores I visited in Vietnam prominently displayed the collected speeches of the Chinese leaders Deng Xiaoping, Jiang Zemin, and Hu Jintao.

Before arriving in Vietnam, I had been in Tokyo, during Chinese Prime Minister Wen Jiabao's 2007 state visit, and I heard a similar refrain. Wen finessed the many points of tension between the two countries and instead accentuated the positive—their booming economic ties. This détente, however, is fragile and points to the principal danger in Beijing's foreign policy—its effort to co-opt nationalism for its own purposes.

In the past, Beijing insisted on keeping relations with Japan tense. Japan's wartime atrocities and reluctance to acknowledge guilt have been a large part of the problem. But Beijing also seemed to actively cultivate tension—bringing up Japan's wartime behavior whenever convenient, refusing to accept Japanese apologies, and teaching a virulently anti-Japanese version of history in its schools. In April 2005, the Chinese government appeared to encourage anti-Japanese protests over history textbooks, only to find them mushroom into mob demonstrations, riots, stone throwing at the Japanese embassy, and widespread calls to boycott Japanese goods.

In strategic terms, assuming a "peaceful rise" policy, it makes little sense for Beijing to be as uncompromising toward Tokyo as it was in the past. Doing so would ensure that China will have a hostile neighbor, one with a formidable military and an economy that is still three times the size of China's. A wiser strategy would be to keep enmeshing Japan with economic ties and greater cooperation, gaining access to its markets, investment, and technology—and achieving dominance over time. There is even an argument for genuine reconciliation. Japan has not behaved perfectly, but it has apologized several times for wartime aggression and paid China more than $34 billion in development aid (reparations, effectively)—something never mentioned by the Chinese. And clearly, a desire for reconciliation was on display when Premier Wen went to Japan in 2007. But it might not last. For China, a domestic problem gets in the way. Having abandoned communism, the Communist Party has been using nationalism as the glue that keeps China together, and modern Chinese nationalism is defined in large part by its hostility toward Japan. Despite his many catastrophic policies, Mao remains a hero in China because he fought the Japanese and unified the country.

The Chinese government has generally assumed it could manage popular sentiment, but it is losing that confidence. Not being a democracy, it has little experience doing so. It deals with public anger and emotions cagily, unsure whether to encourage them or clamp down, for fear of where they might lead. It has no idea what to do with a group like the Patriots Alliance, an Internet-based hypernationalist group that organized the anti-American protests after the 2001 EP-3 plane incident and the anti-Japanese protests of 2005. Both actions were at first encouraged, only to become much more intense than the regime expected. Those incidents appear to have spurred some rethinking, and Beijing has more recently toned down its support of nationalism, more fully embracing a quieter approach to diplomacy and politics.

The danger of external crisis plus internal nationalism looms largest over Taiwan. Beijing, long obsessed with Taiwan, has been uncompromising, as have some Taiwanese politicians—a sometimes combustible combination, as when President Chen Shuibian of Taiwan provoked a flurry of outrage by proposing a national referendum on Taiwan's independence in 2002. For the most part, Beijing has pursued its long-term plan of "normalizing" relations with the island's main opposition party and smothering it with conciliation. But not always. In March 2005, Beijing passed an "anti-secession" law, threatening Taiwan with military force if it dared to anger China in any way. As a result, among other things, the European Union postponed its plan to lift an arms embargo on China.

Taiwan offers the most vivid and important example of how the economic incentives for integration and the political urges for nationalism diverge and yet can be managed. The rational decision making that guides economic policy is not so easily applied in the realm of politics, where honor, history, pride, and anger all play a large role. In recent years, Beijing has switched to a smarter, less aggressive course with regard to Taiwan (and even with Japan), recognizing that time is on its side. Thus it has made several clever moves that have increased Taiwan's dependence on the mainland—most significantly the reduction of tariffs on farm products that come from the most independence-minded parts of Taiwan. All the while, of course, China's military has grown rapidly, its principal strategic objective being to prevail quickly in any conflict over Taiwan. In other words, economic growth and globalization have made Beijing plan for integration and yet given it the power for military and political confrontation.

The Dragon and the Eagle

The importance of China's relations with every country in the world is dwarfed by its relations with one—the United States of America. Or, to put it differently, none of the potential problems that China faces matter unless they trigger the involvement of America. Without U.S. involvement, a war over Taiwan might be bloody and tragic, but only if it turned into a Sino-U.S. confrontation would it have far-reaching global consequences. The China challenge also has greater implications for the United States than for other countries. Historically, when the world's leading power is challenged by a rising one, the two have a difficult relationship. And while neither side will admit it publicly, both China and the United States are worried and planning for trouble. For three decades, Chinese foreign policy has been geared toward satisfying the United States for a variety of practical reasons. First it was anti-Soviet strategy, then a desire for markets and reform, then rehabilitating the country after Tiananmen Square, membership in the World Trade Organization, and finally the Beijing Olympics. But increasingly, China's younger elites believe that their country needs to think of itself as a competitor to Washington in several senses. In Washington, there have always been those who see China as the next comprehensive threat to American national interests and ideals. To say this is not to assume war or even conflict, but merely to note that there is likely to be tension. How the two countries handle it will determine their future relations—and the peace of the world.

For now, the forces of integration have triumphed, in both Beijing and Washington. The Chinese-American economic relationship is one of mutual dependence. China needs the American market to sell its goods; the United States needs China to finance its debt—it's globalization's equivalent of the nuclear age's Mutual Assured Destruction. (And to add to the forces of stability, the Chinese and American nuclear arsenals also act as deterrents.) The reality of a globalized world forces

America and China into an alliance that pure geopolitics could never countenance. As a result, the Bush administration has been strikingly accommodating to Beijing over Taiwan. George W. Bush is probably the most ideologically hostile president ever to handle U.S.-China relations. He has spent his entire term in office praising democracy, denouncing dictatorship, and promising to use American power to further his goals. But despite all of this, Bush has repeatedly sided with Beijing over Taiwan and warned Taiwan not to attempt secession, a more anti-Taiwanese statement than any ever made by an American president. That's why, despite Bush's speeches on liberty and his meeting with the Dalai Lama, Beijing is largely content with the administration. On the issue it cares about, Bush has been its ally.

Beijing and Washington are wise to try to cooperate. Great-power conflict is something the world has not seen since the Cold War. If it were to return, all the troubles we worry about now—terrorism, Iran, North Korea—would pale in comparison. It would mean arms races, border troubles, rivalries among allies and client-states, local conflicts, and perhaps more. The onward movement of economic and political modernization worldwide would slow, if not cease. Even without those dire scenarios, China will complicate existing power relations. Were the United States and the European Union to adopt fundamentally differing attitudes toward the rise of China, for example, it would put permanent strains on the Western alliance that would make the tensions over Iraq look like a minor spat. But a serious U.S.-Chinese rivalry would define the new age and turn it away from integration, trade, and globalization.

There is a group of Americans, made up chiefly of neoconservatives and some Pentagon officials, that has been sounding the alarms about the Chinese threat, speaking of it largely in military terms. But the facts do not support their case. China is certainly expanding its military, with a defense budget that has been growing 10 percent or more a year. But it is still spending a fraction of what America does—at most 10 percent of the Pentagon's annual bill. The United States has twelve nuclear-powered aircraft carriers that can each field eighty-five attack jets; China's naval engineers are still working on their first. China has twenty nuclear missiles that could reach U.S. shores, according to Pentagon estimates, but these "small and cumbersome" weapons are "inherently vulnerable to a pre-emptive strike." The United States, by comparison, has around nine thousand intact nuclear warheads and around five thousand strategic warheads.[16]

The Chinese understand how lopsided the military balance is. The China challenge, accordingly, will not look like another Soviet Union, with Beijing straining to keep pace in military terms. China is more likely to remain an "asymmetrical superpower." It is already exploring and developing ways to complicate and erode American military supremacy, such as space and Internet-based technology. Even more importantly, it will use its economic strength and its political skills to achieve its objectives without having to resort to military force. China does not want to invade and occupy Taiwan; it is more likely to keep undermining the Taiwanese independence movement, slowly accumulating advantage and wearing out the opponent.

In a paper titled "The Beijing Consensus," which draws heavily on interviews with leading Chinese officials and academics, Joshua Cooper Ramo provides a fascinating picture of China's new foreign policy. "Rather than building a U.S.-style power, bristling with arms and intolerant of others' world views," he writes, "China's emerging power is based on the example of their own model, the strength of their economic system, and their rigid defense of . . . national sovereignty." Ramo describes an elite that understands that their country's rising power and less interventionist style make it an attractive partner, especially in a world in which the United States is seen as an overbearing hegemon. "The goal for China is not conflict but the avoidance of conflict," he writes. "True success in strategic issues involves manipulating a situation so effectively that the outcome is inevitably in favor of Chinese interests. This emerges from the oldest Chinese strategic thinker, Sun Zi, who argued that 'every battle is won or lost before it is ever fought.'"[17]

The United States understands how to handle a traditional military-political advance. After all, this was the nature of the Soviet threat and the Nazi rise to power. The United States has a conceptual framework as well as the tools—weapons, aid packages, alliances—with which to confront such an advance. Were China to push its weight around, anger its neighbors, and frighten the world, Washington would be able to respond with a set of effective policies that would take advantage of the natural balancing process by which Japan, India, Australia, and Vietnam—and perhaps others—would come together to limit China's emerging power. But what if China adheres to its asymmetrical strategy? What if it gradually expands its economic ties, acts calmly and moderately, and slowly enlarges its sphere of influence, seeking only greater weight, friendship, and influence in the world? What if it slowly pushes Washington onto the sidelines in Asia, in an effort to wear out America's patience and endurance? What if it quietly positions itself as the alternative to a hectoring and arrogant America? How will America cope with such a scenario—a kind of Cold War, but this time with a vibrant market society, with the world's largest population, a nation that is not showcasing a hopeless model of state socialism or squandering its power in pointless military interventions? This is a new challenge for the United States, one it has not tackled before, and for which it is largely unprepared.

In thinking through how to approach China, American political elites have fixed their gaze on another rising power, close to, and close on the heels of, China—India.

5

The Ally

I n the fall of 1982, I took an Air India flight from Bombay's Santa Cruz airport to go to college in the United States. The preceding decade had been a rough one in India, marked by mass protests, riots, secessionist movements, insurgencies, and the suspension of democracy. Underneath it all was a dismal economy, one that combined meager growth with ever-worsening inflation. Economic growth barely outpaced population growth. It would have taken the average Indian fifty-seven years to double his income, given the rate of increase in per capita GDP at the time. Many talented and ambitious Indians believed that their only real future lay in leaving the country. Over 75 percent of the graduates of the Indian Institutes of Technology in the 1980s emigrated to America.

The decade since 1997 could not have been more different. India has been peaceful, stable, and prosperous. The fires of secession and militant nationalism have died down. National and state governments changed hands without incident. There was even a thaw in the perennially tense relations with Pakistan. And underpinning it all was the transformation of the Indian economy, which grew at 6.9 percent over the entire decade and 8.5 percent in the second half of it. If this latter rate can be sustained, the average Indian will double his income in less than ten years. Already, the cumulative effect of this new economics is apparent. More Indians have moved out of poverty in the last decade than in the preceding fifty years.

The world has taken note. Every year at the World Economic Forum in Davos, Switzerland, there is a national star— one country that stands out in the gathering of global leaders because of a particularly smart prime minister or finance minister or a compelling tale of reform. In the twelve years that I've been going to Davos, no country has so captured the imagination of the conference or dominated the conversation as India did in 2006. It goes well beyond one conference. The world is courting India as never before. Foreign leaders are now flocking to India pledging to form deeper and stronger relations with the once exotic land.

Yet most foreign observers are still unsure of what to make of India's rise to prominence. Will it become the next China? And what would that mean, economically and politically? Will a richer India bump up against China? Will it look on the United States as an ally? Is there such a thing as a "Hindu" worldview? Perplexed foreigners might be comforted to know that Indians themselves remain unsure of the answers to these questions. India is too full of exuberance right now for much serious reflection.

Exuberance worked well enough at the World Economic Forum. As you got off the plane in Zurich, you saw large billboards extolling *Incredible India!* The town of Davos itself was plastered with signs. "World's Fastest Growing Free Market Democracy," proclaimed the local buses. When you got to your room, you found a pashmina shawl and an iPod shuffle loaded with Bollywood songs, gifts from the Indian delegation. When you entered the meeting rooms, you were likely to hear an Indian voice, one of dozens of CEOs of world-class Indian companies in attendance. And then there were the government officials, India's "Dream Team"—all intelligent and articulate, and all intent on selling their country. The forum's main social event was an Indian extravaganza, with a bevy of Indian beauties dancing to pulsating Hindi tunes against an electric blue Taj Mahal. The impeccably dressed chairman of the forum, Klaus Schwab, donned a colorful Indian turban and shawl, nibbled on chicken tikka, and talked up the country's prospects with Michael Dell. *India Everywhere*, said the logo. And it was.

The success of this marketing strategy ensured that it was used again, and again. On the sixtieth anniversary of India's independence, New York was overrun with glamorous concerts, galas, champagne receptions, and seminars celebrating the country's cultural, political, and economic success. The slogan *India@60* reflected the driving force behind it, India's technology companies. The event contrasted markedly with the fiftieth-anniversary celebrations ten years earlier, which culminated in a dull reception at the Indian consulate—with fruit juice only, because of the Gandhian taboo on alcohol—and a speech extolling India's diversity. Of course, today's jazzy campaigns wouldn't work if there were no substance behind them. Over the past fifteen years, India has been the second-fastest-growing country in the world, behind only China, and it seems on track to continue this high-octane growth for the next decade. Like China's, its sheer size—one billion people—means that, once on the move, the country casts a long shadow across the globe.

While China's rise is already here and palpable, India's is still more a tale of the future. Its per capita GDP is still only $960.* But that future is coming into sharp focus. The Goldman Sachs BRIC study projects that, by 2015, India's economy will be equal to the size of Italy's and, by 2020, will have caught up to Britain's. By 2040, India will boast the world's third-largest economy. By 2050, its per capita income will have risen to twenty times its current level.[1] Predictions like these are a treacherous business, and trends often peter out. But still, it's worth noting that India's current growth rate is much higher than the study assumes, and, crucially, the country has a promising demographic profile. As the industrial world ages, India will continue to have *lots* of young people—in other words, workers. China faces a youth gap because of its successful "one-child" policies; India faces a youth bulge because, ironically, its own family-planning policies of the past failed. (The lesson here is that all social engineering has unintended consequences.) If demography is destiny, India's future is secure.

Even the here and now is impressive. India's poverty rate is half what it was twenty years ago. Its private sector is astonishingly vibrant, posting gains of 15, 20, and 25 percent year after year. The private sector's strength goes well beyond just outsourcing firms like Infosys, the main association of many in the United States with the Indian economy. The Tata Group is a far-flung conglomerate that makes everything from cars and

---

* Unadjusted for purchasing power. The PPP figure is $2,100. The comparable numbers for China are $2,500 (market) and $4,100 (PPP).

steel to software and consulting systems. In 2006, its revenues rose from $17.8 billion to $22 billion, a 23 percent gain. The more dynamic Reliance Industries, India's largest company, saw its profits double between 2004 and 2006. The total revenues of the auto-parts business, made up of hundreds of small companies, grew from under $6 billion in 2003 to more than $15 billion in 2007. Over the next three years, General Motors alone will import $1 billion worth of Indian-made auto-parts.[2] And India now has more billionaires than any other Asian country, and most of them are self-made.

Bottoms Up

At this point, anyone who has actually been to India will probably be puzzled. "India?" he or she would ask. "With its dilapidated airports, crumbling roads, vast slums and impoverished villages? Are you talking about that India?" Yes, that, too, is India. The country might have several Silicon Valleys, but it also has three Nigerias within it—that is, more than 300 million people living on less than a dollar a day. It is home to 40 percent of the world's poor and has the world's second-largest HIV-positive population. But even if the India of poverty and disease is the familiar India, the moving picture is more telling than the snapshot. India is changing. Mass poverty persists, but the new economic vigor is stirring things up everywhere. You can feel it even in the slums.

To many visitors, India does not look pretty. Western businessmen go to India expecting it to be the next China. It never will be that. China's growth is overseen by a powerful government. Beijing decides that the country needs new airports, eight-lane highways, gleaming industrial parks—and they are built within months. It courts multinationals and provides them with permits and facilities within days. One American CEO recalled how Chinese officials took him to a site they proposed for his new (and very large) facility. It was central, well located, and met almost all his criteria—except that it was filled with existing buildings and people, making up a small township. The CEO pointed that out to his host. The official smiled and said, "Oh, don't worry, they won't be here in eighteen months." And they weren't.

India does not have a government that can or will move people for the sake of foreign investors. New Delhi and Mumbai do not have the gleaming infrastructure of Beijing and Shanghai, nor do any of India's cities have the controlled urbanization of China's cities. When I asked the chief minister of India's most industrialized state, Vilasrao Deshmukh, whether India could learn something from the Chinese planned model of city development, he replied, "Yes, but with limits. China has often required that people have proof of a job before they can move to a city. This ensures that they don't get millions of job-seekers who crowd into slums ringing around the city. I can't do that. The Constitution of India guarantees freedom of movement. If someone wants to come and look for a job in Mumbai, he's free to do so."

India's growth is taking place not because of the government but despite it. It is not top-down but bottom-up—messy, chaotic, and largely unplanned. The country's key advantages are a genuine private sector, established rights of property and contract, independent courts, and the rule of law (even if it is often abused). India's private sector is the backbone of its growth. In China, private companies did not exist twenty years ago, in India, many date back a hundred years. And somehow they overcome obstacles, cut through red tape, bypass bad infrastructure—and make a buck. If they cannot export large goods because of bad highways and ports, they export software and services, things you can send over wires rather than roads. Gurcharan Das, former CEO of Procter & Gamble in India, quips, "The government sleeps at night and the economy grows."

The most striking characteristic of India today is its human capital—a vast and growing population of entrepreneurs, managers, and business-savvy individuals. They are increasing in number, faster than anyone might have imaged, in part because they have easy access to the language of modernity, English. Unwittingly, Britain's bequest of the English language might prove to be its most consequential legacy. Because of it, India's managerial and entrepreneurial class is intimately familiar with Western business trends, with no need for translators or cultural guides. They read about computers, management theory, marketing strategy, and the latest innovations in science and technology. They speak globalization fluently.

The result is a country that looks like no other developing nation. India's GDP is 50 percent services, 25 percent industry, and 25 percent agriculture. The only other countries that fit this profile are Portugal and Greece—middle-income countries that have passed through the first phases of mass industrialization and are entering the postindustrial economy. India is behind such economies in manufacturing and agriculture but ahead of them in services—a combination that no one could have planned. The role of the consumer in India's growth has been similarly surprising. Most Asian success stories have been driven by government measures that force the people to save, producing growth through capital accumulation and market-friendly policies. In India, the consumer is king. Young Indian professionals don't wait to buy a house at the end of their lives with savings. They take out mortgages. The credit-card industry is growing at 35 percent a year. Personal consumption makes up a staggering 67 percent of GDP in India, much higher than in China (42 percent) or any other Asian country. The only country in the world where consumption is higher is America, at 70 percent.[3]

While Indian infrastructure is improving, and further additions and renovations to the country's airports, highways, and ports are planned, India will not look like China. Democracy may bring certain advantages for long-term development, but autocratic governments are able to plan and execute major infrastructure projects with unrivaled efficiency. This is apparent whether one compares China with India or with Britain. The architect Norman Foster pointed out to me that in the time it took for the environmental review process for *one* new building at Heathrow, Terminal Five, he will have built—start to finish—the entire new Beijing airport, which is larger than all five of Heathrow's terminals combined.

Yet even if great infrastructure pleases foreign travelers and investors and signals a country on the move, its economic impact can be exaggerated. When China was growing at its fastest, in the 1980s and early 1990s, it had terrible roads, bridges, and airports—far worse than India does today. Even in the developed world, the country with the best infrastructure does not always win. France has trains and roads that gleam next to America's creaky system. But it's the U.S. economy that has edged ahead for the last three decades. A vibrant private sector can deliver extraordinary growth even when traveling on bad roads.

Some scholars argue that India's path has distinct advantages. MIT's Yasheng Huang points out that Indian companies use their capital far more efficiently than Chinese companies, in part because they do not have access to almost unlimited supplies of it.[4] They benchmark to global standards and are better managed than Chinese firms. Despite starting its reforms later (and thus being earlier in the development cycle) than China, India has produced many more world-class companies, including Tata, Infosys, Ranbaxy, and Reliance. And its advantage is even more apparent at the lower levels. Every year, Japan awards the coveted Deming Prizes for managerial innovation. Over the last five years, they have been awarded more often to Indian companies than to firms from any other country, including Japan. India's financial sector is at least as transparent and efficient as any in developing Asia (that is, excluding Singapore and Hong Kong).

"The statistics don't capture the shift in mentality," says Uday Kotak, the founder of a booming financial services firm. "The India I grew up in is another country. The young people whom I work with today are just so much more confident and excited about what they can do here." The old assumption that "made in India" means second-rate is disappearing. Indian companies are buying stakes in Western companies because they think they can do a better job of managing them. Indian investment in Britain in 2006 and 2007 was larger than British investment in India.

And it's not just business. Urban India is bursting with enthusiasm. Fashion designers, writers, and artists talk about extending their influence across the globe. Bollywood movie stars are growing their audience from its domestic "base" of half a billion by winning new fans outside of India. Cricket players are working on revamping the game to attract crowds abroad. It is as if hundreds of millions of people had suddenly discovered the keys to unlock their potential. As a famous Indian once put it, "A moment comes, which comes but rarely in history, when we step out from the old to the new, when an age ends and when the soul of a nation, long suppressed, finds utterance."

Those words, which Indians of a certain generation know by heart, were spoken by the country's first prime minister, Jawaharlal Nehru, just after midnight on August 15, 1947, when Britain transferred power to India's Constituent Assembly. Nehru was referring to the birth of India as an independent state. What is happening today is the birth of India as an independent society—boisterous, colorful, open, vibrant, and, above all, ready for change. India is diverging not only from its own past but also from the paths of other countries in Asia. It is not a quiet, controlled, quasi-authoritarian country that is slowly opening up according to plan. It is a noisy democracy that has finally empowered its people economically.

Indian newspapers reflect this shift. For decades their pages were dominated by affairs of the state. Usually written in cryptic insiders' jargon (PM TO PROPOSE CWC EXPANSION AT AICC MEET), they reported on the workings of the government, major political parties, and bureaucratic bodies. A small elite understood them, everyone else pretended to. Today, Indian papers are booming—a rare oasis of growth for print journalism—and overflowing with stories about businessmen, technological fads, fashion designers, shopping malls, and, of course, Bollywood (which now makes more movies a

year than Hollywood). Indian television has exploded, with
new channels seeming to spring up every month. Even in the
news business, the number and variety are bewildering. By
2006, India had almost two dozen all-news channels.[5]

There's more here than just glitz and glamour. Consider the
response to the 2005 tsunami. In the past, the only response
in India worth noting would have been the government's,
which would have involved little more than coordinating foreign aid. In 2005, New Delhi refused offers of help from
abroad (one more indication of growing national pride). But
the more striking shift was elsewhere. Within two weeks after
the tidal wave hit, Indians had privately donated $80 million
to the relief effort. Four years earlier, in 2001, it had taken a
year to collect the same amount of money after a massive (7.9
Richter) earthquake in Gujarat. Private philanthropy in Asia
has typically been a thin stream. When the rich give, they give
to temples and holy men. But that seems to be changing. One
of India's richest men, Azim Premji, a technology multibil-
lionaire, has said he will leave the bulk of his fortune in a
foundation, much as Bill Gates has. Anil Aggarwal, another
self-made billionaire, has announced plans to donate $1 bil-
lion toward setting up a new private university in Orissa, one
of India's poorest regions. Private and nonprofit groups are
getting involved in health care and education, taking on functions that should be the responsibility of the state. By some
measures, more than 25 percent of schools and 80 percent of
the health system in India now lie outside the state sector.[6]
The software firm Infosys Technologies has started its own
corporate foundation to provide rural areas with hospitals,
orphanages, classrooms, and schoolbooks.

All this sounds familiar. In one key regard, India—one of

the poorest countries in the world—looks strikingly similar to the wealthiest one, the United States of America. In both places, society has asserted its dominance over the state. Will that formula prove as successful in India as it has in America? Can society fill in for the state?

The Necessity for Government

The Indian state is often maligned, but on one front it has been a roaring success. India's democracy is truly extraordinary. Despite its poverty, India has sustained democratic government for almost sixty years. If you ask the question "What will India look like politically in twenty-five years?" the answer is obvious: "As it does today—a democracy." Democracy makes for populism, pandering, and delays. But it also makes for long-term stability.

India's political system owes much to the institutions put in place by the British over two hundred years ago. In many other parts of Asia and in Africa, the British were a relatively temporary presence. They were in India for centuries. They saw it as the jewel in their imperial crown and built lasting institutions of government throughout the country—courts, universities, administrative agencies. But perhaps even more importantly, India got very lucky with the vehicle of its independence, the Congress Party, and its first generation of post-independence leaders, who nurtured the best traditions of the British and drew on older Indian customs to reinforce them. Men like Jawaharlal Nehru may not have gotten their economics right, but they understood political freedom and how to secure it.

The fact that a political and institutional framework

already exists is an important strength for India. Of course, pervasive corruption and political patronage have corroded many of these institutions, in some cases to the point of making them unrecognizable. India has a remarkably modern administrative structure—in theory. It has courts, bureaucracies, and agencies with the right makeup, mandate, and independence—in theory. But whatever the abuses of power, this basic structure brings tremendous advantages. India has not had to invent an independent central bank; it already had one. It will not need to create independent courts; it can simply clean up the ones it has. And some of India's agencies, like its national Election Commission, are already honest, efficient, and widely respected.

If the Indian state has succeeded on some dimensions, however, it has failed on many others. In the 1950s and 1960s, India tried to modernize by creating a "mixed" economic model between capitalism and communism. The product was a shackled and overregulated private sector and a massively inefficient and corrupt public sector. The results were poor, and in the 1970s, as India became more socialist, they became disastrous. In 1960, India's per capita GDP was higher than China's and 70 percent that of South Korea; today, it is less than two-fifths of China's. South Korea's is twenty times larger.

Perhaps most depressing is India's score on the United Nations Human Development Index, which gauges countries not just by income but by health, literacy, and other such measures as well. India ranks 128 out of 177 countries—behind Syria, Sri Lanka, Vietnam, and the Dominican Republic. Female literacy is a shockingly low 48 percent. Despite mountains of rhetoric about helping the poor, India's government has done little for them, even when compared with the governments of many other poor countries. It has made too few investments in human beings—in their health and education—and when budgeted, the money has rarely been well spent. In the 1980s, Prime Minister Rajiv Gandhi estimated that, of every ten rupees that was supposed to be spent on the poor, just one actually got to the person in need.

Can these problems be blamed on democracy? Not entirely. Bad policies and administration produce failure whether pursued by dictators or by democrats. Still, certain aspects of democracy can prove problematic, especially in a country with rampant poverty, feudalism, and illiteracy. Democracy in India too often means not the will of the majority but the will of organized minorities—landowners, powerful castes, rich farmers, government unions, local thugs. (Nearly a fifth of the members of the Indian parliament have been accused of crimes, including embezzlement, rape, and murder.) These organized minorities are richer than most of their countrymen, and they plunder the state's coffers to stay that way. India's Communist Party, for example, campaigns not for economic growth to benefit the very poor but rather to maintain the relatively privileged conditions of unionized workers and party apparatchiks. In fact, India's left-wing is largely opposed to the policies that have finally reduced mass poverty. In all this ideological and political posturing, the interests of the 800 million Indians who earn less than two dollars a day often fall through the cracks.

But democracy can also right wrongs, as India's democracy has done on one crucial issue. In the 1990s, an ugly Hindu nationalism raged through the country and captured its politics, through the Bharatiya Janata Party (BJP). It whipped up Hindu animosities against Muslims and also exploited the

stark political reality that India's Muslim population is disem-
powered, almost by definition. Since those areas of British
India where Muslims were a majority became Pakistan and
Bangladesh, Muslims are almost everywhere in India a weak
minority. Over time, though, the BJP's incitement of hatred
and violence produced a backlash. A thoroughly secular government came to power in 2004, headed by Manmohan Singh,
the former finance minister who opened up India's economy in
the summer of 1991. In an act of wisdom and restraint, Sonia
Gandhi, who led the ruling coalition to victory in the polls,
chose to appoint Singh prime minister rather than take the job
herself. As a result, quite unexpectedly, India's chaotic and
often corrupt democratic system produced for its head of government a man of immense intelligence, unimpeachable
integrity, and deep experience. Singh, an Oxford Ph.D., had
already run the country's central bank, planning ministry, and
finance ministry. His breadth, depth, and decency as a person
are unmatched by any Indian prime minister since Nehru.

But Singh's stellar credentials and character haven't helped
the country much. The pace of India's reforms has disap-
pointed its well-wishers. Ever since the initial burst of reforms
in the 1990s, governments in both New Delhi and in the states
have been cautious in eliminating subsidies and protections.
Nor have they pushed new pro-growth initiatives such as the
creation of large economic zones or infrastructure projects.
They have sometimes proposed new programs that look suspi-
ciously like programs that have had little success in the past.
But this paralysis cannot be blamed entirely upon the government. A change in the ruling party will not bring about
Chinese-style reforms. Economic reforms produce growth,
but they also produce dislocation—and those hurt by change

always protest more loudly than those who benefit. Add to that the messy politics of coalitions—someone, somewhere can always block a proposed reform—and you have a recipe for slow movement, one step forward and three-quarters of a step back. It is the price of democracy.

Despite the lack of far-reaching new policies, there is a quiet determination in both the public and the private sectors to keep moving forward. Behind the cacophony of Indian politics, there is actually a broad consensus on policy among the major players. The major opposition party, the BJP, criticizes the Singh government on two fronts—economic reforms and pro-Americanism. In fact, it took exactly the same positions as Singh when it was in government. The arrow may be moving slowly, but it moves in the right direction. Every week in India, one reads about a new set of regulations being eased or permissions being eliminated. These "stealth reforms"—too small to draw vigorous opposition from the unreconstructed left—add up. And India's pro-reform constituency keeps growing. The middle class is already 300 million strong. Urban India is not all of India, but it is a large and influential chunk of it. And the vibrancy of the Indian private sector compensates in some measure for the stasis in the state sector.

In any event, there is no other way. Democracy is India's destiny. A country so diverse and complex cannot really be governed any other way. The task for a smart Indian politician is to use democracy to the country's advantage. In some ways this is already happening. The government has recently begun investing in rural education and health, and is focusing on improving agricultural productivity. Good economics can sometimes make for good politics—or at least that is the Indian hope. Democracy has also been broadened since 1993 to give villages greater voice in their affairs. Village councils must reserve 33 percent of their seats for women, and there are now one million elected women in villages across the country—giving them a platform from which to demand better education and health care. Freedom of information is also being expanded in the hope that people will insist on better government from their local leaders and administrators. It is bottom-up development, with society pushing the state.

Will the state respond? Built during the British Raj, massively expanded in India's socialist era, it is filled with bureaucrats who are in love with their petty powers and privileges. They are joined by politicians who enjoy the power of patronage. Still others are wedded to ideas of Third World socialism and solidarity. In these views they are joined by many intellectuals and journalists, who are all well schooled in the latest radical ideas—circa 1968, when they were in college. As India changes, these old elites are being threatened and redoubling their efforts. Many in India's ruling class are uncomfortable in the modern, open, commercial society they see growing around them.

In the end, government matters. Even India's great success, its private companies, could not flourish without a well-regulated stock market and a financial system that has transparency, adjudication, and enforcement—all government functions. The booming telecommunications industry was created by intelligent government deregulation and reregulation. The Indian Institutes of Technology were created by the state. The private sector cannot solve India's AIDS crisis or its rural education shortfalls or its environmental problems. Most Indians, particularly the poor, have only miserable interactions with their government. They find it inefficient or corrupt, and often both. That might be why anti-incumbent sentiment has been the strongest force in Indian elections over the last three decades: Indians keep throwing the bums out, in the hope that government will get better. And voters have a point. If India's governance does not improve, the country will never fully achieve its potential.

This is perhaps the central paradox of India today. Its society is open, eager, and confident, ready to take on the world. But its state—its ruling class—is hesitant, cautious, and suspicious of the changing realities around it. Nowhere is this tension more obvious than in the realm of foreign policy, the increasingly large and important task of determining how India should fit into the new world.

Blind and Toothless

After winning its independence, India was eager to play a large role on the world stage. This ambition was inherited from Britain, which ran a great deal of its empire from New Delhi. It was from India that Britain administered Iraq in the decades after the First World War. It was Indian soldiers who carried out Britain's imperial crusades in the Middle East and elsewhere. The India Office was a critical center of world power, the most important extension of the British Empire, and Indians watched and learned the great-power game from the superpower of the age.

India's first prime minister, Nehru, was comfortable in that tradition. He had been educated like an English gentleman, at Harrow and Cambridge, traveled and read widely, and written extensively about world affairs. His grasp of history was extraordinary. During one of many spells in the prisons of British India, this time from 1930 to 1933, he wrote a series of letters to his daughter that outlined the entire sweep of human history, from 6000 B.C. to the present day, detailing the rise and fall of empires, explaining wars and revolutions, and profiling kings and democrats—all without any access to a library. In 1934, the letters were collected and released as a book, *Glimpses of World History*, to international acclaim. The *New York Times* described it as "one of the most remarkable books ever published."

Not surprisingly, Nehru became the towering figure in Indian foreign policy. For his entire tenure as prime minister, from 1947 to 1964, he was his own foreign minister. One of India's first foreign secretaries,* K. P. S. Menon, explains in his autobiography, "We had no precedents to fall back upon, because India had no foreign policy of her own until she became independent. We did not even have a section for historical research until I created one. . . . Our policy therefore necessarily rested on the intuition of one man, who was Foreign Minister, Jawaharlal Nehru." This meant that India's early foreign policy was driven by Nehru's principles and prejudices, which were distinctive. Nehru was an idealist, even a moralist. He was for nonalignment and against the Cold War. His mentor, Mahatma Gandhi, was an unyielding pacifist. "An eye for an eye, a tooth for a tooth," Gandhi used to say, "and soon the world will be blind and toothless." The mahatma was revered in India almost like a god, and his strategy of nonviolence had brought down an empire. Like many of his followers, Nehru was determined to chart a new course in international affairs that lived up to those ideals.

---

* The foreign secretary is the senior-most foreign service officer (bureaucrat) in the ministry.

Nehru rooted India's foreign policy in abstract ideas rather than a strategic conception of national interests. He disdained alliances, pacts, and treaties, seeing them as part of the old rules of realpolitik, and was uninterested in military matters. He asked his friend Lord Mountbatten, the last British viceroy (who briefly served as India's first head of state), to organize the defense bureaucracy and intervened only to resist any recommendation that would give the uniformed military too much power, which reminded Nehru too much of Britain's imperial structure. When Mountbatten suggested that there be a powerful chief of defense staff, Nehru turned down the recommendation, since he wanted to have a civilian minister as the unrivaled boss. A week into his new government, he walked over to the defense ministry and was furious to find military officers working there (as they do in every defense ministry in the world). Since then, all armed service personnel who work in New Delhi's "South Block" wear civilian clothes. For much of Nehru's tenure, his defense minister was a close political confidant, V. K. Krishna Menon, who was even less interested in military matters, much preferring long-winded ideological combat in parliament to strategic planning.

Indian foreign policy in its early decades had an airy quality, full of rhetoric about peace and goodwill. Many Western observers believed these pieties to be a smoke screen behind which the nation was cannily pursuing its interests. But sometimes what you see is what you get. In many of his dealings, Nehru tended to put hope above calculation.* When he was

* In a recent book, *Nehru: The Inventor of India*, the UN diplomat and scholar Shashi Tharoor writes that, in 1952, Nehru refused a U.S. overture that it take over the permanent seat on the UN Security Council then held by Taiwan. Instead, he suggested that the seat be given to China.

warned that Communist China would probably seek to annex Tibet, for example, he doubted it, arguing that it would be a foolish and impractical adventure. And even after Beijing did annex Tibet, in 1951, Nehru would not reassess the nature of Chinese interests along India's northern border. Rather than negotiate the disputed boundary with China, he announced the Indian position unilaterally, convinced of its rightness. And so he was shattered when China invaded India in 1962, settling the dispute decisively in its favor. "We were getting out of touch with reality in the modern world and we were living in an artificial atmosphere of our creation," Nehru said in a national address. He was never the same again, and two years later died in office.

Although the rhetoric often remained sanctimonious, India's policies have become more realistic over the years. Ironically, they were especially tough-minded and shrewd during the reign of Nehru's daughter, Indira Gandhi. There was a quiet maturation of the country's foreign policy elite. And yet New Delhi was still not able to play a larger role in the world. Nehru and Indira Gandhi were international figures, but India operated under severe constraints. Conflict in the neighborhood— with Pakistan, China, Sri Lanka—kept it tied down and limited in its scope. In the Cold War, it ended up loosely allied with the Soviet Union and thus on the losing side of that long struggle. Finally and crucially, India's economic performance went from bad to worse, which placed deep limits on its resources, attractiveness, stature, and influence.

As the scholar C. Raja Mohan has pointed out, over the last decade, most of these conditions changed.[7] The Cold War ended, India began booming, and relations with its neighbors —from China to Pakistan to tiny Bhutan—improved markedly. The result is that India has begun to play a much larger role in the world. It is poised to become a great power at last. And at the center of its new role is a much closer relationship with the United States of America.

The Eagle and the Cow

Most Americans would probably be surprised to learn that India is, by at least one measure, the most pro-American country in the world. The Pew Global Attitudes Survey released in June 2005 asked people in sixteen countries whether they had a favorable impression of the United States. A stunning 71 percent of Indians said yes. Only Americans had a more favorable view of America (83 percent). The numbers are somewhat lower in other surveys, but the basic finding remains true: Indians are extremely comfortable with and well disposed toward America.

One reason for this may be that for decades India's government tried to force anti-Americanism down its people's throats. (When explaining away India's miseries in the 1970s, politicians spoke so often of the "hidden hand"—by which they meant the CIA or American interference generally—that the cartoonist R. K. Laxman took to drawing an actual hand descending to cause all kinds of havoc.) But more important is the fact that Indians understand America. It is a noisy, open society with a chaotic democratic system, like theirs. Its capitalism looks distinctly like America's free-for-all. Many urban Indians are familiar with America, speak its language, and actually know someone who lives there, possibly even a relative.

The Indian American community has been a bridge

between the two cultures. The term often used to describe Indians leaving their country is "brain drain." But it has been more like brain gain, for both sides. Indians abroad have played a crucial role in opening up the mother country. They return to India with money, investment ideas, global standards, and, most important, a sense that Indians can achieve anything. An Indian parliamentarian once famously asked the then prime minister Indira Gandhi, "Why is it that Indians seem to succeed everywhere except in their own country?" Stories of Indians scaling the highest peaks in America have generated pride and emulation in India. Americans, for their part, have more readily embraced India because they have had a positive experience with Indians in America.

If Indians understand America, Americans understand India. They are puzzled and disturbed by impenetrable decision-making elites like the Chinese Politburo or the Iranian Council of Guardians. But a quarrelsome democracy that keeps moving backward, forward, and sideways—*that* they understand. During negotiations on nuclear issues, Americans watched what was going on in New Delhi—people opposed to the deal leaking negative stories from inside the government, political adversaries using the issue to score points on unrelated matters—and found it all very familiar. Similar things happen every day in Washington.

Most countries have relationships that are almost exclusively between governments. Think of the links between the United States and Saudi Arabia, which exist almost solely among a few dozen high officials. But sometimes bonds develop not merely between states but also between societies. The United States has developed relationships that are much more than just strategic in two other cases: with Britain and later with Israel. In both, the ties were broad and deep, going well beyond government officials and diplomatic negotiations. The two countries knew each other and understood each other—and, as a result, became natural and almost permanent partners.

Such a relationship between the United States and India is, on some level, almost inevitable. Whether or not the two states sign new treaties, the two *societies* are becoming increasingly intertwined. A common language, a familiar worldview, and a growing fascination with each other is bringing together businessmen, nongovernmental activists, and writers. This doesn't mean that the United States and India will agree on every policy issue. After all, Roosevelt and Churchill disagreed about several issues during their close wartime alliance, most notably India's independence, and America broke with Britain over the Suez crisis in 1956. Ronald Reagan, a staunch supporter of Israel, condemned its invasion of Lebanon in 1978. Washington and New Delhi are big powers with complex foreign commitments and concerns. They have different interests and thus will inevitably have disputes over policy. Also, unlike Britain and America, they have different outlooks on the world. Indian history, religion, and culture will pull it away from a purely American view of the world.

The Hindu Worldview

Despite a growing sense of competition, India is actually moving closer to China in a certain respect, one that relates to the two countries' entries onto the global stage. India has moved away from the self-righteousness of the Nehru era as well as the combativeness of Indira Gandhi's years. It is instead making development its overriding national priority, informing its foreign affairs as well as its domestic policies. Prime Minister Manmohan Singh has repeatedly articulated a goal for Indian foreign policy—peace and stability to allow for development—that sounds similar to the one articulated in Beijing. Indian politicians have become much more aware than ever before of the deep challenges of developing a vast society—especially a democratic one where domestic pressures are felt quickly and deeply—and so are focusing almost entirely on matters internal. External affairs are seen as a way to help with these paramount concerns. This tension—a country that is a world power and at the same time *very poor*—will tend to limit India's activism abroad. It will especially mean that India will not want to be seen as actively involved in a balancing strategy against China, which is becoming its chief trading partner.

There is also Indian culture, which has its own fundamental perspective and outlook on the world. Hindus, like Confucians, don't believe in God. They believe in *hundreds of thousands* of them. Every sect and subsect of Hinduism worships its own God, Goddess, or holy creature. Every family forges its own distinct version of Hinduism. You can pay your respects to some beliefs and not to others. You can believe in none at all. You can be a vegetarian or eat meat. You can pray or not pray. None of these choices determines whether you are a Hindu. There is no heresy or apostasy, because there is no core set of beliefs, no doctrine, and no commandments. Nothing is required, nothing is forbidden.

Sir Monier Monier-Williams, the Boden Professor of Sanskrit at Oxford University from 1860 to 1899, was perhaps the first Westerner to study Hinduism comprehensively. Born in

Bombay, he founded Oxford's Indian Institute, which became a training ground for future leaders of the British Raj. His book *Hinduism*, first published in 1877, drew on ancient Sanskrit texts as well practical knowledge of contemporary Hinduism. He wrote,

> [Hinduism] is all tolerant. . . . It has its spiritual and its material aspect, its esoteric and exoteric, its subjective and objective, its rational and its irrational, its pure and its impure. It may be compared to a huge polygon. . . . It has one side for the practical, another for the severely moral, another for the devotional and imaginative, another for the sensuous and sensual, and another for the philosophical and speculative. Those who rest in ceremonial observances find it all-sufficient; those who deny the efficacy of works, and make faith the one requisite, need not wander from its pale; those who are addicted to sensual objects may have their tastes gratified; those who delight in meditating on the nature of God and Man, the relation of matter and spirit, the mystery of separate existence, and the origin of evil, may here indulge their love of speculation. And this capacity for almost endless expansion causes almost endless sectarian divisions even among the followers of any particular line of doctrine.

The most striking example of Hinduism's absorptive powers is the way it incorporated Buddhism. Buddha was Indian, and Buddhism was founded in India, but there are virtually no Buddhists in the country today. This is not a consequence of persecution. In fact, the opposite. Hinduism so fully absorbed the message of Buddhism that it simply enveloped the creed. Now, if you want to find Buddhists, you must go thousands of miles from where it was founded, to Korea, Indonesia, and Japan.

The Bengali writer Nirad Chaudhuri was driven to exasperation by Hinduism's complexity. "The more one studies the details of the religion the more bewildering does it seem," he wrote. "It is not simply that one cannot form a clear-cut intellectual idea of the whole complex, it is not possible even to come away with a coherent emotional reaction."[8] Hinduism is not really a "religion" in the Abrahamic sense of the word but a loose philosophy, one that has no answers but merely questions. The only clear guiding principle is *ambiguity*. If there is a central verse in Hinduism's most important text, the *Rig Veda*, it is the Creation Hymn. It reads, in part,

> Who really knows, and who can swear,
> How creation came, when or where!
> Even gods came after creation's day,
> Who really knows, who can truly say
> When and how did creation start?
> Did He do it? Or did He not?
> Only He, up there, knows, maybe;
> Or perhaps, not even He.

Compare that with the certainties of the Book of Genesis.

So what does all of this mean for the real world? Hindus are deeply practical. They can easily find an accommodation with the outside reality. Indian businessmen—who are still largely Hindu—can thrive in almost any atmosphere that allows for trade and commerce. Whether in America, Africa, or East Asia, Indian merchants have prospered in any country they live in. As long as they can place a small idol somewhere in their home for worship or meditation, their own sense of Hinduism is fulfilled. As with Buddhism, Hinduism promotes tolerance of differences but also absorption of them. Islam in India has been altered through its contact with Hinduism, becoming less Abrahamic and more spiritual. Indian Muslims worship saints and shrines, celebrate music and art, and have a more practical outlook on life than many of their coreligionists abroad. While the rise of Islamic fundamentalism over the last few decades has pushed Islam in India backward, as it has everywhere, there are still broader societal forces pulling it along with the Indian mainstream. That may explain the remarkable statistic (which may prove to be an exaggeration) that though there are 150 million Muslims in India who watched the rise of the Taliban and Al Qaeda in neighboring Afghanistan and Pakistan, not one Indian Muslim has been found to be affiliated with Al Qaeda.

And what of foreign policy? It is clear that Indians are fundamentally more comfortable with ambiguity and uncertainty than many Westerners, certainly than Anglo-Americans. Indians are not likely to view foreign policy as a crusade or to see the conversion of others to democracy as a paramount national aspiration. The Hindu mind-set is to live and let live. So, Indians are also averse to public and binding commitments of the country's basic orientation. India will be uncomfortable with a designation as America's "chief ally" in Asia or as part of a new "special relationship." This discomfort with stark and explicit definitions of friend and foe might be an Asian trait. NATO might have been the perfect alliance for a group of Western countries—a formal alliance against Soviet expansionism, with institutions and military exercises. In Asia most nations will resist such explicit balancing mechanisms.

They might all hedge against China, but *none will ever admit it*. Whether because of culture or circumstance, it will be the power politics that dare not speak its name.

As in China, however, in India cultural DNA has to be layered with more recent history. In fact, India has lived through a unique Western experience as a part of the British Empire—learning English, adopting British political and legal institutions, running imperial policies. Liberal ideas now permeate Indian thought, to the point that they have become in many ways local. Nehru had his worldview and foreign policy formed of influences that were predominantly Western, liberal, and socialist. The debate about human rights and democracy that courses through the West today is one that finds a comfortable place in New Delhi, Mumbai, and Chennai. Indian newspapers and NGOs raise the same concerns and alarms as Western ones do. They make the same critiques of government policy as those in London, Paris, and Washington. But these attitudes are most true of India's English-speaking elite—still a minority in the country—that is in some ways more comfortable in the West's world than in its own. (Ask an educated Indian businessman, scholar, scientist, or bureaucrat what was the last book he read in a language other than English.) Mahatma Gandhi was a more distinctly Indian figure. His foreign policy ideas were a mixture of Hindu nonviolence and Western radicalism, topped up with a shrewd practicality that was probably shaped by his merchant class background. When Nehru called himself the "last" Englishman to rule India, he sensed that as the country developed, its own cultural roots would begin showing more clearly and would be ruled by more "authentic" Indians. These crosscutting Western and Indian influences are playing themselves out on a very modern and fast-changing world stage, where economics and politics are pulling in sometimes different directions.

Nuclear Power

The proposed nuclear agreement between America and India offers a fascinating illustration of tension between a purely economic view of globalization, on the one hand, and power politics, on the other. In 2007, Washington put its relations with India onto a higher plane of cooperation with the negotiation of a nuclear agreement. This might sound like an issue for policy wonks, but the nuclear deal is actually a big deal. If successful, it will alter the strategic landscape, bringing India firmly and irrevocably onto the global stage as a major player, normalizing its furtive nuclear status, and cementing its partnership with the United States. It puts India on par with the other members of the nuclear club, America, Britain, France, Russia, and China.

According to the Nuclear Nonproliferation Treaty, a country that had nuclear weapons in 1968 is a legitimate nuclear-weapon state, and any country that developed them later is an outlaw. (It was the mother of all grandfather clauses.) India, which exploded a nuclear device in 1974, is the most important country, and the only potential global power, that lies outside the nonproliferation system. The Bush administration has argued that bringing it in is crucial to the system's survival. For similar reasons, Mohamed ElBaradei, head of the International Atomic Energy Agency (which is charged with monitoring and enforcing nonproliferation), has been a staunch

supporter of the Indo-U.S. agreement.[9] The nuclear nonproliferation regime has always tempered idealism with a healthy
dose of realism. The United States, after all, goes around the
world telling countries that a few more nuclear warheads are
dangerous and immoral—while holding on to thousands of
nuclear weapons of its own.

For India, the nuclear deal comes down to something quite
simple: Is India more like China or more like North Korea?
New Delhi argues that the world should accept that India is a
nuclear power, while India should in return be willing to make
its program as safe and secure as possible. Until the Bush
administration, for decades American policy was to try to
reverse India's weapons program, a fruitless task. India has
spent thirty-three years under American sanctions without
budging—even when it was a much poorer country—and anyone who understands the country knows that it would happily
spend many more before even thinking about giving up its
nuclear weapons.

From an economic point of view, the nuclear deal is not that
crucial for India. It would provide the country with greater
access to civilian nuclear technologies, which is important to
its energy needs. But that's a small part of its overall development trajectory. The incentives of globalization would seem to
push New Delhi to stop wasting its time on this matter, focus
on development while pushing off these concerns until a later
date. There are many forms of alternative energy, and both
Germany and Japan have managed to achieve great-power
status without nuclear weapons.

India's nuclear aspirations, however, are about national
pride and geopolitical strategy. Many Indian politicians and
diplomats resent the fact that India will always have second-

class status compared with China, Russia, and the other major nuclear powers. In all those countries, not one reactor is under any inspection regime whatsoever, yet India would place at least two-thirds of its program under the eye of the International Atomic Energy Agency. The inequity with China especially offends New Delhi. Indian officials will quietly point out that China has a long history of abetting nuclear proliferation, most clearly through Pakistan. Yet the United States has an arrangement to share civilian nuclear technology with Beijing. India, they argue, is a democratic, transparent country with a perfect record of nonproliferation. Yet it has been denied such cooperation for the past thirty-three years.

On this issue, globalization and geopolitics operate on different levels. Many American advocates of nuclear disarmament—whom the Indians call "nonproliferation ayatollahs"—oppose the deal, or would settle for one only if India were to cap its production of fissile material. But, New Delhi says, look at a map: India is bordered by China and Pakistan, both nuclear-weapons states, neither of which has agreed to a mandatory cap. (China appears to have stopped producing plutonium, as have the other major powers, but this is a voluntary decision, made largely because it is awash in fissile material already.) India sees a mandatory cap as a one-sided nuclear freeze. This strategic reality figures into American calculations as well. The United States has long been opposed to a single hegemon dominating either Europe or Asia. Were India to be forced to cap its nuclear force—without corresponding constraints on China—the result would be a vast and growing imbalance of power in China's favor. A former U.S. ambassador to India, Robert Blackwill, has asked, Why is it in the United States' long-term national interest to favor an arrangement by which China would become Asia's dominant and unchallenged nuclear power?[10]

Bizarrely, the real stumbling block to the deal has come not from Washington but from New Delhi. On being handed the offer of a lifetime, some leading Indian politicians and intellectuals have refused. "We don't seem to know how to take yes for an answer," a commentator observed on the Indian all-news channel NDTV. While the Indian prime minister and some others at the top of the Indian government saw the immense opportunities the deal would open up for India, others were blinded by old nostrums and prejudice. Many Indian elites have continued to view the world through a Nehruvian prism—India as a poor, virtuous Third World country, whose foreign policy was neutral and detached (and, one might add, unsuccessful). They understand how to operate in that world, whom to beg from and whom to be belligerent with. But a world in which India is a great power and moves confidently across the global stage, setting rules and not merely being shaped by them, and in which it is a partner of the most powerful country in history—that is an altogether new and unsettling proposition. "Why is the United States being nice to us now?" several such commentators have asked me. In 2007, they were still searching for the hidden hand.

China's mandarin class has been able to rethink its country's new role as a world power with skill and effectiveness. So far, India's elites have not shown themselves the equals of their neighbors. Whichever way the nuclear deal goes, the difficulties of its passage in New Delhi highlight the central constraint on the exercise of Indian power in the years ahead. India is a strong society with a weak state. It cannot harness its national power for national purpose.

A Geographic Expression

You can tell that India is a strange land not by looking at snake charmers but by observing its election results: In what other country would sizzling economic growth make you unpopular? In 2004, the ruling BJP coalition went to the polls with the economic wind at its back—the country was growing 9 percent. But the BJP lost the election. A cottage industry of intellectuals, many of them socialist in orientation, quickly explained that the prosperity had been hollow, that growth hadn't trickled down, and that the BJP had forgotten about the real India. But this explanation simply does not bear close examination. Poverty rates in India had fallen rapidly in the 1990s, in numbers large enough to be visible to all. And in any event, the puzzle continued after 2004. The Congress coalition (currently in power) has sustained growth over 8 percent for three years, and yet it has fared poorly in every regional election held since it took office. Even with legitimate concerns over inequality and the distribution of wealth, there is a connection between robust growth and government popularity in almost every country in the world. Why not in India?

India is Thomas (Tip) O'Neill's dreamland. "All politics is local," the former Speaker of the House of Representatives famously said. In India, that principle can be carved in stone. India's elections are not really national elections at all. They are rather simultaneous regional and local elections that have no common theme.

India's diversity is four thousand years old and deeply rooted in culture, language, and tradition. This is a country with seventeen languages and 22,000 dialects that was for centuries a collection of hundreds of separate principalities, king-doms, and states. When the British were leaving India, in 1947, the new government had to negotiate individual acces-sion agreements with over five hundred rulers—bribing them, threatening them, and, in some cases, militarily coercing them into joining the Indian union. Since the decline of the Indian National Congress in the 1970s, no party in India has had a national footprint. Every government formed for the last two decades has been a coalition, comprising an accumulation of regional parties with little in common. Ruchir Sharma, who runs Morgan Stanley's $35 billion emerging-markets portfolio, points out that a majority of the country's twenty-eight states have voted for a dominant regional party at the expense of a so-called national party.

Uttar Pradesh in 2007 provides a perfect example. U.P., as it is called in India, is the country's largest state. (Were it inde-pendent, its population would make it the sixth-largest coun-try in the world.) During the 2007 campaign, the two national parties tried to run on what they saw as the great national issues. The BJP worked assiduously to revive Hindu national-ism; the Congress stressed its secularist credentials and boasted of the country's growth rate. The two parties came in a distant third and fourth, behind local parties that stressed purely local issues—in this case, the empowerment of the lower castes. What worked in U.P. might not work in the south, or even in Mumbai. The Hindu-Muslim divide might be crucially important in one set of states, but it is absent in others. Political leaders who are strong in Tamil Nadu have no following whatsoever in the north. Punjab has its own distinct political culture that relates to Sikh issues and the history of Hindu-Sikh relations. Politicians from Rajasthan have no appeal in Karnataka. They cannot speak each other's language —literally. It would be like holding elections across Europe and trying to talk about the same issues with voters in Poland, Greece, France, and Ireland. Winston Churchill once said that India was "just a geographic term, with no more political personality than Europe." Churchill was usually wrong about India, but on this issue, he had a point.

This diversity and division has many advantages. It adds to India's variety and societal energy, and it prevents the country from succumbing to dictatorship. When Indira Gandhi tried to run the government in an authoritarian and centralized manner in the 1970s, it simply didn't work, provoking violent revolts in six of its regions. Over the last two decades, Indian regionalism has flourished, and the country has found its natural order. Even hypernationalism becomes difficult in a diverse land. When the BJP tries to unleash Hindu chauvinism as a political weapon against India's Muslim minority, it often finds that lower-caste Hindus, as well as south Indians, are alienated and rattled by the rhetoric, which sounds exclusionary and upper-caste to them.

But this diversity and division also complicate the work of the Indian state. The constraints of the past decade are not transient phenomena that will fade; they are expressions of a structural reality in Indian politics. They make it difficult for New Delhi to define a national interest, mobilize the country behind it, and then execute a set of policies to achieve its goals, whether in economic reform or foreign policy. The prime minister cannot command national power the way that Nehru did, and in all probability no prime minister will ever do so again. The office has gone from commander in chief to chairman of the board, and the ruling party has become first among equals in a coalition. The central government often gives in to the prerogatives and power of the regional governments, which are increasingly assertive and independent. In economic terms, this means a future of muddling along, minor reforms, and energy and experimentation at the state level. In foreign policy, it means no large shifts in approach, few major commitments, and a less active and energetic role on the world stage. India will have a larger role in international affairs than ever before. It will dominate South Asia. But it may not become the global power that some hope for and others fear. At least not for a while.

If there ever was a race between India and China, it's over. China's economy is three times the size of India's and is still growing at a faster clip. The law of compounding tells us that India can overtake China economically only if there are drastic and sustained shifts in both countries' trajectories that last for decades. The more likely scenario is that China will stay well ahead of India. But India can still capitalize on its advantages— a vast, growing economy, an attractive political democracy, a vibrant model of secularism and tolerance, a keen knowledge of both East and West, and a special relationship with America. If it can mobilize these forces and use them to its advantage, India will still make for a powerful package, whether it is technically number two, or three, or four in the world.

One experience relevant to India today is that of the United States of America in the late nineteenth century. Domestic constraints substantially slowed America's political rise to world power. By 1890, America had overtaken Britain as the world's leading economy, but in diplomatic and military terms, it was a second-rung power. Its army ranked fourteenth in the world, after Bulgaria's. Its navy was one-eighth the size of

Italy's, even though its industrial strength was by then thirteen times bigger. It participated in few international meetings or congresses, and its diplomats were small-time players in global affairs. Washington was a small, parochial town, its government had limited powers, and the presidency was not generally regarded as a pivotal post. That America was a weak state in the late nineteenth century was undeniable, and it took decades, large domestic changes, and deep international crises for this to change. In the aftermath of depressions and world wars, the American state—Washington—grew, centralized, and gained unquestioned precedence over the states. And presidents from Theodore Roosevelt to Woodrow Wilson began defining America as a world power.

Ultimately, the base of American power—a vibrant American society—was its greatest strength and its weakness. It produced America's gigantic economy and vibrant society. But it also made its rise halting, its course erratic, and its involvement on the world stage always fragile. Perhaps India will have a similar experience: it will have a society able to respond superbly to the opportunities of a globalized world, one that will grow and prosper in the global economy and society. But India's political system is weak and porous and thus not well equipped to play its rightful role in this new world. A series of crises might change all this, but absent a shock to the system, India's society will stay ahead of the Indian state in the new global game.

This tension between society and the state persists in America to this day. In fact, it's worth keeping in mind as we turn to the single most important player in the twenty-first century and ask how America itself will react to a post-American world.

6

American Power

On June 22, 1897, about four hundred million people around the world, one-fourth of humanity, got the day off. It was the sixtieth anniversary of Queen Victoria's ascension to the British throne. The Diamond Jubilee stretched over five days on land and sea, but its high point was the parade and thanksgiving service on June 22. The eleven premiers of Britain's self-governing colonies were in attendance, along with princes, dukes, ambassadors, and envoys from the rest of the world. A military procession of fifty thousand soldiers included hussars from Canada, cavalrymen from New South Wales, carabineers from Naples, camel troops from Bikaner, Gurkhas from Nepal, and many, many others. It was, as one historian wrote, "a Roman moment."

The jubilee was marked with great fanfare in every corner of the empire. "In Hyderabad every tenth convict was set free," wrote James Morris. "There was a grand ball at Rangoon, a dinner at the Sultan's palace in Zanzibar, a salute of gunboats in Table Bay, a 'monster Sunday-school treat' at Freetown, a performance of the Hallelujah Chorus in Happy Valley at Hong Kong." Bangalore erected a statue of the queen, and Vishakapattnam got a new town hall. In Singapore, a statue of Sir Stamford Raffles was placed in the middle of Padang, and a fountain was built in the middle of the public gardens in Shanghai (not even a colony). Ten thousand schoolchildren marched through the streets of Ottawa waving British flags. And on and on.[1]

Back in London, young Arnold Toynbee, an eight-year-old boy, was perched on his uncle's shoulders, eagerly watching the parade. Toynbee, who grew up to become the most famous historian of his age, recalled that watching the grandeur of the day it felt as if the sun were "standing still in the midst of Heaven, as it had once stood still there at the bidding of Joshua." "I remember the atmosphere," he wrote. "It was: 'Well, here we are on top of the world, and we have arrived at this peak to stay there forever. There is, of course, a thing called history, but history is something unpleasant that happens to other people. We are comfortably outside all of that I am sure.'"[2]

But, of course, history did happen to Britain. The question for the superpower of our own age is, Will history happen to America as well? Is it already happening? No analogy is exact, but Britain in its heyday is the closest any nation in the modern age has come to the American position today. When we consider whether and how the forces of change will affect America, it's worth paying close attention to the experience of Great Britain.

There are many contemporary echoes of Britain's dilemmas. America's recent militarily interventions in Somalia, Afghanistan, and Iraq all have parallels with Britain's military interventions there decades ago. The basic strategic dilemma of being the only truly global player on the world stage is strikingly similar. But there are also fundamental differences between Britain then and America now. In Britain, as it tried to maintain its superpower status, the largest challenge was *economic* rather than *political*. In America, it is the other way around.

Britain's Reach

In today's world, it is difficult even to imagine the magnitude of the British Empire. At its height, it covered about a quarter of the earth's land surface and included a quarter of its population. London's network of colonies, territories, bases, and ports spanned the entire globe, and the empire was protected by the Royal Navy, the greatest seafaring force in history. During the Diamond Jubilee, 165 ships carrying forty thousand seamen and three thousand guns were on display in Portsmouth—the largest fleet ever assembled.* Over the preceding quarter century, the empire had been linked by 170,000 nautical miles of ocean cables and 662,000 miles of aerial and buried cables, and British ships had facilitated the development of the first global communications network via the telegraph. Railways and canals (the Suez Canal, most importantly) deepened the connectivity of the system.

---

* Observers from fourteen foreign navies were in attendance, eagerly taking in the spectacle. One of them, the German rear admiral Prince Henry of Prussia, looked on enviously from the deck of his British-built battleship, which had recently been downgraded to a cruiser. He and his brother, Kaiser Wilhelm II, desperately hoped to catch up with Britain in naval power—a story that ended badly.

Through all of this, the British Empire created the first truly global market.

Americans talk about the appeal of our own culture and ideas, but "soft power" really began with Britain in the nineteenth century. Thanks to the empire, English spread as a global language, spoken from the Caribbean to Cairo and from Cape Town to Calcutta. English literature became familiar everywhere—Shakespeare, Sherlock Holmes, *Alice in Wonderland*, *Tom Brown's School Days*. Britain's stories and characters became more securely a part of international culture than any other nation's.

So, too, did many English values. The historian Claudio Véliz points out that in the seventeenth century, the two imperial powers of the day, Britain and Spain, both tried to export their ideas and practices to their Western colonies. Spain wanted the Counter-Reformation to take hold in the New World; Britain wanted religious pluralism and capitalism to flourish. As it turned out, Britain's ideas proved more universal than Spain's. In fact, modern society's modes of work and play are suffused with the values of the world's first industrial nation. Britain has arguably been the most successful exporter of its culture in human history. We speak today of the American dream, but before it there was an "English way of life"—one that was watched, admired, and copied throughout the world. For example, the ideas of fair play, athleticism, and amateurism propounded by the famous English educator Dr. Thomas Arnold, headmaster of Rugby (where *Tom Brown's School Days* was set), heavily influenced the Frenchman Baron de Coubertin—who, in 1896, launched the modern Olympic games. The writer Ian Buruma has aptly described the Olympics as "an English Bucolic fantasy."

Not all of this was recognized in June 1897, but much of it was. The British were hardly alone in making comparisons between their empire and Rome. Paris' *Le Figaro* declared that Rome itself had been "equaled, if not surpassed, by the Power which in Canada, Australia, India, in the China Seas, in Egypt, Central and Southern Africa, in the Atlantic and in the Mediterranean rules the peoples and governs their interests." The *Kreuz-Zeitung* in Berlin, which usually reflected the views of the anti-English Junker elite, described the empire as "practically unassailable." Across the Atlantic, the *New York Times* gushed, "We are a part, and a great part, of the Greater Britain which seems so plainly destined to dominate this planet."

Britain's Descent

Britain's exalted position was more fragile than it appeared. Just two years after the Diamond Jubilee, the United Kingdom entered the Boer War, a conflict that, for many scholars, marks the moment when its global power began to decline. London was sure that it would win the fight with little trouble. After all, the British army had just won a similar battle against the dervishes in Sudan, despite being outnumbered by more than two to one. In the Battle of Omdurman, it inflicted 48,000 dervish casualties in just five hours, while losing only 48 soldiers of its own.[3] Many in Britain imagined an even easier victory against the Boers. After all, as one member of Parliament put it, it was "the British empire against 30,000 farmers."

The war was ostensibly fought for virtuous reasons: the rights of South Africa's English-speaking people, who were treated as second-class citizens by the ruling Dutch migrants, the Boers (*Boer* is the Dutch, and Afrikaans, word for "farmer"). But it did not escape the attention of London that, after the discovery of gold in the region in 1886, South Africa had been producing a quarter of the world's gold supply. And in any event, the Afrikaners launched a preemptive strike, and war began in 1899.

Things went badly for Britain from the beginning. It had more men and better weapons and was fielding its best generals (including Lord Kitchener, the hero of Omdurman). But the Boers were passionate in defending themselves, knew the land, had the support of much of the white population, and adopted successful guerrilla tactics that relied on stealth and speed. Britain's enormous military superiority meant little on the ground, and the British commanders resorted to brutal tactics—burning down villages, herding civilians into concentration camps (the world's first), sending in more and more troops. Eventually, Britain had 450,000 troops in southern Africa fighting a militia of 45,000.

The Boers could not hold Britain back forever, and in 1902 they surrendered. But in a larger sense, Britain lost the war. It had sacrificed 45,000 men, spent half a billion pounds, stretched its army to the breaking point, and discovered enormous incompetence and corruption in its war effort. Its brutal wartime tactics, moreover, gave it a black eye in the view of the rest of the world. At home, all of this created, or exposed, deep divisions over Britain's global role. Abroad, every other great power—France, Germany, the United States—opposed London's actions. "They were friendless," the historian Lawrence James wrote of the British in 1902.[4]

Fast forward to today. Another all-powerful superpower, militarily unbeatable, wins an easy victory in Afghanistan and then takes on what it is sure will be another simple battle, this one against Saddam Hussein's isolated regime in Iraq. The result: a quick initial military victory followed by a long, arduous struggle, filled with political and military blunders and met with intense international opposition. The analogy is obvious; the United States is Britain, the Iraq War is the Boer War—and, by extension, America's future looks bleak. Whatever the outcome in Iraq, the costs have been massive. The United States has been overextended and distracted, its army stressed, its image sullied. Rogue states like Iran and Venezuela and great powers like Russia and China are taking advantage of Washington's inattention and bad fortunes. The familiar theme of imperial decline is playing itself out one more time. History is happening again.

But whatever the apparent similarities, the circumstances are not really the same. Britain was a strange superpower. Historians have written hundreds of books explaining how London could have adopted certain foreign policies to change its fortunes. If only it had avoided the Boer War, say some. If only it had stayed out of Africa, say others. Niall Ferguson provocatively suggests that, had Britain stayed out of World War I (and there might not have been a world war without British participation), it might have managed to preserve its great-power position. There is some truth to this line of reasoning (World War I did bankrupt Britain), but to put things properly in historical context, it is worth looking at this history from another angle. Britain's immense empire was the product of unique circumstances. The wonder is not that Britain declined, but that its dominance lasted as long as it did.[5] Understanding how Britain played its hand—one that got weaker over time—might help illuminate America's path forward.

The Strange Rise of British Power

Britain has been a rich country for centuries (and a great power for most of that time), but it was an economic *superpower* for little longer than a generation. We often make the mistake of dating Britain's apogee by the great imperial events, such as the Diamond Jubilee, that were seen at the time as the markers of power. In fact, by 1897, Britain's best years were already behind it. Britain's true apogee was a generation earlier, from 1845 to 1870. At the time, Britain was producing more than 30 percent of global GDP. Its energy consumption was five times that of the United States and Prussia and 155 times that of Russia. It accounted for one-fifth of the world's trade and two-fifths of its manufacturing trade.[6] And all this with just 2 percent of the world's population!

In 1820, when population and agriculture were the main determinants of GDP, France's economy was larger than Britain's. By the late 1870s, the United States had equaled Britain on most industrial measures and actually surpassed it by the early 1880s, as Germany would about fifteen years later. By World War I, the American economy was twice the size of Britain's, and together France's and Russia's were larger as well. In 1860, Britain produced 53 percent of the world's iron (then a sign of supreme industrial strength); in 1914, it made less than 10 percent.

There are, of course, many ways of measuring power. Politically, London was still the capital of the world at the time of World War I. Across the globe beyond Europe, London's writ was unequaled and largely unchallenged. Britain had acquired an empire in a period before the onset of nationalism, and so there were few obstacles to creating and maintaining control in far-flung places. Its sea power was unrivaled for over a century. It had also proved to be highly skilled at the art of empire. As a result of the empire, it remained dominant in banking, shipping, insurance, and investments. London was still the center of global finance and the pound still the reserve currency of the world. Even in 1914, Britain invested twice as much capital abroad as its closest competitor, France, and five times as much as the United States. The economic returns of these investments and other "invisible trades" in some ways masked Britain's decline.

The reality, however, was that Britain's economy was sliding. In those days, manufacturing still accounted for the bulk of a national economy, and the goods Britain was producing represented the past rather than the future. In 1907, it manufactured four times as many bicycles as the United States did, but the United States manufactured twelve times as many cars. The gap was visible in the chemical industry, the production of scientific instruments, and many other areas. The overall trend was clear: British growth rates had dropped from 2.6 percent in its heyday to 1.9 percent from 1885 onward, and falling. The United States and Germany, meanwhile, were growing at around 5 percent. Having spearheaded the first industrial revolution, Britain had been less adept at moving into the second.

Scholars have debated the causes of Britain's decline since shortly after that decline began. Some have focused on geopolitics; others, on economic factors like low investment in new plants and equipment, bad labor relations, and a loss of marketing skills. British capitalism had remained old-fashioned and rigid. British industries were set up as small cottage-scale enterprises with skilled craftsmen rather than the rationally organized mass factories that sprang up in Germany and the United States. There were signs of broader cultural problems as well. A wealthier Britain was losing its focus on practical education. Science and geography were subordinated to literature and philosophy. British society retained a feudal cast, given to it by its landowning aristocracy. This elite disdained manufacturing and technology, so much so that successful entrepreneurs would set themselves up as faux aristocrats, with country houses and horses, and hide every trace of where the money had come from. Rather than study chemistry or electrical engineering, their sons spent their days at Oxbridge ingesting the history and literature of ancient Greece and Rome.[7]

Perhaps none of these failings were actually crucial. Paul Kennedy points out that Britain's dominance in the nineteenth century was the product of a series of highly unusual circumstances. Given its portfolio of power—geography, population, resources—it could reasonably have expected to have 3 to 4 percent of global GDP, but its share rose to around *ten times* that figure. As those unusual circumstances abated—as other Western countries caught up with industrialization, as Germany united, and as the United States resolved its North-South divide—Britain was bound to decline. The British statesman Leo Amery saw this clearly in 1905. "How can these little islands hold their own in the long run against such great and rich empires as the United States and Germany are rapidly becoming?" he asked. "How can we with forty millions of people compete with states nearly double our size?" It is a question that many Americans are now asking about the United States in the face of China's ascent.

Good Politics, Bad Economics

Britain managed to maintain its position as the leading world power for decades after it lost its economic dominance, thanks to a combination of shrewd strategic outlook and good diplomacy. Early on, as it saw the balance of power shifting, London made one critical decision that extended its influence by decades: it chose to accommodate itself to the rise of America rather than to contest it. In the decades after 1880, on issue after issue London gave in to a growing and assertive Washington. It was not easy for London to concede control to its former colony, a country with which it had fought two wars (the Revolutionary War and the War of 1812) and in whose recent Civil War it had sympathized with the secessionists. Still, Britain ultimately ceded the Western Hemisphere to its former colony, despite having vast interests of its own there.*

It was a strategic masterstroke. Had Britain tried to resist the rise of the United States, on top of all its other commitments, it would have been bled dry. For all of its mistakes over the next half century, London's strategy toward Washington—one followed by every British government since the 1890s—meant that Britain could focus its attention on other critical fronts. As a result, it remained the master of the seas, controlling its lanes and pathways with "five keys" that were said to

---

* During one of the crises in which Britain eventually gave in, over a boundary between Venezuela and British Guiana in 1895, the colonial secretary, Joseph Chamberlain, angrily pointed out, "Britain is an American power with a territorial area greater than the United States itself and with title acquired prior to the independence of the United States." (He was referring to Canada.)

lock up the world—Singapore, the Cape of Africa, Alexandria, Gibraltar, and Dover.

Britain maintained its control of the empire and worldwide influence with relatively little opposition for many decades. In the settlement after World War I, it took over 1.8 million square miles of territory and thirteen million new subjects, mostly in the Middle East. Still, the gap between its political role and its economic capacity was growing. While the empire might originally have been profitable, by the twentieth century it was an enormous drain on the British treasury. And this was no time for expensive habits. The British economy was reeling. World War I cost over $40 billion, and Britain, once the world's leading creditor, had debts amounting to 136 percent of domestic output afterwards.[8] The tenfold rise in government debt meant that by the mid-1920s interest payments alone sucked up half the government's budget. Britain wanted to keep up militarily and, after World War I, bought up the German fleet at fire-sale prices and momentarily retained its status as the leading naval power. But, by 1936, Germany's defense spending was three times higher than Britain's.[9] The same year that Italy invaded Abyssinia, Mussolini also placed fifty thousand troops in Libya—ten times the number of British troops guarding the Suez Canal.[10] It was these circumstances—coupled with the memory of a recent world war that killed more than seven hundred thousand young Britons—that led the British governments of the 1930s, facing the forces of fascism, to prefer wishful thinking and appeasement to confrontation.

Financial concerns now dictated strategy. The decision to turn Singapore into a "massive naval base" is a perfect illustration of this. Britain saw this "eastern Gibraltar" as a strategic bottleneck between the Indian and Pacific oceans that could

stop the westward movement of Japan. (Britain had the option
of maintaining its alliance with Tokyo—more accommodation
—but the United States and Australia had objected.) The strategy was sensible. Given Britain's precarious finances, however,
there was not enough money to fund it. The dockyards were too
small for a fleet that could have taken on the Japanese, the fuel
insufficient, the fortifications modest. When the Japanese
attack came in 1942, Singapore fell in one week.

World War II was the final nail in the coffin of British economic power. (In 1945, American GDP was *ten times* that of
Britain.) Even then, however, Britain remained remarkably
influential, at least partly because of the almost superhuman
energy and ambition of Winston Churchill. When you consider that the United States was paying most of the Allies' economic costs, and Russia was bearing most of the casualties, it
took extraordinary will for Britain to remain one of the three
major powers deciding the fate of the postwar world. The pho-
tographs of Roosevelt, Stalin, and Churchill at the Yalta Conference in February 1945 are somewhat misleading. There was
no "big three" at Yalta. There was a "big two" plus one brilliant
political entrepreneur who was able to keep himself and his
country in the game, so that Britain maintained many elements of great powerdom well into the late twentieth century.

Of course, it came at a cost. In return for its loans to Lon-
don, the United States took over dozens of British bases in the
Caribbean, Canada, the Indian Ocean, and the Pacific. "The
British empire is handed over to the American pawnbroker—
our only hope," said one member of Parliament. The econo-
mist John Maynard Keynes was more enraged, describing the
Lend-Lease Act as an attempt to "pick out the eyes of the
British empire." Less emotional observers saw that it was

inevitable. Arnold Toynbee, by then a distinguished historian, consoled Britons that America's "hand will be a great deal lighter than Russia's, Germany's, or Japan's, and I suppose these are the alternatives."

The fundamental point is that Britain was undone as a great global power not because of bad politics but because of bad economics. It had great global influence, but its economy was structurally weak. And it made matters worse by attempting ill-advised fixes—going off and on the gold standard, imposing imperial tariffs, running up huge war debts. After World War II, it adopted a socialist economic program, the Beveridge Plan, which nationalized and tightly regulated large parts of the economy. This may have been understandable as a reaction to the country's battered condition, but by the 1960s and 1970s it had condemned Britain to stagnation—until Margaret Thatcher helped turn the British economy around in the 1980s.

Despite a seventy-year-long decline in its relative economic place, London played its weakening hand with impressive political skill. Its history offers some important lessons for the United States.

America's Long Run

First, however, it is essential to note that the central feature of Britain's decline—irreversible economic deterioration—does not really apply to the United States today. Britain's unrivaled economic status lasted for a few decades; America's has lasted more than 130 years. The U.S. economy has been the world's largest since the middle of the 1880s, and it remains so today. In fact, America has held a surprisingly constant share of global GDP ever since. With the brief exception of the late 1940s and 1950s—when the rest of the industrialized world had been destroyed and America's share rose to 50 percent!—the United States has accounted for roughly a quarter of world output for over a century (32 percent in 1913, 26 percent in 1960, 22 percent in 1980, 27 percent in 2000, and 26 percent in 2007).* It is likely to slip but not significantly in the next two decades. In 2025, most estimates suggest that the U.S. economy will still be twice the size of China's in terms of nominal GDP (though in terms of purchasing power, the gap will be smaller).[11]

This difference between America and Britain can be seen in the burden of their military budgets. Britannia ruled the seas but never the land. The British army was sufficiently small that the German chancellor Otto von Bismarck once quipped that, were the British ever to invade Germany, he would simply have the local police force arrest them. Meanwhile, London's advantage over the seas—it had more tonnage than the next two navies put together—came at ruinous cost to its treasury. The American military, in contrast, dominates at every level—land, sea, air, space—and spends more than the next fourteen countries put together, accounting for almost 50 percent of global defense spending. Some argue that even this understates America's military lead against the rest of the world because it does not take into account the U.S. scientific and technological edge. The United States spends more on defense research and development than the rest of the world

---

* These numbers are based on market exchange rates, not adjusted for living standards. The numbers in PPP dollars would be 19 percent in 1913, 27 percent in 1950, 22 percent in 1973, 22 percent in 1998, and 19 percent in 2007. The PPP numbers also show the same pattern, of American power being relatively stable at around 20 percent of global GDP.

put together. And, crucially, it does all this without breaking the bank. Defense expenditure as a percent of GDP is now 4.1 percent, lower than it was for most of the Cold War. (Under Eisenhower, it rose to 10 percent of GDP.) The secret here is the denominator. As U.S. GDP grows larger and larger, expenditures that would have been backbreaking become affordable. The Iraq War may be a tragedy or a noble endeavor, depending on your point of view. Either way, however, it will not bankrupt the United States. The war has been expensive, but the price tag for Iraq and Afghanistan together—$125 billion a year—represents less than 1 percent of GDP. Vietnam, by comparison, cost 1.6 percent of American GDP in 1970 and tens of thousands more soldiers' lives.

American military power is not the cause of its strength but the consequence. The fuel is America's economic and technological base, which remains extremely strong. The United States does face larger, deeper, and broader challenges than it has ever faced in its history, and the rise of the rest does mean that it will lose some share of global GDP. But the process will look nothing like Britain's slide in the twentieth century, when the country lost the lead in innovation, energy, and entrepreneurship. America will remain a vital, vibrant economy, at the forefront of the next revolutions in science, technology, and industry—as long as it can embrace and adjust to the challenges confronting it.

The Future Is Here

When trying to explain how America will fare in the new world, I sometimes say, "Look around." The future is already

here. Over the last twenty years, globalization has been gaining breadth and depth. More countries are making goods,
communications technology has been leveling the playing
field, capital has been free to move across the world. And
America has benefited massively from these trends. Its economy has received hundreds of billions of dollars in investment
—a rarity for a country with much capital of its own. Its companies have entered new countries and industries with great
success and used new technologies and processes, all to keep
boosting their bottom lines. Despite two decades of a very
expensive dollar, American exports have held ground.

GDP growth, the bottom line, has averaged just over 3 percent for twenty-five years, significantly higher than in Europe.
(Japan's averaged 2.3 percent over the same period.) Productivity growth, the elixir of modern economics, has been over
2.5 percent for a decade now, again a full percentage point
higher than the European average. The United States is currently ranked as the most competitive economy in the world
by the World Economic Forum. These rankings have been
produced every year since 1979, and the U.S. position has
been fairly constant, slipping sometimes in recent years to
small northern European countries like Sweden, Denmark,
and Finland (whose collective population is twenty million,
less than that of the state of Texas). America's superior growth
trajectory might be petering out, and perhaps its growth will
be more "normal" for an advanced industrial country for the
next few years. But the general point—that America is a highly
dynamic economy at the cutting edge, despite its enormous
size—still holds.

Look at the industries of the future. Nanotechnology—
applied science dealing with the control of matter at the

atomic or molecular scale—is considered likely to lead to fundamental breakthroughs over the next fifty years. At some point in the future, or so I'm told, households will construct products out of raw materials, and businesses will simply create the formulas that turn atoms into goods. Whether this is hype or prescience, what is worth noticing is that by every conceivable measure, the United States dominates the field. It has more dedicated nanocenters than the next three nations (Germany, the United Kingdom, and China) combined, and many of its new centers focus on narrow subjects with a high potential for practical, marketable applications— such as the Emory-Georgia Tech Nanotechnology Center for Personalized and Predictive Oncology. At market exchange rates, government nanotech funding in the United States is almost double that of its closest competitor, Japan. And while China, Japan, and Germany contribute a fair share of journal articles on nanoscale science and engineering topics, the United States has issued more patents for nanotechnology than the rest of the world combined, highlighting America's unusual strength in turning abstract theory into practical products.

The firm Lux, led by Dr. Michael Holman, constructed a matrix to assess countries' overall nanotech competitiveness. Their analysis looked not just at nanotechnology activity but also at the ability to "generate growth from scientific innovation."[12] It found that certain countries that spend much on research can't turn their science into business. These "Ivory Tower" nations have impressive research funding, journal articles, and even patents, but somehow don't manage to translate this into commercial goods and ideas. China, France, and even Britain fall into this category. A full 85 percent of venture capital investments in nanotechnology went to U.S. companies.

Biotechnology—a broad category that describes the use of biological systems to create medical, agricultural, and industrial products—is already a multibillion-dollar industry. It, too, is dominated by the United States. More than $3.3 billion in venture financing went to U.S. biotech companies in 2005, while European companies received just half that amount. Follow-on equity offerings (that is, post-IPO) in the United States were more than seven times those in Europe. And while European IPOs attracted more cash in 2005, IPO activity is highly volatile—in 2004, U.S. IPO values were more than four times Europe's. As with nanotechnology, American companies excel at turning ideas into marketable and lucrative products. U.S. biotech revenues approached $50 billion in 2005, five times greater than those in Europe and representing 76 percent of global revenues.*

Manufacturing has, of course, been leaving the United States, shifting to the developing world and turning America into a service economy. This scares many Americans and Europeans, who wonder what their countries will make if everything is "made in China." But Asian manufacturing must be viewed in the context of a global economy in which countries like China have become an important part of the supply chain—but still just a part.

---

* Of course, information from public companies represents only part of the picture, because more than three-quarters of the world's 4,203 biotech companies are held privately. Europe has a larger share of the world's private biotech companies, representing 42 percent of the total (compared with 31 percent in America). The United States, by contrast, is home to a greater share of public biotech companies (50 percent versus Europe's 18 percent), perhaps indicating the greater maturity of the U.S. market.

The *Atlantic Monthly* writer James Fallows spent a year in China watching that manufacturing juggernaut up close, and he provides a persuasive explanation—one well understood by Chinese businessmen—of how outsourcing has strengthened American competitiveness. Most Americans, even management experts, have not heard of the "smiley curve." But Chinese manufacturers know it well. Named for the U-shaped smile on the simple 1970s cartoon of a happy face, ☺, the curve illustrates the development of a product, from conception to sale. At the top left of the curve one starts with the idea and high-level industrial design—how the product will look and work. Lower down on the curve comes the detailed engineering plan. At the bottom of the U is the actual manufacturing, assembly, and shipping. Then rising up on the right of the curve are distribution, marketing, retail sales, service contracts, and sales of parts and accessories. Fallows observes that, in almost all manufacturing, China takes care of the bottom of the curve and America the top— the two ends of the U—which is where the money is. "The simple way to put this—that the real money is in the brand name, plus retail—may sound obvious," he writes, "but its implications are illuminating."[13] A vivid example of this is the iPod: it is manufactured mostly outside the United States, but the majority of value added is captured by Apple, Inc. in California. The company made $80 in gross profit on a 30-gigabyte video iPod that retailed (in late 2007) for $299. Its profit was 36 percent of the estimated wholesale price of $224. (Add to that the retail profit if it was sold in an Apple store.) The total cost of parts was $144.[14] Chinese manufacturers, by contrast, have margins of a few percent on their products.

America's Best Industry

"Ah yes," say those who are more worried, "but you're look-ing at a snapshot of today. America's advantages are rapidly eroding as the country loses its scientific and technological base." For some, the decline of science is symptomatic of a larger cultural decay. A country that once adhered to a Puri-tan ethic of delayed gratification has become one that revels in instant pleasures. We're losing interest in the basics—math, manufacturing, hard work, savings—and becoming a postindustrial society that specializes in consumption and leisure. "More people will graduate in the United States in 2006 with sports-exercise degrees than electrical-engineering degrees," says General Electric's CEO, Jeffrey Immelt. "So, if we want to be the massage capital of the world, we're well on our way."[15]

No statistic seems to capture this anxiety better than those showing the decline of engineering. In 2005, the National Academy of Sciences released a report warning that the United States could soon lose its privileged position as the world's science leader. In 2004, the report said, China graduated 600,000 engineers, India 350,000, and the United States 70,000. These numbers were repeated in hun-dreds of articles, books, and blogs, including a *Fortune* cover story, the *Congressional Record*, and speeches by technology titans like Bill Gates. And indeed, the figure does seem like cause for despair. What hope does the United States have if for every qualified American engineer there are 11 Chinese and Indian ones? For the cost of one chemist or engineer in the United States, the report pointed out, a company could hire 5 well-trained and eager chemists in China or 11 engineers in India.

The only problem is that the numbers are wildly off the mark. A journalist, Carl Bialik of the *Wall Street Journal*, and several academics investigated the matter. They quickly realized that the Asian totals included graduates of two- and three-year programs—people getting diplomas in simple technical tasks. A group of professors at the Pratt School of Engineering at Duke University traveled to China and India to collect data from governmental and nongovernmental sources and interview businessmen and academics. They concluded that eliminating graduates of two- or three-year programs halves the Chinese figure, to around 350,000 graduates, and even this number is probably significantly inflated by differing definitions of "engineer" that often include auto mechanics and industrial repairmen. Bialik notes that the National Science Foundation, which tracks these statistics in the United States and other nations, puts the Chinese number at about 200,000 degrees per year. Ron Hira, a professor of public policy at the Rochester Institute of Technology, puts the number of Indian graduates at 120,000–130,000 a year. That means the United States actually trains more engineers per capita than either India or China does.[16]

And the numbers don't address the issue of quality. As someone who grew up in India, I have a healthy appreciation for the virtues of its famous engineering academies, the Indian Institutes of Technology (IIT). Their greatest strength is that they administer one of the world's most ruthlessly competitive entrance exams. Three hundred thousand people take it, five thousand are admitted—an acceptance rate of 1.7 percent (compared with 9 to 10 percent for Harvard, Yale, and Prince-

ton). The people who make the mark are the best and brightest out of one billion. Place them in any educational system,
and they will do well. In fact, many of the IITs are decidedly
second-rate, with mediocre equipment, indifferent teachers,
and unimaginative classwork. Rajiv Sahney, who attended IIT
and then went to Caltech, says, "The IITs' core advantage is
the entrance exam, which is superbly designed to select
extremely intelligent students. In terms of teaching and facilities, they really don't compare with any decent American technical institute." And once you get beyond the IITs and other
such elite academies—which graduate under ten thousand
students a year—the quality of higher education in China and
India remains extremely poor, which is why so many students
leave those countries to get trained abroad.

The data affirm these anecdotal impressions. In 2005, the
McKinsey Global Institute did a study of "the emerging global
labor market" and found that a sample of twenty-eight low-
wage countries had approximately 33 million young professionals* at their disposal, compared with just 15 million in a
sample of eight higher-wage nations (the United States,
United Kingdom, Germany, Japan, Australia, Canada, Ireland, and South Korea).[17] But how many of these young professionals in low-wage countries had the skills necessary to
compete in a global marketplace? "Only a fraction of potential
job candidates could successfully work at a foreign company,"
the study reported, pointing to several explanations, chiefly
poor educational quality. In both India and China, it noted,

---

* MGI's figure includes graduates trained in engineering, finance and accounting, life
science research, and "professional generalists," such as call center operatives. Young
professionals are defined as graduates with up to seven years of experience.

beyond the small number of top-tier academies, the quality and quantity of education is low. Only 10 percent of Indians get any kind of postsecondary education. Thus, despite enormous demand for engineers, there are relatively few well-trained ones. Wages of trained engineers in both countries are rising by 15 percent a year, a sure sign that demand is outstripping supply. (If you were an employer and had access to tens of thousands of well-trained engineers coming out of colleges every year, you would not have to give your employees 15 percent raises year after year.)

Higher education is America's best industry. There are two rankings of universities worldwide. In one of them, a purely quantitative study done by Chinese researchers, eight of the top ten universities in the world are in the United States. In the other, more qualitative one by London's *Times Higher Educational Supplement*, it's seven. The numbers flatten out somewhat after that. Of the top twenty, seventeen or eleven are in America; of the top fifty, thirty-eight or twenty-one. Still, the basic story does not change. With 5 percent of the world's population, the United States absolutely dominates higher education, having either 42 or 68 percent of the world's top fifty universities (depending which study you look at). In no other field is America's advantage so overwhelming.*

A 2006 report from the London-based Centre for European Reform, "The Future of European Universities," points out that the United States invests 2.6 percent of its GDP in higher education, compared with 1.2 percent in Europe and 1.1 per-

---

* The right-wing attack on American universities as being out-of-touch ivory towers has always puzzled me. In a highly competitive global environment, these institutions dominate the field.

cent in Japan. The situation in the sciences is particularly striking. A list of where the world's 1,000 best computer scientists were educated shows that the top ten schools are all American. U.S. spending on R&D remains higher than Europe's, and its collaborations between business and educational institutions are unmatched anywhere in the world. America remains by far the most attractive destination for students, taking 30 percent of the total number of foreign students globally. All these advantages will not be erased easily, because the structure of European and Japanese universities—mostly state-run bureaucracies—is unlikely to change. And while China and India are opening new institutions, it is not that easy to create a world-class university out of whole cloth in a few decades. Here's a statistic about engineers that you might not have heard. In India, universities graduate between 35 and 50 Ph.D.'s in computer science each year; in America, the figure is 1,000.

Learning to Think

If American universities are first-rank, few believe that the same can be said about its schools. Everyone knows that the American school system is in crisis and that its students do particularly badly in science and math, year after year, in international rankings. But the statistics here, while not wrong, reveal something slightly different. America's real problem is one not of excellence but of access. Since its inception in 1995, the Trends in International Mathematics and Science Study (TIMSS) has become the standard for comparing educational programs across nations. The most recent results, from 2003, put the United States squarely in the middle of the pack. The United States beat the average score of the twenty-four countries included in the study, but many of the countries ranked below it were developing nations like Morocco, Tunisia, and Armenia. Eighth-graders did better than fourth-graders (the two grades measured) but still lagged behind their counterparts in countries like Holland, Japan, and Singapore. The media reported the news with a predictable penchant for direness: "Economic time bomb: U.S. teens are among worst at math," declared the *Wall Street Journal*.

But even if the U.S. scores in math and science fall well below leaders like Singapore and Hong Kong, the aggregate scores hide deep regional, racial, and socioeconomic variation. Poor and minority students score well below the American average, while, as one study noted, "students in affluent suburban U.S. school districts score nearly as well as students in Singapore, the runaway leader on TIMSS math scores."[18] These are the students who then go on to compete for and fill the scarce slots in America's top universities. The difference between average science scores in poor and wealthy school districts *within* the United States, for instance, is *four to five times greater* than the difference between the U.S. and Singaporean national averages. In other words, America is a large and diverse country with a real inequality problem. This will, over time, translate into a competitiveness problem, because if we cannot educate and train a third of the working population to compete in a knowledge economy, it will drag down the country. But we do know what works. The large cohort of students in the top fifth of American schools rank along with the world's best. They work hard and have a highly scheduled academic and extracurricular life, as anyone who has recently been to an Ivy League campus can attest.

I went to elementary, middle, and high school in Mumbai, at an excellent institution, the Cathedral and John Connon School. Its approach (thirty years ago) reflected the teaching methods often described as "Asian," in which the premium is placed on memorization and constant testing. This is actually the old British, and European, pedagogical method, one that now gets described as Asian. I recall memorizing vast quantities of material, regurgitating it for exams, and then promptly forgetting it. When I went to college in the United States, I encountered a different world. While the American system is too lax on rigor and memorization—whether in math or poetry—it is much better at developing the critical faculties of the mind, which is what you need to succeed in life. Other educational systems teach you to take tests; the American system teaches you to think.

It is surely this quality that goes some way in explaining why America produces so many entrepreneurs, inventors, and risk takers. In America, people are allowed to be bold, challenge authority, fail, and pick themselves up. It's America, not Japan, that produces dozens of Nobel Prize winners. Tharman Shanmugaratnam, until recently Singapore's minister of education, explains the difference between his country's system and America's. "We both have meritocracies," Shanmugaratnam says. "Yours is a talent meritocracy, ours is an exam meritocracy. We know how to train people to take exams. You know how to use people's talents to the fullest. Both are important, but there are some parts of the intellect that we are not able to test well—like creativity, curiosity, a sense of adventure, ambition. Most of all, America has a culture of learning that challenges conventional wisdom, even if it means challenging authority. These are the areas where Singapore must learn from America."

This is one reason that Singaporean officials recently visited U.S. schools to learn how to create a system that nurtures and rewards ingenuity, quick thinking, and problem solving. As the *Washington Post* reported in March 2007, researchers from Singapore's best schools came to the Academy of Science, a public magnet school in Virginia, to examine U.S. teaching methods.[19] As the students "studied tiny, genetically altered plants one recent afternoon, drawing leaves and jotting data in logbooks," the Singaporean visitors "recorded how long the teacher waited for students to answer questions, how often the teenagers spoke up and how strongly they held to their views." Har Hui Peng, a visitor from Singapore's Hwa Chong Institution, was impressed, as the *Post* noted. "Just by watching, you can see students are more engaged, instead of being spoon-fed all day," said Har. The *Post* article continued, "[In Singapore], she said, the laboratories are fully stocked but stark, and the students are bright but reluctant to volunteer answers. To encourage spontaneity, Hwa Chong now bases 10 percent of each student's grade on oral participation."

While America marvels at Asia's test-taking skills, Asian countries come to America to figure out how to get their kids to think. Top high schools in Beijing and Shanghai are emphasizing independent research, science competitions, and entrepreneur clubs. "I like the way your children are able to communicate," said Rosalind Chia, another Singaporean teacher on tour in the States. "Maybe we need to cultivate that more—a conversation between students and teachers." Such change does not come easily. Indeed, Japan recently attempted to improve the flexibility of its national education system by eliminating mandatory Saturday classes and increasing the time dedicated to general studies, where students and teachers can pursue their own interests. "But the Japanese shift to *yutori kyoiku*, or relaxed education," the *Post* says, "has fueled a back-to-basics backlash from parents who worry that their children are not learning enough and that test scores are slipping." In other words, simply changing curricula —a top-down effort—may lead only to resistance. American culture celebrates and reinforces problem solving, questioning authority, and thinking heretically. It allows people to fail and then gives them a second and third chance. It rewards self-starters and oddballs. These are all bottom-up forces that cannot be produced by government fiat.

America's Secret Weapon

America's advantages might seem obvious when compared with Asia, which is still a continent of mostly developing countries. Against Europe, the margin is slimmer than many Americans believe. The Eurozone has been growing at an impressive clip, about the same pace per capita as the United States since 2000. It takes in half the world's foreign investment, boasts labor productivity often as strong as that of the United States, and posted a $30 billion trade surplus in 2007 from January through October. In the WEF Competitiveness Index, European countries occupy seven of the top ten slots. Europe has its problems—high unemployment, rigid labor markets—but it also has advantages, including more efficient and fiscally sustainable health care and pension systems. All in all, Europe presents the most significant short-term challenge to the United States in the economic realm.

But Europe has one crucial disadvantage. Or, to put it more accurately, the United States has one crucial advantage over Europe and most of the developed world. The United States is demographically vibrant. Nicholas Eberstadt, a scholar at the American Enterprise Institute, estimates that the U.S. population will increase by 65 million by 2030, while Europe's will remain "virtually stagnant." Europe, Eberstadt notes, "will by that time have more than twice as many seniors older than 65 than children under 15, with drastic implications for future aging. (Fewer children now means fewer workers later.) In the United States, by contrast, children will continue to outnumber the elderly. The U.N. Population Division estimates that the ratio of working-age people to senior citizens in western Europe will drop from 3.8:1 today to just 2.4:1 in 2030. In the U.S., the figure will fall from 5.4:1 to 3.1:1. Some of these demographic problems could be ameliorated if older Europeans chose to work more, but so far they do not, and trends like these rarely reverse."[20] The only real way to avert this demographic decline is for Europe to take in more immigrants. Native Europeans actually stopped replacing themselves as early as 2007, so even maintaining the current population will require modest immigration. Growth will require much more. But European societies do not seem able to take in and assimilate people from strange and unfamiliar cultures, especially from rural and backward regions in the world of Islam. The question of who is at fault here—the immigrant or the society—is irrelevant. The political reality is that Europe is moving toward taking in fewer immigrants at a time when its economic future rides on its ability to take in many more. America, on the other hand, is creating the first universal nation, made up of all colors, races, and creeds, living and working together in considerable harmony.

Surprisingly, many Asian countries—with the exception of India—are in demographic situations similar to or even worse than Europe's. The fertility rates in Japan, Taiwan, Korea, Hong Kong, and China* are well below the replacement level of 2.1 births per female, and estimates indicate that major East Asian nations will face a sizable reduction in their working-age population over the next half century. The working-age population in Japan has already peaked; by 2010, Japan will have three million fewer workers than in 2005. Worker populations in China and Korea are also likely to peak within the next decade. Goldman Sachs predicts that China's median age will rise from thirty-three in 2005 to forty-five in 2050, a remarkable graying of the population. By 2030, China may have nearly as many senior citizens sixty-five years of age or older as children under fifteen. And Asian countries have as much trouble with immigrants as European ones. Japan faces a large prospective worker shortage because it can neither take in enough immigrants nor allow its women to fully participate in the labor force.

The effects of an aging population are considerable. First, there is the pension burden—fewer workers supporting more gray-haired elders. Second, as the economist Benjamin Jones

---

* Birthrates in China could be underreported owing to the government's one-child policy. However, the demographic consensus holds that the total fertility rate has been below replacement level in China for fifteen years or more.

has shown, most innovative inventors—and the overwhelming majority of Nobel laureates—do their most important work between the ages of thirty and forty-four. A smaller working-age population, in other words, means fewer technological, scientific, and managerial advances. Third, as workers age, they go from being net savers to being net spenders, with dire ramifications for national saving and investment rates. For advanced industrial countries—which are already comfortable, satisfied, and less prone to work hard—bad demographics are a killer disease.

The native-born, white American population has the same low fertility rates as Europe's. Without immigration, U.S. GDP growth over the last quarter century would have been the same as Europe's. America's edge in innovation is overwhelmingly a product of immigration. Foreign students and immigrants account for 50 percent of the science researchers in the country and, in 2006, received 40 percent of the doctorates in science and engineering and 65 percent of the doctorates in computer science. By 2010, foreign students will get more than 50 percent of all Ph.D.'s awarded in every subject in the United States. In the sciences, that figure will be closer to 75 percent. Half of all Silicon Valley start-ups have one founder who is an immigrant or first-generation American. America's potential new burst of productivity, its edge in nanotechnology, biotechnology, its ability to invent the future—all rest on its immigration policies. If America can keep the people it educates in the country, the innovation will happen here. If they go back home, the innovation will travel with them.

Immigration also gives America a quality rare for a rich country—hunger and energy. As countries become wealthy, the drive to move up and succeed weakens. But America has found a way to keep itself constantly revitalized by streams of people who are looking to make a new life in a new world. These are the people who work long hours picking fruit in searing heat, washing dishes, building houses, working night shifts, and cleaning waste dumps. They come to the United States under terrible conditions, leave family and community, only because they want to work and get ahead in life. Americans have almost always worried about such immigrants—whether from Ireland or Italy, China or Mexico. But these immigrants have gone on to become the backbone of the American working class, and their children or grandchildren have entered the American mainstream. America has been able to tap this energy, manage diversity, assimilate newcomers, and move ahead economically. Ultimately, this is what sets the country apart from the experience of Britain and all other historical examples of great economic powers that grow fat and lazy and slip behind as they face the rise of leaner, hungrier nations.

The Macro Picture

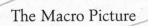

Many experts, scholars, and even a few politicians worry about a set of statistics that bode ill for the United States. The savings rate is zero, the current-account deficit, trade deficit, and budget deficit are high, median income is flat, and commitments for entitlements are unsustainable. These are all valid concerns and will have to be addressed by Washington. If America's economic system is its core strength, its political system is its core weakness. But the numbers might not tell us everything we need to know. The economic statistics that we rely on give us only an approximate, antiquated measure of an economy. Many of them were developed in the late nineteenth century to describe an industrial economy with limited cross-border activity. We now live in an interconnected global market, with revolutions in financial instruments, technology, and trade. It is possible that we're not measuring things correctly.

It used to be a law of macroeconomics, for example, that in an advanced industrial economy there is such a thing as NAIRU—the nonaccelerating inflation rate of unemployment. Basically, this meant that unemployment could not fall below a certain level, usually pinned at 6 percent, without driving inflation up. But for the last two decades, many Western countries, especially the United States, have had unemployment rates well below levels economists thought possible. Or consider that America's current-account deficit—which in 2007 reached $800 billion, or 7 percent of GDP—was supposed to be unsustainable at 4 percent of GDP. The current-account deficit is at dangerous levels, but we should also keep in mind that its magnitude can be explained in part by the fact that there is a worldwide surplus of savings and that the United States remains an unusually stable and attractive place in which to invest.

Harvard University's Richard Cooper even argues that the American savings rate is miscalculated, painting an inaccurate picture of massive credit card debt and unaffordable mortgages. While many households do live beyond their means, the picture looks healthier at the aggregate level, Cooper argues. Private U.S. savings, which includes both household saving (the "often-cited" low figure of about 2 percent of personal income) and corporate saving, reached 15 percent in 2005. The decrease in personal saving, in other words, has been largely offset by an increase in corporate saving. More important, the whole concept of "national saving" might be outdated, not reflecting the reality of new modes of production. In the new economy, growth comes from "teams of people creating new goods and services, not from the accumulation of capital," which was more important in the first half of the twentieth century. Yet we still focus on measuring capital. The national accounts, which include GDP and traditional measures of national saving, were, Cooper writes, "formulated in Britain and the United States in the 1930s, at the height of the industrial age."[21]

Economists define saving as the income that, instead of going toward consumption, is invested to make possible consumption in the future. Current measures of investment focus on physical capital and housing. Cooper argues that this measure is misleading. Education expenditures are considered "consumption," but in a knowledge-based economy, education functions more like savings—it is spending forgone today in order to increase human capital and raise future income and spending power. Private R&D, meanwhile, isn't included in national accounts at all, but rather considered an intermediate business expense—even though most studies suggest that R&D on average has a high payoff, much higher than investing in bricks and mortar, which counts under the current measures as savings. So Cooper would also count as savings expenditure on consumer durables, education, and R&D—which would give the United States a significantly higher savings rate. The new metric worldwide would raise the figure for other nations as well, but the contribution of education, R&D,

and consumer durables to total savings "is higher in the United States than in most other countries, except perhaps for a few Nordic countries."*

With all these caveats, the United States still has serious problems. Many trends relating to the macroeconomic picture are worrisome. Whatever the savings rate, it has fallen fast over the past two decades. By all calculations, Medicare threatens to blow up the federal budget. The swing from surpluses to deficits between 2000 and 2008 has serious implications. For most families, moreover, incomes are flat or rising very slowly. Growing inequality is the signature feature of the new era fueled by a triple force—the knowledge economy, information technology, and globalization. Perhaps most worryingly, Americans are borrowing 80 percent of the world's surplus savings and using it for consumption. In other words, we are selling off our assets to foreigners to buy a couple more lattes a day. These problems have accumulated at a bad time because, for all its strengths, the American economy now faces its strongest challenge in history.

Everyone Is Playing the Game

Let me begin with an analogy drawn from my favorite sport, tennis. American tennis enthusiasts have noted a worrying recent trend: the decline of America in championship tennis. The *New York Times*' Aron Pilhofer ran the numbers. Thirty

---

* Consumer durables, education, and R&D amount to 8.6 percent, 7.3 percent, and 2.8 percent of GDP, respectively. Adding this to the 15 percent saved by more traditional means yields just over 33 percent of GDP in national savings.

years ago, Americans made up half the draw (the 128 players selected to play) in the U.S. Open. In 1982, for example, 78 of the 128 players selected were Americans. In 2007, only 20 Americans made the draw, a figure that accurately reflects the downward trend over twenty-five years. Millions of pixels have been devoted to wondering how America could have slipped so far and fast. The answer lies in another set of numbers. In the 1970s, about twenty-five countries sent players to the U.S. Open. Today, about thirty-five countries do, a 40 percent increase. Countries like Russia, South Korea, Serbia, and Austria are now churning out world-class players, and Germany, France, and Spain are training many more players than ever before. In the 1970s, three Anglo-Saxon nations—America, Britain, and Australia—utterly dominated tennis. In 2007, the final-sixteen players came from ten different countries. In other words, it's not that the United States has been doing badly over the last two decades. It's that, all of a sudden, everyone is playing the game.

If tennis seems trivial, consider a higher-stakes game. In 2005, New York City got a wake-up call. Twenty-four of the world's twenty-five largest initial public offerings (IPOs) that year were held in countries other than the United States. This was stunning. America's capital markets have long been the biggest, deepest, and most liquid in the world. They financed the turnaround in manufacturing in the 1980s, the technology revolution of the 1990s, and the ongoing advances in bioscience. It was the fluidity of these markets that had kept American business nimble. If America was losing this distinctive advantage, it was very bad news. The worry was great enough that Mayor Michael Bloomberg and Senator Chuck Schumer of New York commissioned McKinsey and Company to do a report assessing the state of New York's financial competitiveness. It was released late in 2006.[22]

Much of the discussion around the problem focused on America's overregulation, particularly with post-Enron laws like Sarbanes-Oxley, and the constant threat of litigation that hovers over business in the United States. These findings were true enough, but they did not really get at what had shifted business abroad. America was conducting business as usual. But others were joining in the game. Sarbanes-Oxley and other such regulatory measures would not have had nearly the impact they did had it not been for the fact that *there are now alternatives*. What's really happening here, as in other areas, is simple: the rise of the rest. America's sum total of stocks, bonds, deposits, loans, and other instruments—its financial stock, in other words—still exceeds that of any other region, but other regions are seeing their financial stock grow much more quickly. This is especially true of the rising countries of Asia—at 15.5 percent annually between 2001 and 2005—but even the Eurozone's is outpacing America's, which clips along at 6.5 percent. Europe's total banking and trading revenues, $98 billion in 2005, have nearly pulled equal to U.S. revenues of $109 billion. In 2001, 57 percent of high-value IPOs occurred on American stock exchanges; in 2005, just 16 percent did. In 2006, the United States hosted barely a third of the number of total IPOs it did in 2001, while European exchanges expanded their IPO volume by 30 percent, and in Asia (minus Japan) volume doubled. IPOs are important because they generate "substantial recurring revenues for the host market" and contribute to perceptions of market vibrancy.

IPOs and foreign listings are only part of the story. New derivatives based on underlying financial instruments like stocks or interest-rate payment are increasingly important for hedge funds, banks, insurers, and the overall liquidity of international markets. And the dominant player on the international derivatives market (estimated at a notional value of $300 trillion) is London. London exchanges account for 49 percent of the foreign-exchange derivatives market and 34 percent of the interest-rate derivatives market. (The United States accounts for 16 percent and 4 percent of these markets, respectively.) European exchanges as a whole represent greater than 60 percent of the interest rate, foreign exchange, equity, and fund-linked derivatives. McKinsey's interviews with global business leaders indicate that Europe dominates not only in existing derivatives products but also in the innovation of new ones. The only derivatives product in terms of which Europe trails the U.S. is commodities, which accounts for the lowest overall revenue among major derivatives categories.

There were some specific reasons for the fall. Many of the massive IPOs in 2005 and 2006 were privatizations of state-owned companies in Europe and China. The Chinese ones naturally went to Hong Kong, and the Russian and Eastern European ones to London. In 2006, the three biggest IPOs all came from emerging markets. But this is all part of a broader trend. Countries and companies now have options that they never had before. Capital markets outside America—chiefly Hong Kong and London—are well regulated and liquid, which allows companies to take other factors, such as time zones, diversification, and politics, into account.

The United States is not doing worse than usual. It functions as it always has—perhaps subconsciously assuming that
it is still leagues ahead of the pack. American legislators rarely
think about the rest of the world when writing laws, regulations, and policies. American officials rarely refer to global
standards. After all, for so long the United States *was* the
global standard, and when it chose to do something different,
it was important enough that the rest of the world would cater
to its exceptionality. America is the only country in the world,
other than Liberia and Myanmar, that is not on the metric system. Other than Somalia, it is alone in not ratifying the international Convention on the Rights of the Child. In business,
America didn't need to benchmark. It was the one teaching
the world how to be capitalist. But now everyone is playing
America's game, and playing to win.

For the last thirty years, America had the lowest corporate
tax rates of the major industrialized countries. Today, it has the
second highest. American rates have not gone up; others have
come down. Germany, for example, long a staunch believer in
its high-taxation system, cut its rates (starting in 2008) in
response to moves by countries to its east, like Slovakia and
Austria. This kind of competition among industrialized countries is now widespread. It is not a race to the bottom—
Scandinavian countries have high taxes, good services, and
strong growth—but a quest for growth. American regulations
used to be more flexible and market friendly than all others.
That's no longer true. London's financial system was over-
hauled in 2001, with a single entity replacing a confusing mish-
mash of regulators, one reason that London's financial sector
now beats out New York's on some measures. The entire
British government works aggressively to make London a

global hub. Washington, by contrast, spends its time and energy thinking of ways to tax New York, so that it can send its revenues to the rest of the country. Regulators from Poland to Shanghai to Mumbai are moving every day to make their systems more attractive to investors and manufacturers all over the world. Even on immigration, the European Union is creating a new "blue card," to attract highly skilled workers from developing countries.

Being on top for so long has its downsides. The American market has been so large that Americans have always known that the rest of the world would take the trouble to understand it and them. We have not had to reciprocate by learning foreign languages, cultures, and markets. Now that could leave America at a competitive disadvantage. Take the spread of English worldwide as a metaphor. Americans have delighted in this process because it makes it so much easier for them to travel and do business abroad. But for the locals, it gives them an understanding of and access to two markets and cultures. They can speak English but also Mandarin or Hindi or Portuguese. They can penetrate the American market but also the internal Chinese, Indian, or Brazilian one. (And in all these countries, the non-English-speaking markets remain the largest ones.) Americans, by contrast, can swim in only one sea. They have never developed the ability to move into other peoples' worlds.

We have not noticed how fast the rest has risen. Most of the industrialized world—and a good part of the nonindustrialized world as well—has better cell phone service than the United States. Broadband is faster and cheaper across the industrial world, from Canada to France to Japan, and the United States now stands sixteenth in the world in broadband penetration per capita. Americans are constantly told by their politicians that the only thing we have learn from other countries' health care systems is to be thankful for ours. Most Americans ignore the fact that a third of the country's public schools are totally dysfunctional (because their children go to the other two-thirds). The American litigation system is now routinely referred to as a huge cost to doing business, but no one dares propose any reform of it. Our mortage deduction for housing costs a staggering $80 billion a year, and we are told it is crucial to support home ownership. Except that Margaret Thatcher eliminated it in Britain, and yet that country has the same rate of home ownership as the United States. We rarely look around and notice other options and alternatives, convinced that "we're number one." But learning from the rest is no longer a matter of morality or politics. Increasingly it's about competitiveness.

Consider the automobile industry. For a century after 1894, most of the cars manufactured in North America were made in Michigan. Since 2004, Michigan has been replaced by Ontario, Canada. The reason is simple: health care. In America, car manufacturers have to pay $6,500 in medical and insurance costs for every worker. If they move a plant to Canada, which has a government-run health care system, the cost to the manufacturer is around $800 per worker. In 2006, General Motors paid $5.2 billion in medical and insurance bills for its active and retired workers. That adds $1,500 to the cost of every GM car sold. For Toyota, which has fewer American retirees and many more foreign workers, that cost is $186 per car. This is not necessarily an advertisement for the Canadian health care system, but it does make clear that the costs of the American health care system have risen to a point that there is a significant competitive disadvantage to hiring American workers. Jobs are going not to countries like Mexico but to places where well-trained and educated workers can be found: it's smart benefits, not low wages, that employers are looking for. Tying health care to employment has an additional negative consequence. Unlike workers anywhere else in the industrialized world, Americans lose their health care if they lose their job, which makes them far more anxious about foreign competition, trade, and globalization. The Pew survey found greater fear of these forces among Americans than among German and French workers, perhaps for this reason.

For decades, American workers, whether in car companies, steel plants, or banks, had one enormous advantage over all other workers: privileged access to American capital. They could use that access to buy technology and training that no one else had—and thus produce products that no one else could, and at competitive prices. That special access is gone. The world is swimming in capital, and suddenly American workers have to ask themselves, what can we do better than others? It's the dilemma not just for workers but for companies as well. What's critical now is not how a company compares with its own past (are we doing better than we were?), but how it compares with the present elsewhere (how are we doing relative to others?). The comparison is no longer along a vertical dimension of time but along a horizontal one of space.

When American companies went abroad, they used to bring with them capital and know-how. But when they go abroad now, they discover that the natives already have money and already know how. There really isn't a Third World anymore. So what do American companies bring to India or Brazil? What is America's competitive advantage? It's a question few

American businessmen thought they would ever have to answer. The answer lies in something the economist Martin Wolf noted. Describing the changing world, he wrote that economists used to discuss two basic concepts, *capital* and *labor*. But these are now commodities, widely available to everyone. What distinguishes economies today are *ideas* and *energy*. A country must be a source of either ideas or energy (meaning oil, natural gas, coal, etc.). The United States has been and can be the world's most important, continuing source of new ideas, big and small, technical and creative, economic and political. But to do that, it has to make some significant changes.

A Do-nothing Politics

The United States has a history of worrying that it is losing its edge. This is at least the fourth wave of such concern since 1945. The first was in the late 1950s, a result of the Soviet Union's launch of the *Sputnik* satellite. The second was in the early 1970s, when high oil prices and slow growth in the United States convinced Americans that Western Europe and Saudi Arabia were the powers of the future, and President Nixon heralded the advent of a multipolar world. The most recent one arrived in the mid-1980s, when most experts believed that Japan would be the technologically and economically dominant superpower of the future. The concern in each of these cases was well founded, the projections intelligent. But none of these scenarios came to pass. The reason is that the American system was proved be flexible, resourceful, and resilient, able to correct its mistakes and shift its attention. A focus on American economic decline ended up preventing it. The problem today is that the American political system seems to have lost its ability to create broad coalitions that solve complex issues.

The economic dysfunctions in America today are real, but, by and large, they are not the product of deep inefficiencies within the American economy, nor are they reflections of cultural decay. They are the consequences of specific government policies. Different policies could quickly and relatively easily move the United States onto a far more stable footing. A set of sensible reforms could be enacted tomorrow to trim wasteful spending and subsidies, increase savings, expand training in science and technology, secure pensions, create a workable immigration process, and achieve significant efficiencies in the use of energy.* Policy experts do not have wide disagreements on most of these issues, and none of the proposed measures would require sacrifices reminiscent of wartime hardship, only modest adjustments of existing arrangements. And yet, because of politics, they appear impossible. The American political system has lost the ability for large-scale compromise, and it has lost the ability to accept some pain now for much gain later on.

As it enters the twenty-first century, the United States is not fundamentally a weak economy, or a decadent society. But it has developed a highly dysfunctional politics. An antiquated and overly rigid political system to begin with—about 225

---

* I would not add fixing health care to this list, because that is not an easy problem with an easy fix. Most problems in Washington have simple policy solutions but face political paralysis. Health care is an issue that is complex in both policy and political terms. That doesn't mean it doesn't need to be fixed, far from it. But solving it would have been difficult under any circumstances, as it is today.

years old—has been captured by money, special interests, a sensationalist media, and ideological attack groups. The result is ceaseless, virulent debate about trivia—politics as theater—and very little substance, compromise, and action. A "can-do" country is now saddled with a "do-nothing" political process, designed for partisan battle rather than problem solving. By every measure—the growth of special interests, lobbies, pork-barrel spending—the political process has become far more partisan and ineffective over the last three decades.

It is clever contrarianism to be in favor of sharp party politics and against worthy calls for bipartisanship. Some political scientists have long wished that America's political parties were more like European ones—ideologically pure and tightly disciplined. Well, it has happened—there are fewer and fewer moderates on either side—and the result is gridlock. Europe's parliamentary systems work well with partisan parties. In them, the executive branch always controls the legislative branch, and so the party in power can implement its agenda easily. The British prime minister doesn't need any support from the opposition party; he has a ruling majority by definition. The American system, by contrast, is one of shared power, overlapping functions, and checks and balances. Progress requires broad coalitions between the two parties and politicians who will cross the aisle. That's why James Madison distrusted political parties, lumping them together with all kinds of "factions" and considering them a grave danger to the young American Republic.

I know that these complaints all sound very high-minded and squishy. And I know there has long been nasty partisanship in America, even in Madison's own era. But there has also been a lot of bipartisanship, especially over the past century. Reacting to the political bitterness of the late nineteenth century—the last time there were two close elections in succession—many American leaders tried to create forces for good, problem-solving government. Robert Brookings established the Brookings Institution in Washington in 1916 because he wanted an organization "free from any political or pecuniary interest . . . to collect, interpret, and lay before the country in a coherent form, the fundamental economic facts." The Council on Foreign Relations, founded five years later, also consciously reached across party lines. The first editor of its magazine, *Foreign Affairs*, told his deputy that if one of them became publicly identified as a Democrat, the other should immediately start campaigning for the Republicans. Contrast that with a much more recently founded think tank, the conservative Heritage Foundation, whose former senior vice president Burton Pines has admitted, "Our role is to provide conservative policymakers with arguments to bolster our side."

The trouble is that progress on any major problem—health care, Social Security, tax reform—will require compromise from both sides. In foreign policy, crafting a strategic policy in Iraq, or one on Iran, North Korea, or China, will need significant support from both sides. It requires a longer-term perspective. And that's highly unlikely. Those who advocate sensible solutions and compromise legislation find themselves marginalized by the party's leadership, losing funds from special-interest groups, and being constantly attacked by their "side" on television and radio. The system provides greater incentives to stand firm and go back and tell your team that you refused to bow to the enemy. It's great for fund-raising, but it's terrible for governing.

The real test for the United States is, in some ways, the

opposite of that faced by Britain in 1900. Britain's economic power waned while it managed to maintain immense political influence around the world. The American economy and American society, in contrast, are capable of responding to the economic pressures and competition they face. They can adjust, adapt, and persevere. The real test for the United States is political—and it rests not just with America at large but with Washington in particular. Can Washington adjust and adapt to a world in which others have moved up? Can it respond to shifts in economic and political power? This challenge is even more difficult in foreign policy than in domestic policy. Can Washington truly embrace a world with a diversity of voices and viewpoints? Can it thrive in a world it cannot dominate?

7

American Purpose

W hen historians try to understand the world of the early twenty-first century, they should take note of the Parsley crisis. In July 2002, the government of Morocco sent twelve soldiers to a tiny island called Leila, a few hundred feet off its coast, in the Straits of Gibraltar, and planted its flag there. The island is uninhabited, except for some goats, and all that thrives on it is wild parsley, hence its Spanish name, Perejil. But its sovereignty had long been contested by Morocco and Spain, and the Spanish government reacted forcefully to the Moroccan "aggression." Within a couple of weeks, seventy-five Spanish soldiers had been airlifted onto the island. They pulled down the Moroccan flag, hoisted two Spanish flags, and sent the Moroccans home. The Moroccan government denounced the "act of war" and organized rallies, where scores of young men chanted, "Our souls and our blood are sacrifices to you, Leila!" Spain kept its military helicopters hovering over the island and its warships off the coast of Morocco. From afar, the whole affair looked like a comic opera. But however absurd it may have seemed, someone was going to have to talk the two countries down.

That role fell not to the United Nations, or to the European Union, or to a friendly European country like France, which has good relations with both sides. It fell to the United States. "I kept thinking to myself, 'What do I have to do with any of this? Why are we—the United States—in the middle of it?'" then–Secretary of State Colin Powell recalled amusedly. Once it became clear that nothing else was working, he began a hectic round of telephone diplomacy, placing more than a dozen calls to the Moroccan king and foreign minister late into Friday night and Saturday morning. "I decided that I had to push for a compromise fast because otherwise pride takes over, positions harden, and people get stubborn," said Powell. "It was getting to be evening in the Mediterranean. And my grandkids were going to come over soon for a swim!" So Powell drafted an agreement on his home computer, got both sides to accept it, then signed for each side himself, and faxed it over to Spain and Morocco. The countries agreed to leave the island unoccupied and begin talks, in Rabat, about its future status. The two governments issued statements thanking the United States for helping to resolve the crisis. And Colin Powell got to go swimming with his grandkids.

It is a small example, but a telling one. The United States has no interests in the Strait of Gibraltar. Unlike the European Union, it has no special leverage with Spain or Morocco. Unlike the United Nations, it cannot speak for the international community. But it was the only country that could resolve the dispute, for a simple, fundamental reason. In a unipolar world, it is the single superpower.

The summer of 2002 will be seen as the high-water mark of

unipolarity, America's Roman moment. The decade leading up to it was a heady time. The economy was roaring, productivity growth was higher than it had been in decades, Washington was churning out massive surpluses, the dollar was sky-high, and American CEOs were global superstars. Then the world saw the United States brutally attacked in September 2001, producing feelings of sympathy as well as some quiet glee that even a superpower could be humbled. But soon, while America felt weak and vulnerable, the world watched it respond to 9/11 on a scale that was unimaginable for any other country. Washington immediately increased its defense budget by $50 billion, a sum greater than the total annual defense budgets of Britain and Germany. It single-handedly put terrorism at the top of the global agenda, making every country reorient its foreign policy accordingly. Pakistan, which was allied with the Taliban for years, turned against it within a week. Within a month, the United States had attacked Afghanistan, seven thousand miles away, almost entirely from the air, and quickly toppled the regime.

That was then. America remains the global superpower today, but it is an enfeebled one. Its economy has troubles, its currency is sliding, and it faces long-term problems with its soaring entitlements and low savings. Anti-American sentiment is at an all-time high everywhere from Great Britain to Malaysia. But the most striking shift between the 1990s and now has to do not with America but rather with the world at large. In the 1990s, Russia was completely dependent on American aid and loans. Now, it posts annual budget surpluses in the tens of billions of dollars. Then, East Asian nations desperately needed the IMF to bail them out of their crises. Now, they have massive foreign-exchange reserves, which they are using to finance America's debt. Then, China's economic growth was driven almost entirely by American demand. In 2007, China contributed more to global growth than the United States did—the first time any nation has done so since at least the 1930s—and surpassed it as the world's largest consumer market in several key categories.

In the long run this secular trend—the rise of the rest—will only gather strength, whatever the temporary ups and downs. At a military-political level, America still dominates the world, but the larger structure of unipolarity—economic, financial, cultural—is weakening. Washington still has no true rival, and will not for a very long while, but it faces a growing number of constraints. Polarity is not a binary condition. The world will not stay unipolar for decades and then, one day, suddenly switch and become bipolar or multipolar. There will be a slow shift in the nature of international affairs. While unipolarity continues to be a defining reality of the international system for now, every year it becomes weaker and other nations and actors grow in strength.

This power shift could be broadly beneficial. It is a product of good things—robust economic growth and stability around the world. And it is good for America, if approached properly. The world is going America's way. Countries are becoming more open, market friendly, and democratic. As long as we keep the forces of modernization, global interaction, and trade growing, good governance, human rights, and democracy all move forward. That movement is not always swift. There are often setbacks, but the basic direction is clear. Look at Africa, which is often seen as the most hopeless continent in the world. Today two-thirds of the continent is democratic and growing economically.

These trends provide an opportunity for the United States to remain the pivotal player in a richer, more dynamic, more exciting world. But grasping that opportunity will take a substantial shift in America's basic approach to the world. There is only so much America can do about its relative power. As others grow from low starting points, its relative weight will slip. But there is a great deal that Washington can do to redefine America's purpose.

The Virtues of Competition

How did the United States blow it? The United States has had an extraordinary hand to play in global politics—the best of any country in history. Yet, by almost any measure—problems solved, success achieved, institutions built, reputation enhanced—Washington has played this hand badly. America has had a period of unparalleled influence. What does it have to show for it?

Beyond specific personalities and policies, about which much has been written, the condition that made such errors possible was, ironically, America's immense power. Americans firmly believe in the virtues of competition. We believe that individuals, groups, and corporations perform better when they are in a competitive environment. When it comes to the international arena, we have forgotten this fact. Ever since the collapse of the Soviet Union, the United States has walked the world like a colossus, unrivaled and unchecked. This has had its benefits, but it has also made Washington arrogant, careless, and lazy. Its foreign policy has at times resembled General Motors' business strategy in the 1970s—an approach driven by internal factors, with little sense of the broader environment in which it was operating. It didn't work so well for GM, and it hasn't for the United States.

We didn't start out careless. Most politicians and policy experts, American and foreign, were slow to embrace unipolarity. In 1990, as the Soviet Union was collapsing, Margaret Thatcher expressed a commonly held view that the world was moving toward three regional groups, "one based on the dollar, one based on the yen, one on the Deutsche mark."[1] George H. W. Bush, steeped in the bipolar order, never acted like the head of the sole superpower. He took a cautious approach to the historic changes in the global system. Rather than triumphantly claiming victory in the Cold War, his administration carefully consolidated the gains of Soviet collapse, always aware that the process could either reverse or end in violence. In waging the first Gulf War, Bush was highly attentive to building an international coalition, getting United Nations approval, and sticking to the mandate that gave the war its legitimacy. With the United States beset by a recession and mounting deficits, Bush sent his secretary of state, James Baker, around the world hat in hand to raise funds for the war. His great foreign policy achievement, German unification, was won not through unilateral force but through collaborative diplomacy—even though the United States held all the trump cards at the time. Germany was unified within the Western alliance, and 340,000 Russians quietly left East Germany—all with Moscow's acquiescence.

Some did recognize that, with the Soviet Union in tatters, the United States was the only "pole" left standing. But they assumed that unipolarity was a passing phase, a "moment," in one columnist's phrase.[2] Talk of American weakness dominated the 1992 presidential election. "The Cold War is over: Japan and Germany won," Paul Tsongas said throughout his campaign for the Democratic nomination. Henry Kissinger, in his 1994 book *Diplomacy*, predicted the emergence of a new multipolar world, a view held by most scholars. Europeans believed that they were on the path to unity and world power, and Asians spoke confidently of the rise of "the Pacific Century."

Despite these claims, foreign problems, no matter how distant, always seemed to end up in Washington's lap. When the crisis in the Balkans began in 1991, the president of the European Council, Jacques Poos of Luxembourg, declared, "This is the hour of Europe. If one problem can be solved by the Europeans it is the Yugoslav problem. This is a European country and it is not up to the Americans." It was not an unusual or an anti-American view; most European leaders, including Thatcher and Helmut Kohl, shared it. But several bloody years later, it was left to America to stop the fighting. When Kosovo erupted later that decade, Europe immediately let Washington take the lead. The same pattern emerged in the East Asian economic crisis, East Timor's struggle for independence, successive Middle East conflicts, and Latin American debt defaults. Other countries were often part of the solution, but, unless America intervened, the crisis persisted. And at the same time, the American economy was in its longest boom since World War II, actually increasing its share of world output as Europe and Japan stagnated.

When Bill Clinton came into office in 1993, he promised to stop worrying about foreign policy and to focus "like a laser beam" on the economy. But the pull of unipolarity was strong. By his second term, he had become a foreign policy president, spending most of his time, energy, and attention on matters like Middle East peace and the Balkan crisis. George W. Bush, reacting to what he saw as a pattern of over-involvement in international affairs—from economic bailouts to nation building—promised on the campaign trail to scale back America's commitments. Then came his presidency and, more important, 9/11.

Through the Clinton years, American power became more apparent, Washington became more assertive, and foreign governments became more resistant. Some of Clinton's economic advisers, like Mickey Cantor and Lawrence Summers, were accused of arrogance in their dealings with other countries. Diplomats like Madeleine Albright and Richard Holbrooke were disparaged in Europe for talking about America as, in Albright's phrase, the "indispensable nation." The French foreign minister Hubert Vedrine devised the term "hyperpower"—which he did not mean as a term of endearment—during the 1990s.[3]

But all these complaints were polite chatter compared with the hostility aroused by George W. Bush. For several years, the Bush administration practically boasted of its disdain for treaties, multilateral organizations, international public opinion, and anything that suggested a conciliatory approach to world politics. By Bush's second term, when the failure of this confrontational approach was clear, the administration had started to change course on many fronts, from Iraq to the Israeli-Palestinian peace process to North Korea. But the new policies were adopted belatedly, with considerable muttering and grumbling and with elements of the administration utterly unreconciled to the new strategy.

To understand the Bush administration's foreign policy, it is not enough to focus on Dick Cheney's and Donald Rumsfeld's "Jacksonian" impulses or Bush's Texas background or the nefarious neoconservative conspiracy. The crucial enabling factor for the Bush policies was 9/11. For a decade prior to the attacks, the United States had been unchecked on the world stage. But several domestic constraints—money, Congress, public opinion—made it difficult for Washington to pursue a unilateral and combative foreign policy. Military interventions and foreign aid were both unpopular, as the public wanted the United States to retreat from the world after the rigors of the Cold War. The Balkan interventions, NATO expansion, aid to Russia, all required considerable effort from the Clinton administration, often pushing uphill, despite the fact that these were relatively small ventures that cost little in resources. But 9/11 changed all that. It broke the domestic constraints on American foreign policy. After that terrible attack, Bush had a united country and a largely sympathetic world. The Afghan War heightened the aura of American omnipotence, emboldening the most hard-line elements in the administration, who used that success as an argument for going to war with Iraq quickly and doing so in a particularly unilateral manner. The United States didn't need the rest of the world or the old mechanisms of legitimacy and coopera-tion. It was the new global empire that would create a new reality—so the argument went. The formula to explain Bush's foreign policy is simple:

Unipolarity + 9/11 + Afghanistan = Unilateralism + Iraq.*

* It is not a subject for this book, but I was in favor of the effort to oust Saddam Hus-sein, though I argued from the start for a much larger force and an internationally sanc-tioned intervention and occupation. My reasoning was mostly related to the fact that

It was not just the substance of American policy that changed in the unipolar era. So did the style, which has become imperial and imperious. There is much communication with foreign leaders, but it's a one-way street. Other governments are often simply informed of U.S. policy. Senior American officials live in their own bubbles, rarely having any genuine interaction with their overseas counterparts, let alone other foreigners. "When we meet with American officials, they talk and we listen—we rarely disagree or speak frankly because they simply can't take it in. They simply repeat the American position, like the tourist who thinks he just needs to speak louder and slower and then we will all understand," a senior foreign policy adviser in a major European government told me.

"Even for a senior foreign official dealing with the US administration," writes the solidly pro-American Christopher Patten, recounting his experience as Europe's commissioner for external affairs, "you are aware of your role as a tributary: however courteous your hosts, you come as a subordinate bearing goodwill and hoping to depart with a blessing on your endeavours. . . . In the interests of the humble leadership to which President Bush rightly aspires, it would be useful for

---

Western policy toward Iraq had collapsed—sanctions were leaking, countless civillians were dying because of the embargo, Al Qaeda was enraged by our base in Saudi Arabia, from which we operated the no-fly zone—and I believed that a more modern and moderate Iraq in the middle of the Arab world would help break the dysfunctional political dynamics of the Arab world. I opposed, from the first few weeks, Washington's occupation policies. In retrospect, I underestimated not merely the administration's arrogance and incompetence but also the inherent difficulty of the task. I continue to believe that a modern, moderate Iraq would make an important difference in the politics of the Middle East. I hope that Iraq will, in the long run, evolve into such a place, but the costs have been ruinously high—for Americans, for America's reputation, but especially for Iraqis. And foreign policy is a matter of costs and benefits, not theology.

some of his aides to try to get in to their own offices for a meeting with themselves some time!" Patten continues, "Attending any conference abroad, American Cabinet officers arrive with the sort of entourage that would have done Darius proud. Hotels are commandeered; cities are brought to a halt; innocent bystanders are barged into corners by thick-necked men with bits of plastic hanging out of their ears. It is not a spectacle that wins hearts and minds."[4]

President Bush's foreign trips seem designed to require as little contact as possible with the countries he visits. He is usually accompanied by two thousand or so Americans, as well as several airplanes, helicopters, and cars. He sees little except palaces and conference rooms. His trips involve almost no effort to demonstrate respect and appreciation for the country and culture he is visiting. They also rarely involve any meetings with people outside the government—businessmen, civil society leaders, activists. Even though the president's visit must be highly programmed by definition, a broader effort to touch the people in these foreign lands would have great symbolic value. Consider an episode involving Bill Clinton and India. In May 1998, India detonated five underground nuclear devices. The Clinton administration roundly condemned New Delhi, levied sanctions, and indefinitely postponed a planned presidential visit. The sanctions proved painful, by some estimates costing India one percent of GDP growth over the next year. Eventually Clinton relented and went to India in March 2000. He spent five days in the country, visited famous sights, put on traditional clothes, and took part in dances and ceremonies. He communicated the message that he enjoyed and admired India as a country and civilization. The result was a transformation. Clinton is a rock star in India. And George W. Bush, despite being the most pro-Indian president in American history, commands none of this attention, affection, or respect. Policy matters but so does the symbolism surrounding it.

Apart from the resentment that the imperial style produces, it ensures that American officials don't benefit from the experience and expertise of foreigners. The UN inspectors in Iraq were puzzled by how uninterested U.S. officials were in talking to them before the war. The Americans, comfortably ensconced in Washington, lectured the inspectors—who had spent weeks combing through Iraq—on the evidence of weapons of mass destruction. "I thought they would be interested in our firsthand reports on what those supposedly dual-use factories looked like," one inspector told me. "But no, *they* explained to *me* what those factories were being used for."

To foreigners, American officials seem clueless about the world they are supposed to be running. "There are two sets of conversations, one with Americans in the room and one without," says Kishore Mahbubani, who was formerly Singapore's foreign secretary and ambassador to the United Nations. Because Americans live in a "cocoon," they don't see the "sea change in attitudes towards America throughout the world."

This Time It's Different

It is too easy to dismiss the hostility that grew out of the Iraq campaign as just envious anti-Americanism (even if some of it is). American conservatives have claimed that there has been large, popular opposition in Europe every time the United States has taken strong military action—for example, when it deployed Pershing nuclear missiles in Europe in the early

1980s. In fact, the historical record highlights the opposite. The street demonstrations and public protests against the Pershing deployments made for good television, but the reality was that, in most polls, 30 to 40 percent of Europeans, and often more, strongly supported American policies. Even in Germany, where pacifist feelings ran sky-high, 53 percent of the population supported the Pershing deployments, according to a 1981 poll in *Der Spiegel*. A majority of the French supported American policy through much of Ronald Reagan's two terms, even preferring him to the Democratic candidate in the 1984 election, Walter Mondale. Today, in contrast, staggering majorities in most European countries—as high as 80 percent in many places—oppose U.S. foreign policy and even say that the United States is the greatest threat to world peace.

Josef Joffe, one of Germany's leading international affairs commentators, observes that, during the Cold War, anti-Americanism was a left-wing phenomenon. "In contrast to it, there was always a center-right that was anti-communist and thus pro-American," he explains. "The numbers waxed and waned, but you always had a solid base of support for the United States." In short, the Cold War kept Europe pro-American. The year 1968, for example, saw mass protests against American policies in Vietnam, but it was also the year of the Soviet invasion of Czechoslovakia. Europeans (and Asians) could oppose America, but their views were balanced by wariness of the Soviet threat. Again, the polls bear this out. European opposition even to the Vietnam War never approached the level of the opposition to Iraq. This was true outside Europe as well. In Australia, a majority of the public supported that country's participation in the Vietnam War through 1971, when it withdrew its forces.

For most of the world, the Iraq War was not about Iraq. "What does Mexico or Chile care about who rules in Baghdad?" Jorge Castañeda, the former foreign minister of Mexico, told me. "It was about how the world's superpower wields its power. That's something we all care deeply about." Even if Iraq finally works out, that will solve only the Iraq problem. The America problem will remain. People around the globe worry about living in a world in which one country has so much power. Even if they cannot contest this power, they can complicate it. In the case of Iraq, no country could stop the United States from going to war without international sanction, but the rest of the world has made the effort more difficult by largely sitting on the sidelines in the aftermath. As of this writing, not one Arab country has opened an embassy in Baghdad. Non-Arab allies of the United States have not been much more helpful.

Nicolas Sarkozy delights in being called "the American" and even "the neoconservative" in France. He is unabashedly pro-American and makes clear that he wants to emulate the United States in many ways. When he met Condoleezza Rice after his election as France's president, in May 2007, she asked him, "What can I do for you?" His response was revealing. "Improve your image in the world," he said. "It's difficult when the country that is the most powerful, the most successful—that is, of necessity, the leader of our side—is one of the most unpopular countries in the world. It presents overwhelming problems for you and overwhelming problems for your allies. So do everything you can do to improve the way you're perceived—that's what you can do for me."[5]

The neoconservative writer Robert Kagan argues that European and American differences over multilateral cooperation are a result of their relative strengths. When Europe's major countries were the world's great powers, they celebrated realpolitik and cared little for international cooperation. Since Europe is now weak, according to Kagan, it favors rules and restraints. America, for its part, wants complete freedom of action: "Now that the United States is powerful, it behaves as powerful nations do."[6] But this argument misinterprets history and misunderstands the unique place that America occupied in twentieth-century diplomacy. America was the most powerful country in the world when it proposed the creation of the League of Nations to manage international relations after World War I. It was the dominant power at the end of World War II, when it founded the United Nations, created the Bretton Woods system of international economic cooperation, and launched the world's key international organizations. America had the world at its feet, but Franklin Delano Roosevelt and Harry Truman chose not to create an American imperium. Instead, they built an international order of alliances and multilateral institutions and helped get the rest of the world back on its feet by pumping out vast amounts of aid and private investment. The centerpiece of this effort, the Marshall Plan, was worth $100 billion in today's dollars. For most of the twentieth century, in other words, America embraced international cooperation not out of fear and vulnerability but out of confidence and strength.

Central to this approach was the special attention given to diplomacy. Think of what it must have meant for Franklin Roosevelt, at the pinnacle of power, to go halfway across the world to Tehran and Yalta to meet with Churchill and Stalin in 1943 and 1945. Roosevelt was a sick man, paralyzed from the waist down, hauling ten pounds of steel braces on his legs.

Traveling for forty hours by sea and air took the life out of him. He did not have to go. He had plenty of deputies—George Marshall, Dwight Eisenhower—who could have done the job. Or he could have summoned the other leaders to him. But FDR understood that American power had to be coupled with a generosity of spirit. He insisted that British commanders like Montgomery be given their fair share of glory in the war. He brought China into the UN Security Council, even though it was a poor peasant society, because he believed that it was important to have the largest Asian country properly represented within a world body.

The standard set by Roosevelt and his generation endured. When Secretary of State Marshall devised the plan that bears his name, he insisted that the initiative and control lie with Europeans. For decades thereafter, the United States built dams, funded magazines, and provided technical know-how to other countries. It sent its scholars and students abroad so that people got to know America and Americans. It paid deference to its allies, even when they were in no sense equals. It conducted joint military exercises with small nations, even when they added little to U.S. readiness. For half a century, American presidents and secretaries of state circled the globe and hosted their counterparts in a never-ending cycle of diplomacy.

All these exertions served our interests, of course. They produced a pro-American world that was rich and secure. They laid the foundations for a booming global economy in which others could participate and in which America thrived. But it was an enlightened self-interest that took into account the interests of others. Above all, it reassured countries—through word and deed, style and substance—that America's mammoth power was not to be feared.

New Rules for a New Age

Some Americans believe that we should not learn from history but just copy it. If only we could find another Truman administration, many liberals and Democrats seem to pine, it would establish a new set of institutions for a new era. But this is nostalgia, not strategy. When Truman, Acheson, and Marshall built the postwar order, the rest of the world was in tatters. People had seen the devastating effects of nationalism, war, and economic protectionism. As a result, there was strong support everywhere, especially in the United States, for a large and generous effort to engage the world, raise it out of poverty, create global institutions, and ensure international cooperation—so that such a war never took place again. America had the moral high ground that came from defeating fascism, but it also had unrivaled power. American GDP made up almost 50 percent of the global economy. Outside of the Soviet sphere, Washington's lead role in devising new institutions was never really questioned. Today, the world is different, and so is America's position in it. Were Truman and Marshall and Acheson alive, they would face a wholly new set of challenges. The task for today is to construct a new approach for a new era, one that responds to a global system in which power is far more diffuse than ever before and in which everyone feels empowered.

The United States does not have the hand it had in 1945 or even in 2000. Still, it does have a stronger hand than anyone else—the most complete portfolio of economic, political, military, and cultural power—and it will not be replaced in the foreseeable future. Perhaps more importantly, we do not need to invent the world anew. The international order established by the United States after World War II is in urgent need of expansion and repair, but not reconception. As the Princeton scholar John Ikenberry has perceptively noted, the Western-oriented system created in the 1940s and 1950s allows for the expansion of global trade, the rise of new powers, and mechanisms of cooperation and conflict management. It cannot always and easily address certain problems, such as great power conflict and internal human rights tragedies, but those are the limits of international relations, not of these particular structures. Simultaneously, the reality of nuclear weapons and deterrence makes it extremely costly—suicidal—for a rising power to try to assert itself militarily against its peers. "Today's Western order, in short, is hard to overturn and easy to join," writes Ikenberry.[7] That is how modern Japan and Germany have seen their choices and how China and India seem to be viewing their future. They want to gain power and status and respect, for sure, but by growing within the international system, not by overturning it. As long as these new countries feel they can be accommodated, they have every incentive to become "responsible stakeholders" in this system.

The rise of the rest, while real, is a long, slow process. And it is one that ensures America a vital, though different, role. As China, India, Brazil, Russia, South Africa, and a host of smaller countries all do well in the years ahead, new points of tension will emerge among them. Many of these rising countries have historical animosities, border disputes, and contemporary quarrels with one another; in most cases, nationalism will grow along with economic and geopolitical stature. Being a distant power, America is often a convenient partner for many regional nations worried about the rise of a hegemon in their midst. In fact, as the scholar William Wohlforth notes, American influence is strengthened by the growth of a dominant regional power.[8] These factors are often noted in discussions of Asia, but it is true of many other spots on the globe as well. The process will not be mechanical. As one of these countries rises (China), it will not produce a clockwork-like balancing dynamic where its neighbor (India) will seek a formal alliance with the United States. Today's world is more complicated than that. But these rivalries do give the United States an opportunity to play a large and constructive role at the center of the global order. It has the potential to be what Bismarck helped Germany become (briefly) in the late nineteenth-century— Europe's "honest broker," forging close relationships with each of the major countries, ties that were closer than the ones those countries had with one another. It was the hub of the European system. Being the global broker today would be a job involving not just the American government but its society, with all the strengths and perspectives that it will bring to the challenge. It is a role that the United States—with its global interests and presence, complete portfolio of power, and diverse immigrant communities—could learn to play with great skill.

This new role is quite different from the traditional superpower role. It involves consultation, cooperation, and even compromise. It derives its power by setting the agenda, defining the issues, and mobilizing coalitions. It is not a top-down hierarchy in which the United States makes its decisions and then informs a grateful (or silent) world. But it is a crucial role because, in a world with many players, setting the agenda and organizing coalitions become primary forms of power. The chair of the board who can gently guide a group of independent directors is still a very powerful person.

Those who have figured out how best to thrive in a post-American world are America's great multinationals. They are conquering new markets by changing their old ways. Take General Electric, which in the past didn't believe in joint ventures abroad. It wanted to own 100 percent of every foreign involvement it had. Over the last five years, however, as it has watched the growing skill and confidence of the local firms in emerging markets like China, India, Brazil, Russia, and South Africa, GE has come to realize that such a strategy would keep it locked out of the fastest-growing parts of the world. So it changed its approach. GE's CEO Jeffrey Immelt sums it up: "Sure, we could keep buying small companies and G.E.-ize them. But we've learned that it's better to partner with the No. 3 company that wants to be No. 1 than to buy a tiny company or go it alone." The *New York Times* called it a turn away from "managerial imperialism," which has become a "luxury G.E. could no longer afford."[9] Washington, which faces no market test, has not yet figured out that diplomatic imperialism is a luxury that the United States can no longer afford.

There is still a strong market for American power, for both geopolitical and economic reasons. But even more centrally, there remains a strong ideological demand for it. "No one in Asia wants to live in a Chinese-dominated world. There is no Chinese dream to which people aspire," explained Simon Tay, a Singaporean scholar. A former president of Brazil, Fernando Henrique Cardoso, has argued that what the world really wants from America is not that it offer a concession on trade here and there but that it affirm its own ideals. That role, as the country that will define universal ideals, remains one that only America can play.[10] America's soft power, in this sense, is intricately linked to its hard power. But it is the combination of the two that give it a unique role in world affairs.

To describe more concretely what operating in this new world would look like, I have set out six simple guidelines.

1. Choose. American omnipotence has made Washington believe that it is exempt from the need to have priorities. It wants to have it all. It is crucial that the United States be more disciplined about this. On North Korea and Iran, for example, the Bush administration could not decide whether it wanted regime change or policy change (that is, denuclearization). The two work at cross-purposes. If you threaten a country with regime change, it only makes more urgent that government's desire for nuclear weapons, which is an insurance policy in the world of international politics.

Consider what the world looks like to Iran. It is surrounded by nuclear powers (Russia, China, India, Pakistan, Israel), and across two of its borders sit tens of thousands of U.S. troops (in Iraq and Afghanistan). The president of the United States has repeatedly made clear that he regards the regime in Tehran as illegitimate, wishes to overthrow it, and funds various groups whose aims are similar. If you were in Tehran, would this make you feel like giving up your nuclear program? Insisting on both policy change and regime change, we have gotten neither.

Or take American policy toward Russia. We have never been able to prioritize what exactly our core interests and concerns with Moscow are. Is it the danger of its loose nuclear weapons, which can be secured only with its help? Is it Moscow's help in isolating Iran? Or its behavior in Ukraine and Georgia? Or its opposition to the proposed missile shield in Eastern Europe? Or its oil and natural gas policies? Or internal human rights conditions in Russia? Recent U.S. policy has been "all of the above." But to govern is to choose. If we believe that nuclear proliferation and terrorism are the gravest issues we face at present, as President Bush has said, then securing Russia's nuclear arsenal and preventing Iran from developing nuclear weapons are surely the two issues on which we should be seeking Russian cooperation—above all else.

The United States will especially need to choose with regard to China. China is experiencing the largest, swiftest rise to world power of any country in history—larger and swifter even than that of the United States in the past. It will have to be given some substantial political and even military space commensurate with that power. At the same time, its rise should not become a cover for expansionism, aggression, or disruption. How to strike this balance—deterring China, on the one hand, accommodating its legitimate growth, on the other—is the central strategic challenge for American diplomacy. The United States can and should draw lines with China. But it should also recognize that it cannot draw lines everywhere. Unfortunately, the most significant hurdle the United States faces in shaping such a policy is a domestic political climate that tends to view any concessions and accommodations as appeasement.

To the extent that the United States can learn something from the experience of Great Britain, it is the need to make large strategic choices about where it will focus its energies and attention. Britain did so wisely when it faced the rise of the United States. It was less wise about its own empire. In the early twentieth century, London confronted a dilemma much like Washington's today. When a crisis broke somewhere, no matter how remote, the world would look to London and ask,

"What will you do about this?" Britain's strategic blunder was to spend decades—time and money, energy and attention—on vain attempts to stabilize peripheral places on the map. For example, Britain should have expended less effort organizing the constitutional arrangements of Dutch farmers in the Transvaal—and thus fighting the Boer War, which broke the back of the empire—and more facing up to its declining productivity and the rise of Germany in the center of Europe.

British elites pored over Roman histories in part because of their fascination with a previous great empire, but also because they were looking for lessons in managing vast swaths of land on different continents. There was a demand, as it were, for people skilled in language, history, and imperial administration. This, however, ended up trumping the need to develop the engineers of the future. Britain's power and reach also made it intoxicated with a sense of historic destiny, a trend fueled by a Protestant revival. The historian Correlli Barnett wrote (in the 1970s) that a "moral revolution" gripped England in the mid-nineteenth century, moving it away from the practical and reason-based society that had brought about the industrial revolution and toward one dominated by religious evangelicalism, excessive moralism, and romanticism.[11]

The United States could easily fall into a similar imperial trap. Every crisis around the world demands its attention and action. American tentacles and interests are spread as widely today as were Britain's at the height of its empire. For those who believe that America's place in the world is wholly different from that of the British Empire, it is instructive to read the "Base Structure Report" for fiscal year 2006. In it, the Department of Defense boasts of being "one of the world's largest 'landlords' with a physical plant consisting of more than

571,200 facilities (buildings, structures, and utilities) located on more than 3,700 sites, on nearly 30 million acres." The report lists a sprawling network of 766 bases in forty foreign countries, from Antigua to the United Kingdom. These overseas bases were worth at least $127 billion in 2005, housed 197,000 uniform personnel and an equal number of dependents and civilian officials, and employed an additional 81,000 local foreign hires. They covered 687,000 acres (nearly 1,100 square miles) of foreign land and cost taxpayers $13 billion in maintenance alone.

America may be more powerful than Britain was, but it still cannot neglect the lesson that it must make choices. It cannot be involved in everything. Tensions in the Middle East are important, but they have sucked all the resources, energy, and attention out of every other issue in American foreign policy for the last seven years. Washington has to move out of the eighth century A.D., adjudicating claims between Sunnis and Shias in Baghdad, and move into the twenty-first century—to China, India, Brazil—where the future is being made. Every choice to engage in some cause, worthy as it is, is a distraction from the larger strategic issues that confront the United States. In focusing on the seemingly urgent, we will forget the truly important.

2. Build broad rules, not narrow interests. There is a fundamental tension in U.S. foreign policy. Does the country want to push its own particular interests abroad, or does it want to create a structure of rules, practices, and values by which the world will be bound? In an age of rising new powers, the United States' overriding goal should be the latter—so that even as these countries get more powerful, they will continue to live within the framework of the current international system. This is the principal constraint we can construct to ensure that the rise of the rest does not turn into a downward competitive spiral, with great powers freelancing for their own interests and advantage in such a way as to destabilize the whole system. For such a system to work, *we* would have to adhere to these rules as well. If the United States freelances when it suits its purposes, why would China not do the same with regard to Taiwan? Or India with regard to Pakistan? If we are not bound by the rules, why should they be?

First, that means recommitting itself to the institutions and mechanisms for problem solving and adjudication that the United States (largely) created over the last five decades. But this is more than simply about attending more UN meetings and signing treaties. When the United States proclaims universal values, it must phrase its positions carefully. George Bush declared in his second inaugural that it "is the policy of the United States to seek and support the growth of democratic movements and institutions in every nation and culture, with the ultimate goal of ending tyranny in our world." And yet, when democrats in Taiwan and Pakistan and Saudi Arabia were silenced, the United States kept quiet, arguing—perhaps persuasively—that these are special cases. Still, Washington pillories China and scolds India for not being tougher on North Korea and Burma. Diplomats in both countries will tell you that these are special cases for them. Instability in Burma is a remote problem for the United States. But that country shares long borders with China and India. Instability to them means millions of refugees. Washington should recognize that if it has its own exceptions, so do other countries. Or else it should drop its own exceptions. But to do neither, and preach one thing and practice another, is hypocrisy, which is both ineffective and undermining of American credibility.

When it comes to terrorism, the United States has been too narrow-minded. The best systemic protection against the threat of terrorism would be a global set of customs and immigration controls that checks people and cargo around the world, using the same standards and sharing databases. As it is now, America's unilateral approach forces countries and airlines to comply, but only at its own borders—creating chokepoints, with negative consequences for the economy and for America's image in the world. That's why, in the midst of a worldwide tourism boom, travel to the United States has been sluggish ever since 9/11.

The more significant ongoing example of this tension has to do with nuclear proliferation. The United States asks the rest of the world to strictly adhere to the Nuclear Nonproliferation Treaty. The treaty has created a two-tier system: those nations that developed nuclear weapons before 1968 are permitted to have them; those that didn't are not (and must accordingly follow certain guidelines for developing nuclear energy). But even while insisting that nonnuclear powers comply, the United States and other nuclear powers have themselves taken no steps to follow the other injunction in the treaty: to "pursue negotiations in good faith on effective measures relating to cessation of the nuclear arms race . . . and to nuclear disarmament." Thus, when the United States tells countries that to build a single nuclear weapon is a moral, political, and strategic abomination while maintaining an arsenal of thousands of missiles and building and testing new ones, the condemnation rings hollow. Motivated by such concerns, Henry Kissinger, George Shultz, William Perry, and Sam Nunn have proposed that the United States lead an ambitious effort among the nuclear powers—and particularly with Russia, which together with America holds 85 percent of all nuclear weapons—to reduce the numbers of weapons, move them off alert status, and eventually work toward a nonnuclear world. Whether or not we get all the way there—and whether or not a world without nuclear deterrence is a good idea—the United States would gain much credibility if it made some serious efforts in this direction. Or else, once again it appears to be saying to the rest of the world, "Do what I say, not what I do."

3. Be Bismarck not Britain. Josef Joffe has argued that there are two historical analogies that the United States can look to in constructing its grand strategy: Britain and Bismarck.[12] Britain tried to balance against rising and threatening great powers but otherwise kept a low profile on the European continent. Bismarck, by contrast, chose to engage with all the great powers. His goal was to have better relations with all of them than any of them had with each other—to be the pivot of Europe's international system.

For the United States, the British option is not the right one. America has played that role in the past—against Nazi Germany and Soviet Russia—but the circumstances today make such a strategy unwise. The world is not divided into camps, and it is far more connected and interdependent than it was. "Balancing" against a rising power would be a dangerous, destabilizing, and potentially self-fulfilling policy. Were Washington to balance against China, before Beijing had shown any serious inclination to disrupt the international order, it would find itself isolated—and would pay heavy costs economically and politically for itself being the disruptive force. Given America's massive power, not overplaying its hand must be a crucial component of any grand strategy. Otherwise, others will try—in various ways—to balance against it.

Washington is, however, ideally suited to play a Bismarckian role in the current global system. It has better relations with almost all the major powers than they do with each other. In Asia, the Bush administration has done an excellent job of strengthening ties with Japan, Australia, and India. It should try to do the same with Russia and China. While Washington has many differences with Moscow and Beijing, there is no advantage to turning them into permanent adversaries. The virtue of the Bismarckian approach is that it gives the United States the greatest leverage with all parties, maximizing its ability to shape a peaceful and stable world. And if things do not work out, it also gives the United States legitimacy and leeway to move into a balancing role.

4. Order à la carte. Among scholars and practitioners of international relations, there is one predominant theory about how and why international peace endures. It holds that the most stable system is one with a single dominant power that maintains order. Britain and the United States have played this role for two hundred years. In each case, the hegemon was the dominant economic and military player, becoming the market and lender of last resort, home to the world financial center, and holder of the reserve currency. In politico-military terms, each secured the sea lanes, balanced against rising threats, and intervened when it thought necessary to prevent disorder. Although both made many mistakes, the stability of the system and the success of the world economy and the open societies it created are an extraordinary legacy of Anglo-American hegemony.

What if that hegemony is waning? America no longer has the only large market in the world. The dollar is unlikely to retain its totemic position forever as the reserve currency, yielding to a basket that is largely composed of euros and dollars but includes other currencies too. In certain areas—the South China Sea, for example—U.S. military force is likely to be less relevant than that of China. In international negotiations, America will have to bargain and compromise with others. Does all this add up to instability and disorder?

Not necessarily. Two hundred years of Anglo-American hegemony has in fact created a system that is not as fragile as it might have been in the 1920s and 1930s. (When British power waned, America was unwilling to step in, and Europe fell through the cracks.) The basic conception of the current system—an open world economy, multilateral negotiations—has wide acceptance. And new forms of cooperation are growing. Anne-Marie Slaughter has written about how legal systems are constructing a set of transnational standards without anyone's forcing them to do so—creating a bottom-up, networked order.[13] Not every issue will lend itself to such stabilization, but many will. In other words, the search for a superpower solution to every problem may be futile and unnecessary. Smaller work-arounds might be just as effective.

The United States should embrace such an ad hoc order. Richard Haass, the former head of Policy Planning at the State Department, has creatively called for "à la carte multilateralism."[14] No one institution or organization is always right, no one framework ideal. The UN might work for one problem, NATO for another, the OAS for a third. And for a new issue like climate change, perhaps a new coalition that involves private business and nongovernmental groups would make the most sense. International life is only going to get messier. Being accommodating, flexible, and adaptable is likely to produce better results on the ground than insisting on a pure

approach based on the notion that the only way to solve international problems is the way we have solved international
problems in the past, in decades when the state was unusually
strong. A more organic international system in which problems
are addressed through a variety of different structures and
solutions can create its own kind of layered stability. It is not as
appealing as a more formal structure of peace, rooted in and
directed through one or two central organizations in New York
and Geneva. But it might be a more realistic and durable order.

The search for order is not simply an American problem. If
the rise of the rest also brings about a rise in national pride
and interest and assertiveness, it has the potential to produce
disorder everywhere. At the same time, this rise is happening
in a world in which peace and stability pay great rewards—
giving China, India, and even Russia large incentives to keep
the system stable. The problem is that these rising powers do
not have an obvious and immediate incentive to solve the
common problems that this new system generates. National
frictions, climate change, trade disputes, environmental
degradation, and infectious disease might all fester until a crisis hits—and then it might be too late. Solving such problems
and providing global public goods requires a moderator,
organizer, or leader.

5. Think asymmetrically. The United States has the
most powerful military in the history of the world. And yet it
has found it difficult to prevail in Iraq. The Israeli military is
vastly superior to Hezbollah's forces. But it was not able to
win a decisive victory over the latter in its conflict with it.
Why? Because the current era is one in which asymmetrical
responses have become easier to execute and difficult to
defeat. This is true not simply in war. Consider the rise of

drug cartels, money-laundering syndicates, migrant workers, and terrorists, all far smaller and poorer than the governments that oppose them. In an age of constant activity across and within borders, small groups of people with ingenuity, passion, and determination have important advantages.

In working within this context, the first and most important lesson is to not get drawn into traps. In a videotaped message in 2004, Osama bin Laden explained his strategy with astonishing frankness. He termed it "provoke and bait": "All we have to do is send two mujahedin . . . [and] raise a piece of cloth on which is written 'Al Qaeda' in order to make the generals race there, to cause America to suffer human, economic, and political losses." His point has been well understood by ragtag terror groups across the world. With no apparent communication, collaboration, or further guidance from bin Laden, small outfits from Southeast Asia to North Africa to Europe now announce that they are part of Al Qaeda, and so inflate their own importance, bring global attention to their cause—and of course get America to come racing out to fight them. This kind of overreaction also makes the U.S. military presence and policies—its bombings, its collateral damage— the main issue. The local debate moves from terrorism to U.S. imperialism.

Consider the manner in which the United States is considering expanding its presence in Africa. The rhetoric that the Bush administration has used is commendable. "We want to prevent problems from becoming crises, and crises from becoming catastrophes," Theresa Whelan, deputy assistant defense secretary for African affairs, explained in an interview in 2007. "We have in our national interest that Africa is a stable continent." Its solution, however, has been the creation of a new military command for the continent, AFRICOM, with its own commander and staff. But as the *Washington Post* columnist David Ignatius perceptively asks, "Is the U.S. military the right instrument for the nation-building effort that AFRICOM apparently envisions? Will a larger U.S. military presence check terrorism and instability on the continent, or will it instead become a new magnet for anti-Americanism?" The United States has many interests in Africa, from keeping countries stable to checking China's influence to preventing humanitarian tragedies. But is a military command the way to go about this? Or is this simply the response generated because this is how the U.S. government knows to respond— with a military command? The danger here is of wasted resources, a reaction to perceived American imperialism. But the deeper problem is conceptual. It is a misdiagnosis of the problem. "To the man who has a hammer," Mark Twain wrote, "every problem looks like a nail."

The United States should be thinking creatively and asymmetrically. This would allow it to capitalize on one of its key advantages. The United States has a much broader and deeper range of instruments than just its military. An American policy toward Africa, for example, that focused on building up our diplomatic corps, nation-building capacities, and technical assistance teams would be a bit duller than AFRICOM—but it might be more effective in the long run. This would be true outside Africa as well. What the United States is lacking in a place like Pakistan is a broader effort to assist that country in its modernization and an effort that makes it clear that the United States wants to ally with the people of that country and not merely its military. When I was growing up in India, the U.S. Information Services used to serve as ambassadors of

American culture, ideas, and ideals. That entire approach to diplomacy was shuttered after the Cold War and even after 9/11 remains moribund. The U.S. military effort against Islamic extremism has received close to $1 trillion of funding. The generous accounting of the figure for diplomatic and civilian activities would be under $10 billion.

America is also much more than its government. And here there is more promising activity. Foundations, universities, charities, and private individuals are working more deeply and effectively abroad. Washington should learn more from these groups, work more with them, and engage other Americans to get involved. American Muslims, instead of being questioned, harassed, and detained, should be enlisted in the effort to understand the appeal of Islamic fundamentalism. One of America's core strengths—its civil society—has been largely untapped in the war on terror.

6. Legitimacy is power. The United States has every kind of power in ample supply these days except one: legitimacy. In today's world, this is a critical deficiency. Legitimacy allows one to set the agenda, define a crisis, and mobilize support for policies among both countries and nongovernmental forces like private business and grass-roots organizations. Legitimacy was what allowed the rock singer Bono, for example, to change government policy on a crucial issue, debt relief. His power lay in his ability to capture the intellectual and moral high ground.

Legitimacy comes in many forms. The Clinton administration used force on three important occasions—in Bosnia, Haiti, and Kosovo. In none of them did it take the matter to the UN Security Council, but there was little suggestion that it needed to do so. Indeed, Secretary General Kofi Annan even made statements that seemed to justify the action in Kosovo, explaining that state sovereignty should not be used as a cover for humanitarian abuses. The Clinton administration was able to get away with this partly because of a basic sense of trust. While the Clinton administration—or the George H. W. Bush administration—was assertive in many ways, the rest of the world did not need assurances about its intentions. The current Bush administration does not bear all the blame for how dramatic the difference is today. Because of 9/11, it had no choice but to assert American power and act forcefully on the world stage. But that should have given it all the more reason to adopt a posture of consultation and cooperation while doing what needed to be done. It's one thing to scare your enemies; it's another to terrify the rest of the world.

The United States retains considerable ability to set the agenda and thereby confer legitimacy with regard to what constitutes a problem, crisis, or outrage. American ideas and ideals still dominate the debates over Darfur, Iranian nuclear weapons, and Burma. But Washington needs to understand that generating international public support for its view of the world is a core element of power, not merely an exercise in public relations. Other countries, peoples, and groups now have access to their own narratives and networks. They will not quietly accept the version of events handed down to them. Washington will have to make its case, and persuasively. This task has gotten more difficult, but it has also become more vital. In an increasingly empowered and democratized world, in the long run, the battle of ideas is close to *everything*.

The Bush administration never seemed to understand the practical value of legitimacy in the run-up to the Iraq War. American officials would contest the view that they were iso-

lated by pointing to their allies in "new Europe," Asia, and
Africa—many of whom were bribed or cajoled into the coalition. And while the *governments* of Central Europe supported
Washington, its people opposed it in almost the same numbers as in old Europe. Missing this distinction, Washington
misunderstood Turkey, a long-standing and faithful ally that
had become much more democratic over the 1990s. The government wanted to back the United States, but more than 90
percent of the Turkish people opposed it. The result, after a
close parliamentary vote, was that Turkey could not support
the United States—which meant the two-front war against
Saddam became a one-front war, with serious drawbacks. At
the start of the war, the United States had the support of a
majority of the people in only one country in the world, Israel.
And while one might laud Tony Blair for his loyalty, one cannot expect most democratic politicians to ignore the wishes of
vast majorities of their people.

Nationalism in a unipolar world can often become anti-
American. How do you show that you are a staunch Brazilian,
Chinese, or Russian patriot? By standing up to Mr. Big. In the
1970s, many of Indira Gandhi's domestic policies were unpopular. Standing up to America, however, would always get a
cheer on the campaign trail. Why? India was then as now fas-
cinated by America and the American dream. But it was a sign
of strength and courage that Mrs. Gandhi could assert herself
against the hegemon. Americans complain that this is irra-
tional, and that the country is unfairly turned into a punching
bag. They are right. But get over it. There are many, many
advantages to being a superpower. It has some costs as well.
Those costs can be easily lowered by attentive diplomacy.

"It is better to be feared than loved," Machiavelli wrote. It is a motto that Dick Cheney takes to heart. In a 2007 speech, he quoted Bernard Lewis to the effect that, during the Cold War, Middle Eastern dictators learned that they should fear the Soviet Union but not America. Machiavelli and Cheney are wrong. Yes, the Soviet Union was feared by its allies, while the United States was loved, or at least liked. Look who's still around. It is odd and unsettling that Vice President Cheney should cite enviously the thuggish and failed strategies of a totalitarian dictatorship. America has transformed the world with its power but also with its ideals. When China's pro-democracy protesters gathered in Tiananmen Square, they built a makeshift figure that suggested the Statue of Liberty, not an F-16. America's image may not be as benign as Americans think, but it is, in the end, better than the alternatives. That is what has made its immense power tolerable to the world for so long.

Fear and Loathing

Before it can implement any of these specific strategies, however, the United States must make a much broader adjustment. It needs to stop cowering in fear. It is fear that has created a climate of paranoia and panic in the United States and fear that has enabled our strategic missteps. Having spooked ourselves into believing that we have no option but to act fast and alone, preemptively and unilaterally, we have managed to destroy decades of international goodwill, alienate allies, and embolden enemies, while solving few of the major international problems we face. To recover its place in the world, America first has to recover its confidence.

By almost all objective measures, the United States is in a blessed position today. It faces problems, crises, and resistance, but compared with any of the massive threats of the past—Nazi Germany, Stalin's aggression, nuclear war—the circumstances are favorable, and the world is moving our way. In 1933, Franklin Delano Roosevelt diagnosed the real danger for the United States. "The only thing we have to fear is fear itself," he said. "Nameless, unreasoning, unjustified terror." And he was arguing against fear when America's economic and political system was near collapse, when a quarter of the workforce was unemployed, and when fascism was on the march around the world. Somehow we have managed to spook ourselves in a time of worldwide peace and prosperity. Keeping that front and center in our minds is crucial to ensure that we do not miscalculate, misjudge, and misunderstand.

America has become a nation consumed by anxiety, worried about terrorists and rogue nations, Muslims and Mexicans, foreign companies and free trade, immigrants and international organizations. The strongest nation in the history of the world now sees itself as besieged by forces beyond its control. While the Bush administration has contributed mightily to this state of affairs, it is a phenomenon that goes beyond one president. Too many Americans have been taken in by a rhetoric of fear.

The 2008 presidential campaign could have provided the opportunity for a national discussion of the new world we live in. On the Republican side, it has been largely an exercise in chest-thumping hysteria. The contenders may have left the scene but their words both reflect and shape the national consciousness. "They hate you!" Rudy Giuliani repeatedly shouted on the campaign trail, relentlessly reminding audiences of the nasty people out there. "They don't want you to be in this college!" he warned an audience at Oglethorpe University, in Atlanta. "Or you, or you, or you," he added, reportedly jabbing his finger at students. Giuliani urged that America not only stay on the offensive but go on the offensive on new fronts.

In his book *Courage Matters*, Senator John McCain took a far more sensible approach and wrote, "Get on the damn elevator! Fly on the damn plane! Calculate the odds of being harmed by a terrorist. It's still about as likely as being swept out to sea by a tidal wave." Writing in late 2003, he added what seemed like a sound rule of thumb: "Watch the terrorist alert and when it falls below yellow, go outside again." Unfortunately, since 9/11 the alert has never dropped below yellow (which means an "elevated" level of risk from a terrorist attack). At airports, it has been almost permanently at orange—"high risk," the second-highest level of alertness. Yet the Department of Homeland Security admits that "there continues to be no credible information at this time warning of an imminent threat to the homeland." Since 9/11, only two or three *extremely* minor terrorist plots have been uncovered in the entire country, and there is no example of an Al Qaeda sleeper cell having been found in America.

And still, the enemy—as many American politicians describe it—is vast, global, and relentless. Giuliani casually lumped together Iran and Al Qaeda. Mitt Romney went further, banding together all the supposed bad guys. "This is about Shia and Sunni. This is about Hizbullah and Hamas and Al Qaeda and the Muslim Brotherhood," he recently declared. In fact, Iran is a Shiite power and actually *helped* the United States topple the Al Qaeda–backed Taliban regime in

Afghanistan. Al Qaeda–affiliated radical Sunnis slaughtered Shiites in Iraq, and Iranian-backed Shiite militias responded by executing Iraqi Sunnis. We are now repeating one of the central errors of the early Cold War—putting together all our potential adversaries, rather than dividing them. Mao and Stalin were both nasty. But they were nasties who disliked each other, a fact that could be exploited to the great benefit of the free world. To miss this is not strength. It's stupidity.

The competition to be the tough guy has produced new policy ideas—ones that range from bad to insane. Romney, who bills himself as the smart, worldly manager, recently explained that while "some people have said we ought to close Guantánamo, my view is we ought to double [the size of] Guantánamo." Romney asked in 2005, "Are we monitoring [mosques]? Are we wiretapping?" Of course, this proposal is mild compared with what Representative Tom Tancredo, another Republican presidential candidate, suggested that same year. When asked about a possible nuclear strike by Islamic radicals on the United States, he suggested that the U.S. military threaten to "take out" Mecca.

Some praise the Bush administration's aggressive approach for preventing another terrorist attack on U.S. soil after 9/11. Certainly, the administration does deserve credit for dismantling Al Qaeda's infrastructure in Afghanistan and in other countries where it once had branches or supporters—though that success has been more limited than many recognize. But since 9/11 there have occurred terrorist attacks in countries like Britain, Spain, Morocco, Turkey, Indonesia, and Saudi Arabia—most of which are also very tough on terrorism. The common thread in these attacks is that they were launched by local groups. It's easier to spot and stop foreign agents, far more difficult to detect a group of locals.

The crucial advantage that the United States has in this regard is that it does not have a radicalized domestic population. American Muslims are generally middle class, moderate, and well assimilated. They believe in America and the American dream. The first comprehensive poll of U.S. Muslims, conducted in 2007 by the Pew Research Center, found that more than 70 percent believe that if you work hard in America, you get ahead. (That figure for the general U.S. population is only 64 percent.) Their responses to almost all questions were in the American mainstream—and strikingly different from the responses of Muslim populations elsewhere. Some 13 percent of U.S. Muslims believe that suicide bombings can be justified. Too high, for sure, but the figure compares with 42 percent for French Muslims and 88 percent for Jordanians.

This distinct American advantage—testament to the country's ability to assimilate new immigrants—is increasingly in jeopardy. If American leaders begin insinuating that the entire Muslim population be viewed with suspicion, that will change the community's relationship to the United States. Proposals by presidential candidates of wiretapping America's mosques and bombing Mecca are certainly not steps in the right direction.

Though Democrats are more sensible on most of these issues, the party remains consumed by the fear that it will not come across as tough. Its presidential candidates vie with one another to prove that they are going to be just as macho and militant as the fiercest Republican. In a South Carolina presidential debate in 2007, when candidates were asked how they would respond to another terror strike, they promptly vowed to attack, retaliate, and blast the hell out of, well, somebody. Barack Obama, the only one to answer differently, quickly realized his political vulnerability and dutifully threatened retaliation as well. After the debate, his opponents suggested that his original response proved he didn't have the fortitude to be president. (In fact, Obama's initial response was the right one. He said that the first thing he would do was make certain that the emergency response was effective, then ensure we had the best intelligence possible to figure out who had caused the attack, and then move with allies to dismantle the network responsible.)

We will never be able to prevent a small group of misfits from planning some terrible act of terror. No matter how far-seeing and competent our intelligence and law-enforcement officials, people will always be able to slip through the cracks in a large, open, and diverse country. The real test of American leadership is not whether we can make 100 percent sure we prevent the attack, but rather how we respond to it. Stephen Flynn, a homeland-security expert at the Council on Foreign Relations, argues that our goal must be resilience—how quickly can we bounce back from a disruption? In the material sciences, resilience is the ability of a material to recover its original shape after a deformation. If one day bombs do go off, we must ensure that they cause as little disruption—economic, social, political—as possible. This would prevent the terrorist from achieving his main objective. If we are not terrorized, then in a crucial sense we have defeated terrorism.[15]

The atmosphere of fear and panic we are currently engendering is likely to produce the opposite effect. Were there to be another attack, two things can be predicted with near-certainty. The actual effects of the attack would be limited, allowing the country to get back to normal quickly. And Washington would go berserk. Politicians would fall over each other to pledge to pulverize, annihilate, and destroy . . . someone. A retaliatory strike would be appropriate and important—if you could hit the right targets. But what if the culprits were based in Hamburg or Madrid or Trenton? It is far more likely that a future attack will come from countries that are unknowingly and involuntarily sheltering terrorists. Are we going to bomb Britain and Spain because they housed a terrorist cell?

The other likely effect of another terror attack would be an increase in the restrictions on movement, privacy, and civil liberties that have already imposed huge economic, political, and moral costs on America. The process of screening passengers at airports, which costs nearly $5 billion annually, gets more cumbersome every year as new potential "risks" are discovered. The visa system, which has become restrictive and forbidding, will get more so every time one thug is let in. None of these procedures is designed with any consideration of striking a balance between the need for security and the need for openness and hospitality. The incentives are skewed to ensure that anytime, anywhere an official has a concern, he is better off stopping, questioning, arresting, and deporting.

Our fears extend well beyond terrorism. CNN's Lou Dobbs has become the spokesman of a paranoid and angry segment of the country, railing against the sinister forces that are overwhelming us. For many on the right, illegal immigrants have become an obsession. The party of free enterprise has dedicated itself to a huge buildup of the state's police powers *to stop people from working*. The Democrats are worried about the wages of employees in the United States, but these fears are now focused on free trade. Though protecting American firms from competition is a sure path to lower productivity, open economic policies are fast losing support within the party. Bill Clinton's historic realignment of his party—toward the future, markets, trade, and efficiency—is being squandered in the quest for momentary popularity. Whether on terrorism, trade, immigration, or internationalism of any kind, the political dynamic in the United States these days is to hunker down.

Some of foreign policy is what we do, but some of it is also who we are. Hubert Humphrey reputedly said that the Civil Rights Act of 1964 was one of the most important foreign policies of that decade. America *the place* has often been the great antidote to U.S. foreign policy. When American actions across the world have seemed harsh, misguided, or unfair, America itself has always been open, welcoming, and tolerant. I remember visiting the United States as a kid in the 1970s, at a time when, as a country, India was officially anti-American. The reality of the America that I experienced was a powerful refutation of the propaganda and caricatures of its enemies. But today, through inattention, fear, and bureaucratic cowardice, the caricature threatens to become reality.

At the end of the day, openness is America's greatest strength. Many smart policy wonks have clever ideas that they believe will better American productivity, savings, and health care. More power to them all. But historically, America has succeeded not because of the ingenuity of its government programs but because of the vigor of its society. It has thrived because it has kept itself open to the world—to goods and services, to ideas and inventions, and, above all, to people and cultures. This openness has allowed us to respond quickly and flexibly to new economic times, to manage change and diversity with remarkable ease, and to push forward the boundaries of individual freedom and autonomy. It has allowed America to create the first universal nation, a place where people from all over the world can work, mingle, mix, and share in a common dream and a common destiny.

In the fall of 1982, I arrived here as an eighteen-year-old student from India, eight thousand miles away. America was in rough shape. That December, unemployment hit 10.8 percent, higher than at any point since World War II. Interest rates hovered around 15 percent. Vietnam, Watergate, the energy crisis, and the Iranian hostage crisis had all battered American confidence. Images of the helicopters on the roof of the American Embassy in Saigon, of Nixon resigning, of long lines at gas stations, and of the hostages blindfolded were all fresh in people's minds. The Soviet Union was on a roll, expanding its influence far beyond its borders, from Afghanistan to Angola to Central America. That June, Israel invaded Lebanon, making a volatile situation in the Middle East even more tense.

Yet America was a strikingly open and expansive country. Reagan embodied it. Despite record-low approval ratings at the time, he exuded optimism from the center of the storm. In the face of Moscow's rising power, he confidently spoke of a mortal crisis in the Soviet system and predicted that it would end up on "the ash heap of history." Across the political aisle stood Thomas (Tip) O'Neill, the hearty Irish-American Speaker of the House, who personified the generosity and tolerance of old-school liberalism. Everywhere I went, the atmosphere was warm and welcoming. It was a feeling I had never had before, a country wide open to the world, to the future, and to anyone who loved it. To a young visitor, it seemed to offer unlimited generosity and promise.

For America to thrive in this new and challenging era, for it to succeed amid the rise of the rest, it need fulfill only one test. It should be a place that is as inviting and exciting to the young student who enters the country today as it was for this awkward eighteen-year-old a generation ago.

Notes

2. The Cup Runneth Over

1. Ted Robert Gurr and Monty G. Marshall, *Peace and Conflict 2005: A Global Survey of Armed Conflicts, Self-Determination Movements, and Democracy*, Center for International Development and Conflict Management, University of Maryland, College Park (June 2005).

2. Steven Pinker, "A Brief History of Violence" (talk at Technology, Entertainment, Design Conference, Monterey, Calif., March 2007).

3. Kevin H. O'Rourke, "The European Grain Invasion, 1870–1913," *Journal of Economic History* 57, no. 4 (Dec. 1997): 775–801.

4. For a good, accessible discussion of the late nineteenth-century "positive supply shock," see Gary Saxonhouse, "The Integration of Giants into the Global Economy," *AEI: Asian outlook*, no. 1 (Jan. 31, 2006).

5. See a survey from the *Economist* on "The New Titans" in the Sept. 14, 2006, issue.

6. Michael Specter, "The Last Drop," *New Yorker*, Oct. 23, 2006.

7. Larry O'Hanlon, "Arctic Ice Melt Gets Stark Reassessment," *Discovery News*, Sept. 6, 2007, available at http://dsc.discovery.com/news/2007/09/06/arcticice_pla.html?category=earth.

8. Zbigniew Brzezinski, "The Dilemma of the Last Sovereign," *American Interest* 1, no. 1 (Autumn 2005).

9. Benjamin Schwarz, review of Stephen E. Ambrose, *The Good Fight*, in *Atlantic Monthly*, June 2001, p. 103.

10. Naazneen Barma et al., "The World without the West," *National Interest*, no. 90 (July/Aug. 2007): 23–30.

11. Thomas L. Friedman, *The World Is Flat: A Brief History of the Twenty-first Century* (New York: Farrar, Straus and Giroux, 2006), 226. Andy Grove's statement is quoted in Clyde Prestowitz, *Three Billion New Capitalists: The Great Shift of Wealth and Power to the East* (New York: Basic Books, 2005), 8.

12. Gabor Steingart, *The War for Wealth: Why Globalization Is Bleeding the West of Its Prosperity* (New York: McGraw-Hill, 2008).

3. A Non-Western World?

1. The facts of Zheng He's voyages come from a variety of sources, including Gavin Menzies, *1421: The Year China Discovered America* (New York: Harper Perennial, 2004); David Landes, *The Wealth and Poverty of Nations* (New York: W. W. Norton, 1999); and Kuei-Sheng Chang, "The Maritime Scene in China at the Dawn of Great European Discoveries," *Journal of the American Oriental Society* 94, no. 3 (July–Sept., 1974): 347–59.

2. Kenneth Pomeranz, *The Great Divergence: China, Europe, and the Making of the Modern World Economy* (Princeton: Princeton University Press, 2000). Pomeranz dissents from the view that China was as backward as I describe. But Angus Maddison, William McNeil, and David Landes are better guides on this general topic, and Philip Huang (see below) effectively rebuts Pomeranz in great detail.

3. Quoted in Bernard Lewis, "The West and the Middle East," *Foreign Affairs* 76, no. 1 (Jan./Feb. 1997): 114.

4. Daniel J. Boorstin, *The Discoverers* (New York: Vintage Books, 1985), 64. The work of David S. Landes, especially *Revolution in Time: Clocks and the Making of the Modern World* (Cambridge: Harvard University Press, 1983), also uses the development of the clock to contrast the attitudes toward innovation and technological change in Eastern and Western societies.

5. David S. Landes, "Why Europe and the West? Why Not China?" *Journal of Economic Perspectives* 20, no. 2 (Spring 2006): 18.

6. Philip C. C. Huang, "Development or Involution in Eighteenth-Century Britain and China: A Review of Kenneth Pomeranz's *The Great Divergence: China, Europe, and*

the Making of the Modern World Economy," Journal of Asian Studies 61, no. 2 (May 2002): 501–38.

7. Landes, "Why Europe and the West?," 18.

8. Paul Kennedy, *The Rise and Fall of the Great Powers: Economic Change and Military Conflict from 1500 to 2000* (New York: Random House, 1987), 13.

9. J. M. Roberts, *History of the World* (Oxford: Oxford University Press, 1993).

10. This line of reasoning will be familiar to any reader of Jared Diamond's *Guns, Germs, and Steel: The Fates of Human Societies* (New York: W. W. Norton, 2005). David Landes, *The Wealth and Poverty of Nations*, and Eric Jones, *The European Miracle: Environments, Economies, and Geopolitics in the History of Europe and Asia*, 3d ed. (Cambridge: Cambridge University Press, 2003), also consider geography a crucial determinant of societal development.

11. Niall Ferguson, *Empire: The Rise and Demise of the British World Order and the Lessons for Global Power* (New York: Basic Books, 2004).

12. Quoted in Braj B. Kachru, *The Indianization of English: The English Language in India* (Oxford: Oxford University Press, 1983), 59–60.

13. Max Boot, *War Made New: Technology, Warfare, and the Course of History, 1500 to Today* (New York: Gotham Books, 2006). In "The West and the Middle East," Bernard Lewis describes how the effects of military modernization rippled across Ottoman society. Building a more intelligent officer corps meant reforming the educational system, and creating a mobile military meant investing heavily in roads and modern infrastructure. Thus the urge to win battles led to cultural and economic change, too.

14. Samuel P. Huntington, "The West: Unique, Not Universal," *Foreign Affairs* 75, no. 6 (Nov./Dec. 1996): 28–46.

15. Kishore Mahbubani, "Will India Emerge as an Eastern or Western Power?" (Center for the Advanced Study of India, Penn Club, New York, Nov. 9, 2006); Indrajit Basu, "Western Wear Rivals the Indian Sari," *Asia Times Online*, May 10, 2007.

16. Fabrizio Gilardi, Jacint Jordana, and David Levi-Faur, "Regulation in the Age of Globalization: The Diffusion of Regulatory Agencies across Europe and Latin America," IBEI Working Paper, 2006:1.

17. Jason Overdorf, "Bigger Than Bollywood," *Newsweek International*, Sept. 10, 2007.

18. Christian Caryl, "Turning Un-Japanese," *Newsweek International*, Feb. 13, 2006.

19. Diana Crane, "Culture and Globalization: Theoretical Models and Emerging Trends," in *Global Culture: Media, Arts, Policy, and Globalization*, ed. Diana Crane, Nobuko Kawashima, and Kenichi Kawasaki (London: Routledge, 2002).

4. The Challenger

1. Melinda Liu, "Beijing Reborn," *Newsweek International*, Aug. 13, 2007.

2. Jun Ma and John Norregaard, *China's Fiscal Decentralization* (International Monetary Fund, Oct. 1998).

3. Minxin Pei, *China's Trapped Transition: The Limits of Developmental Autocracy* (Cambridge: Harvard University Press, 2006).

4. Ibid.

5. Pan Yue, deputy head of China's State Environmental Protection Agency, quoted in Jamil Aderlini and Mure Dickie, "Taking the Waters," *Financial Times*, July 24, 2007.

6. Joseph Kahn and Jim Yardley, "As China Roars, Pollution Reaches Deadly Extremes," *New York Times*, Aug. 26, 2007.

7. John Thornton, "Long Time Coming: The Prospects for Democracy in China," *Foreign Affairs* 87, no. 1 (Jan./Feb. 2008): 2–22.

8. I am grateful to Mr. Lee Kuan Yew for telling me about this series and then arranging for it to be sent to me. One of Singapore's television stations aired the entire series with English subtitles, so I was able to watch the whole show.

9. Joseph Needham, *Within the Four Seas: The Dialogue of East and West* (London: Allen & Unwin, 1969), 63.

10. Ibid., 90.

11. Thomas Fuchs, "The European China: Receptions from Leibniz to Kant," *Journal of Chinese Philosophy* 33, no. 1 (2006): 43.

12. Email to the author.

13. Robert Gilpin, *War and Change in World Politics* (Cambridge: Cambridge University Press, 1981), 94–95.

14. Ernest Harsch, "Big Leap in China-Africa Ties," *Africa Renewal* 20, no. 4 (Jan. 2007): 3.

15. Carlos H. Conde, "Asean and China Sign Trade and Services Accord," *International Herald Tribune*, Jan. 14, 2007.

16. "Out of Their Silos; China and America," *Economist*, June 10, 2006.

17. Joshua Cooper Ramo, "The Beijing Consensus" (Foreign Policy Centre, London, 2004).

5. The Ally

1. Dominic Wilson and Roopa Purushothaman, *Dreaming with BRICs: The Path to 2050* (Goldman Sachs, Global Economics Paper no. 99, Oct. 1, 2003).

2. "GM to triple parts sourcing from India," *Times of India*, Nov. 20, 2007.

3. Jahangir Aziz and Steven Dunaway, "China's Rebalancing Act," *Finance & Development* 44, no. 3 (Sept. 2007).

4. Yasheng Huang, "Will India Overtake China?" *Foreign Policy*, July/Aug. 2003, pp. 71–81.

5. Manjeet Kripalani, "Read All About It: India's Media Wars," *BusinessWeek*, May 16, 2005.

6. From the World Health Organization, available at http://www.who.int/countries/ind/en/.

7. See, e.g., his article, "India and the Balance of Power," *Foreign Affairs* 85, no. 4 (July/Aug. 2006): 17–32.

8. Chaudhuri explains these ideas further in his *Hinduism: A Religion to Live By* (Oxford: Oxford University Press, 1979).

9. Mohamed ElBaradei, "Rethinking Nuclear Safeguards," *Washington Post*, June 14, 2006.

10. Robert D. Blackwill, "Journalist Roundtable on India" (transcript), hosted by David B. Ensor, Feb. 23, 2006.

6. American Power

1. James Morris, *Pax Britannica: Climax of an Empire* (New York: Harcourt Brace, 1980).

2. Quoted in Karl Meyer, "An Edwardian Warning: The Unraveling of a Colossus," *World Policy Journal* 17, no. 4 (Winter 2000/2001): 47–57.

3. Niall Ferguson, *Empire: The Rise and Demise of the British World Order and the Lessons for Global Power* (New York: Basic Books, 2002), 268.

4. Lawrence James, *The Rise and Fall of the British Empire* (New York: St. Martin's Press, 1996), 212.

5. Paul Kennedy, "Why Did the British Empire Last So Long?" in *Strategy and Diplomacy, 1870–1945: Eight Studies* (London: Allen & Unwin, 1984), 197–218.

6. The facts on Britain's economic situation come largely from Paul Kennedy, *The Rise and Fall of Great Powers* (New York: Random House, 1987), 151–200. Maddison and Barnett (see below) are also useful sources.

7. This theory on the British decline is fleshed out in Correlli Barnett, *The Collapse of British Power* (Gloucestershire: Sutton Publishing, 1997).

8. Niall Ferguson, *The Pity of War* (New York: Penguin Books, 1998).

9. Kennedy, *Rise and Fall of Great Powers*, 317.

10. James, *Rise and Fall of the British Empire*, 464.

11. Dominic Wilson and Roopa Purushothaman, *Dreaming with BRICs: The Path to 2050* (Goldman Sachs, Global Economics Paper no. 99, Oct. 1, 2003). Although this widely cited study is the best source for projections of this kind, it is worth noting that since its publication, the BRICs have been growing at a faster rate than the Goldman economists assumed.

12. Michael W. Holman, *Profiting from International Nanotechnology* (Lux Research, Dec. 2006).

13. James Fallows, "China Makes, the World Takes," *Atlantic Monthly*, July/Aug. 2007.

14. Greg Linden, Kenneth Kraemer, and Jason Dedrick, *Who Captures Value in a Global Innovation System? The Case of Apple's iPod* (Personal Computing Industry Center, June 2007).

15. The Immelt quotation originally appeared in an interview with the *Globalist* magazine, "A CEO's Responsibilities in the Age of Globalization," March 17, 2006.

16. Bialik wrote two columns on the topic in the *Wall Street Journal*: "Outsourcing Fears Help Inflate Some Numbers," Aug. 26, 2005, and "Sounding the Alarm with a Fuzzy Stat," Oct. 27, 2005. The Duke study, called "Framing the Engineering Outsourcing Debate: Placing the United States on a Level Playing Field with China and India," was led by Dr. Gary Gereffi and Vivek Wadhwa.

17. *The Emerging Global Labor Market: Part II—The Supply of Offshore Talent in Services* (McKinsey Global Institute, June 2005).

18. Alan S. Brown and Linda LaVine Brown, "What Are Science & Math Test Scores Really Telling U.S.?" *Bent of Tau Beta Pi*, Winter 2007, pp. 13–17.

19. Michael Alison Chandler, "Asian Educators Looking to Loudoun for an Edge," *Washington Post*, March 19, 2007.

20. Eberstadt's recent articles provide good background on the demographic trends in various regions and their impact on their respective economies: "Born in the USA," *American Interest*, May/June 2007; "Critical Cross-Cutting Issues Facing Northeast Asia: Regional Demographic Trends and Prospects," *Asia Policy* (Jan. 2007); and "Healthy Old Europe," *Foreign Affairs* 86, no. 3 (May/June 2007): 55–68.

21. Richard N. Cooper, "Living with Global Imbalances: A Contrarian View," *Policy Briefs in International Economics* (Institute for International Economics, Nov. 2005).

22. *Sustaining New York's and the U.S.'s Global Financial Services Leadership*, available at www.senate.gov/~schumer/SchumerWebsite/pressroom/special_reports/2007/NY_REPORT%20_FINAL.pdf.

7. American Purpose

1. Speech to the G8 Economic Summit, Houston, Tex., July 11, 1990.

2. Charles Krauthammer, "The Unipolar Moment," *Foreign Affairs* 70, no. 1 (1990/1991): 23–33.

3. Speech to the Association France-Amériques, Paris, France, Feb. 1, 1999.

4. Chris Patten, *Not Quite the Diplomat: Home Truths about World Affairs* (London: Allen Lane, 2005), 229.

5. As recounted by Sarkozy's national security adviser, Jean-David Levitte, in Adam Gopnik, "The Human Bomb," *New Yorker*, Aug. 27, 2007.

6. Robert Kagan, *Of Paradise and Power: America and Europe in the New World Order* (New York: Alfred Knopf, 2003).

7. John Ikenberry, "The Rise of China and the Future of the West," *Foreign Affairs* 87, no. 1 (Jan./Feb. 2008).

8. William C. Wohlforth, "The Stability of a Unipolar World," *International Security* 21, no. 1 (Summer 1999), 5–41.

9. Claudia Deutsch, "The Venturesome Giant," *New York Times*, Oct. 5, 2007.

10. Fernando Henrique Cardoso, "A Collaborative Contract," *Newsweek*: Issues 2008, Special Edition, Dec. 2007.

11. Correlli Barnett, *The Collapse of British Power*, first published in 1972.

12. Josef Joffe, "How America Does It," *Foreign Affairs* 76, no. 5 (Sept./Oct. 1997): 13–27.

13. Anne-Marie Slaughter, "The Real New World Order," *Foreign Affairs* 76, no. 5 (Sept./Oct. 1997): 183–97.

14. Richard N. Haass, "Paradigm Lost," *Foreign Affairs* 74, no. 1 (Jan./Feb. 1995): 43–58.

15. Stephen Flynn, *The Edge of Disaster: Rebuilding a Resilient Nation* (New York: Random House, 2007).

Acknowledgments

This book is the outgrowth of much travel, reading, and reflection over the last few years, but it is also the product of passion. I came to America as a young man, fell in love with the country, and built a life and family here. I want the best for this country and firmly believe that American power and purpose, properly harnessed, benefit both America and the world.

This book has also been a first for me, the first time I've tried to write a book with two children actively demanding my attention. I have professional obligations that are often quite demanding but the hardest part of working on this project—by far—was retreating into my study when my kids wanted to spend time with me. I hope I struck a decent balance between family, work, and the book.

Writing a book while juggling various other commitments takes work—also help, patience, and indulgence from others.

Above all, I want to thank all the smart and generous people at *Newsweek* with whom I work, particularly Rick Smith, Mark Whitaker (now at NBC News), Jon Meacham, Nisid Hajari, and Tony Emerson. Before I came to *Newsweek*, I had always heard that Donald Graham was an extraordinary boss and I'm happy to report from personal experience that it's true. Three years ago, I launched a television show on PBS, *Foreign Exchange*, which I hosted until November 2007. Thanks to Bruce Blair, Mark Sugg, and especially Sujata Thomas for being wonderful colleagues in that venture.

Sharon Sullivan and Patricia Huie have managed the acrobatics of my life with great skill and dedication and made day-to-day work a very pleasant experience, for which I am very grateful.

I had help on the research for this book from four extremely talented young people, all now on to greater things: Robert Wiesenberger, Rukhmini Punoose, Alan Isenberg, and Barrett Sheridan. Barrett worked on the book for the longest period and during its most intense phase and the final product owes a great deal to his hard work, sharp intelligence, and good judgment.

I asked a few friends—Andrew Moravscik, Gideon Rose, Zachary Karabell, and Allison Stanger—to read parts of the manuscript and am greatly indebted to them for their extremely useful comments. Daniel Kurtz-Phelan read the whole thing and smoothened out the prose.

Tina Bennett, my agent, was so enthusiastic about this project at every stage that I didn't quite believe her, and yet it kept me going. Drake McFeely, my editor, is a class act. His comments were well-chosen and apposite. Drake's assistant, Kyle

Frisina, had to turn a manuscript into a book a good bit faster than is the norm and did it without ever complaining. Cullen Stanley has been wonderful at handling the book's foreign rights. When people talk about the old days when agents and publishers were deeply interested in quality and substance, I feel they have not been lucky enough to know the people at Janklow and Nesbit and W. W. Norton.

I have dedicated this book to my brother Arshad, who came to America a year before I did. I suppose if he hadn't enjoyed his first year in the States, I wouldn't be here. Since then we have been friends and companions, through ups and downs. He and I have discussed many of the ideas in this book and I've gained much from his insights. I've benefited from a lifetime of wisdom, encouragement, support, and love from my mother, Fatma Zakaria. My father, Rafiq Zakaria, died three years ago. I wish I had had the chance to talk over the themes of this book with him.

At some point last fall, I gave my wife, Paula, a draft of some chapters and asked for her comments. She read some of it, made comments, and then said to me, "I think my best contribution to this book can be to keep the family life running and the kids out of your hair." In fact she has always been an excellent editor—because she is herself a gifted writer—but in the circumstances she was right. Without her help, I would not have had the peace of mind and mental stamina to write this book. I thank her for her love and friendship.

My daughter, Lila, who turned five as the book was going to the press, informed me that she was delighted that I was done with it because now she could now use my computer to get onto YouTube and listen to songs from *High School Musical*.

My son, Omar, who is eight, was more concerned about the project itself. When I explained to him for the first time what the book was about, he said in a somewhat distressed tone, "Why do you want to write a book about the future? If you're wrong, people won't buy the book anymore." Here's hoping that I don't embarrass him.

Index

Abrahamic religions, 109, 155, 156
Abu Sayyaf, 11
Abyssinia, 178
Academy of Science, 194
Acheson, Dean, 231
Acquaviva, Claudio, 111
affirmative action, 96
Afghanistan, 13, 14, 88, 156, 168–69,
        182, 217, 223, 235, 252, 254,
        258
Afghan War, 13, 156, 217, 223, 235,
        252, 254
Africa:
    agriculture in, 57
    Chinese influence in, 116–19, 246
    Christian population of, 85
    colonization of, 52, 66, 67, 116, 140
    corruption in, 117–19
    debt relief in, 247
    economies of, 20n, 38, 55, 116, 117,
        218
    geography of, 64
    instability of, 12–13, 18, 26–27, 38,
        52, 55
    national debts of, 117
    natural resources of, 116–19

    North, 12–13, 18, 67
    slaves from, 66
    sub-Saharan, 67
    U.S. influence in, 245–46, 248–49
    see also specific countries
AFRICOM, 245–46
Aggarwal, Anil, 139
aging populations, 197–98
agriculture, 19, 28, 30, 52–54, 57,
        58–59, 87, 93–94, 99, 123, 135,
        144
Agtmael, Antoine van, 2
Ahmadinejad, Mahmoud, 15
AIDS, 133, 146
air conditioners, 89
air pollution, 98
airport security, 256
Akbar, 62
Albright, Madeleine, 222
Alembert, Jean Le Rond d', 110
alerts, terrorist, 232
algebra, 54
Algeria, 12–13
algorithm, 54
Al-Jabr wa-al-Muqabilah, 54
Al Jazeera, 83

al-Khwarizmi, 54
Al Qaeda, 4, 10–17, 156, 224n, 245,
        252–53, 254
Ambrose, Stephen, 34
American Enterprise Institute, 196
Amery, Leo, 176
Amsterdam, 54
Anglo-Chinese Wars, 68–69
Angola, 258
Annan, Kofi, 247–48
anti-Americanism, 13, 32, 36–37,
        39–40, 47–48, 150, 217, 221,
        226–30, 249–50, 257
Apple, Inc., 186
Arab culture, 54, 62, 63, 65, 67, 85
Arab-Israeli conflict, 6–7, 83, 222
arbitrage, 24–25
architecture, 82, 85, 90, 92, 136
Argentina, 2, 24, 102
Armenia, 192
Arnold, Thomas, 170
Arroyo, Gloria, 120
art, modern, 82
Asia:
    agriculture in, 57
    Chinese influence in, 119–23, 127,
        156–57, 160–61, 234, 243
    colonization of, 66, 67–69, 140
    demographics of, 197–98
    East, 22, 27, 30, 40, 42, 51n, 52,
        109, 120, 197, 217–18, 221
    economies of, 42, 62, 135–36, 204
    education in, 191–95
    financial markets of, 204–5
    geography of, 63–64
    global influence of, 221, 233
    India's influence in, 135–36, 140,
        156–57, 165
    manufacturing sector of, 185–86
    South, 19, 20n, 42, 47–48
    technology sector of, 183–91
    U.S. influence in, 77, 217–18, 221,
        234–35, 242, 243, 248–49
    Western influence in, 77, 80, 86
    see also specific countries
assets, 27, 202
Association of Southeast Asian Nations
        (ASEAN), 119, 120
Atatürk, Kemal, 71

Australia, 65, 119, 127, 179, 227, 242
Austria, 206
automobile industry, 31, 97–98, 133,
        175, 188, 208–9, 219–20

Bacon, Francis, 73
Baker, James A., III, 36, 220
balance of power, 66–67
Bali bombings (2002), 11, 16
Balkans, 18, 26, 104–5, 221, 222, 223
Bangalore, 40
Bangladesh, 48, 143
banking industry, 40, 68, 93, 94, 96, 97,
        114, 136–37, 141
Barma, Naazneen, 36
Barnett, Correlli, 237
"Base Structure Report" (2006), 237–38
Bay of Pigs invasion (1961), 19
BBC, 83, 107
Beijing, 58, 90, 92, 98, 124, 134, 194
"Beijing Consensus, The" (Ramo),
        126–27
Beijing Olympic Games (2008), 90, 92,
        124
Belgium, 38
Berlin, 90
Berlin Wall, 22
Beveridge Plan, 180
Bharatiya Janata Party (BJP), 142–43,
        144, 162, 163, 164
Bhutan, 149
Bialik, Carl, 188
Bible, 155
bicycles, 175
bin Laden, Osama, 12, 13, 72, 245
biological weapons, 16
biotechnology, 185, 198, 202, 204
bipolar order, 4
Bismarck, Otto von, 181, 233, 241–42
Blackwill, Robert, 160–61
Blair, Tony, 249
Bloomberg, Michael, 203–4
"blue card," 207
blue jeans, 75, 77, 78
Boer War, 171–73, 237
Bollywood, 77–78, 81, 131, 137–39
bonds, 27
Bono, 247
Boorstin, Daniel, 56

Bosnia, 247

Brahmans, 61

"brain drain," 150–51

brand names, 186

Brazil, 2, 3, 18, 22, 24, 26, 37, 44, 48,
    66, 82, 85, 232, 234, 238

Bretton Woods Conference (1944), 229

British East India Company, 47–48, 67,
    69–70

British Empire, 33, 35, 45, 47–48, 52,
    66, 67–70, 71, 76, 81, 84–85,
    135, 138, 140, 143, 145, 146–47,
    148, 154, 157, 163, 167–82,
    213–14, 236–38, 241, 243

British Guiana, 177n

broadband service, 25, 207–8

Brookings, Robert, 213

Brookings Institution, 213

Brzezinski, Zbigniew, 33–34

Buck, Pearl, 87

Buddhism, 111, 154–55, 156

budget deficits, 202, 217–18, 220

Bulgaria, 165

Burma, 24, 66, 108, 206, 239, 248

Burns, Ken, 34

Buruma, Ian, 170

Bush, George H. W., 35, 220, 248

Bush, George W., 37, 39–40, 46–47,
    125, 159, 222–26, 235, 236, 239,
    245–46, 248–50, 251, 253, 254

Calcutta, 69–70

Cambodia, 9

Canada, 29, 208–9

Canary Wharf, 90

cannons, 56, 60

Cantor, Mickey, 222

capital, 19–20, 23, 27, 29–30, 52–54,
    57n, 62, 63, 80–81, 135–36, 183,
    184–85, 198–99, 201, 202–10

capitalism, 19–22, 23, 25, 27, 29–30,
    48, 61, 80–81, 86, 92–94,
    100–102, 107, 136–37, 141, 150,
    170, 175–76, 183–85, 202–10

Capra, Frank, 72

Cardoso, Fernando Henrique, 234

Caribbean, 66

Caryl, Christian, 78–79

casinos, gambling, 3, 85

Castañeda, Jorge, 228

caste system, 61, 163, 164

Cathedral and John Connon School,
    193

Catholic Church, 111

cell phones, 21, 25, 74, 91, 207

cement, 91

Center for International Development
    and Conflict Management, 8–9

Central America, 258

Central Asia, 42

central banks, 40, 114

Central Intelligence Agency (CIA), 150

central planning, 93–104, 133–34, 136

Centre for European Reform, 190–91

Chamberlain, Joseph, 177n

Chaudhuri, Nirad, 155

Chávez, Hugo, 6, 18

Chechnya, 12

chemicals industry, 175

Cheney, Dick, 47, 222–23, 249–50

Chen Shuibian, 122

Chia, Rosalind, 194–95

Chicago, 90

"Chicago Boys," 22–23

Chile, 2, 18, 22–23, 228

China, 87–128
    African policy of, 116–19, 246
    agriculture in, 52–54, 58–59, 87,
        93–94, 99, 123
    Asian policy of, 119–23, 127,
        156–57, 160–61, 243
    as "asymmetrical superpower,"
        126–28
    automobiles in, 31, 97–98
    banking system of, 93, 94, 96, 97,
        114, 137
    British influence in, 68–69
    capitalism in, 92–94, 137
    Central Bank of, 114
    central planning in, 93–104, 133–34,
        136
    coal power in, 31
    Communist regime of, 88, 89,
        93–104, 106–7, 113–16, 120–22,
        124, 126–28, 133–34, 151
    Confucianism in, 60–61, 84, 85,
        109–14, 153
    corruption in, 97, 101

China (*continued*)
    Cultural Revolution in, 104, 116
    culture of, 78, 80, 82, 86, 108–14
    currency of, 114
    democratic reform in, 97, 99–104,
        121, 122, 250
    as developing country, 89, 93, 95,
        98, 105–6, 137
    domestic market of, 91–92, 98, 105,
        117, 123, 128, 218
    economic reforms in, 88–97, 102,
        103–4, 105, 113–14, 143
    economy of, 2, 20–21, 27, 35–36, 38,
        41, 52–54, 74, 87–97, 103–6,
        113–14, 124, 128, 136, 137, 141,
        143, 165, 218
    education in, 95–96, 121, 187–91,
        194
    as emerging market, 26, 43, 105, 234
    energy needs of, 28, 31, 35, 115, 118
    engineers trained in, 187–91
    environmental problems of, 98
    fertility rate of, 132, 197
    foreign aid by, 116–19, 120
    foreign exchange reserves of, 26, 92
    foreign investment in, 91, 95,
        185–86
    foreign policy of, 105–23, 124
    foreign trade of, 56, 65, 68–69, 89,
        91–92, 116–19, 120
    free-market approach in, 93–95,
        102
    geography of, 63–64
    global influence of, 32, 43, 87–88,
        104–28, 156–57, 176, 232, 233,
        234, 235, 241, 242, 244
    Great Leap Forward in, 104, 116
    Great Wall of, 63–64
    gross domestic product (GDP) of,
        20, 53, 91–92, 97, 98, 105–6,
        129, 132, 136, 141, 181
    growth rate for, 89–93, 97–99, 105,
        113–14, 136, 141, 165, 218
    "harmonious society" plan for, 98
    human rights in, 84, 108–14, 250
    Imperial, 49–61, 63–64, 65, 71, 73,
        109–12
    income levels in, 100–101
    incremental approach of, 105–8

    India compared with, 51, 95, 97, 98,
        100, 130, 131–34, 136, 141, 143,
        151, 152, 153, 159–61, 165, 233
    Indian relations of, 120, 127,
        148–49, 152, 156–57, 233
    industrialization of, 3, 93–94, 97
    infrastructure of, 133–34, 136
    Japan compared with, 91–92
    Japan's relations with, 88, 107,
        121–22, 127
    Korean relations of, 17
    legal system of, 101
    living conditions in, 53–54
    manufacturing sector of, 20–21, 89,
        91–92, 185–86
    middle class in, 102
    military forces of, 73, 92, 104, 121,
        123, 124–27, 158, 159–61, 235,
        252
    military spending of, 92, 126
    modernization of, 89, 96–97, 101–2,
        113–14
    nationalism in, 32, 88, 121–22, 127
    natural resources needed by, 116–19
    naval forces of, 49–51, 57, 58,
        59–60, 64, 126
    nuclear weapons of, 124, 126, 158,
        159–61, 235
    oil needs of, 28, 35, 115, 118
    one-child policy of, 132, 197n
    "peaceful rise" policy of, 106–7,
        114–23
    peasants of, 52–53, 87, 93–94, 99
    population of, 21, 52–53, 87, 97–98,
        99, 128, 129, 132, 197
    poverty in, 3, 20n, 52–53, 87, 89,
        93–94, 98, 100–101, 104, 108,
        130
    privatization in, 94, 97, 134–35, 136,
        137, 205
    productivity in, 58–59
    protests in, 97, 100, 121, 122
    road safety in, 97–98
    savings rate of, 91–92
    shopping malls in, 3
    social change in, 97, 99–104
    Soviet relations of, 120, 124, 126
    Taiwan policy of, 105, 106, 119,
        122–23, 124, 125, 126, 239

taxation in, 51, 95
technology sector of, 54–55, 56,
    59–60, 88, 105, 108, 184–85,
    187–91
television in, 106–7
as UN member, 105, 118, 148n, 230
urbanization of, 89–90, 93–94, 97,
    134
U.S. compared with, 87, 90, 95, 176,
    218, 239
U.S. relations with, 87, 91, 92–93,
    95, 105, 123–28, 160–61, 173,
    213, 230, 235, 238, 239, 241,
    242, 244
wealth of, 52–54
Western influence in, 68–69, 71, 82,
    86, 113–14
Chinese opera, 78
Chomsky, Noam, 72
Chongqing, 90
"Christian Confucians," 114
Christianity, 63, 68, 74, 75, 84–85, 109,
    111, 112, 114, 155, 156, 237
Christmas, 75
Churchill, Winston S., 152, 164, 179,
    229–30
Civil Rights Act (1964), 257
Civil War, U.S., 177
Clark, Gregory, 54
climate change, 30–31, 37, 72
Clinton, Bill, 221–22, 223, 225–26,
    247–48, 257
clocks, 56, 58, 111n
clothing, 75–77
CNN, 83
coal, 31, 52, 91
Cold War, 4, 8–9, 19, 35–36, 125, 127,
    128, 147–50, 179, 182, 220–21,
    223, 227, 229–30, 231, 247, 250,
    253, 258–59
collectivization, 104
colonialism, 33, 35, 45, 47–48, 52,
    65–70, 116, 140, 146, 178
Columbus, Christopher, 49, 67
commodity prices, 28
communism, 10, 12, 22, 23, 35–36, 88,
    89, 93–104, 106–7, 113–16,
    120–22, 124, 126–28, 133–34,
    141, 142, 151, 227

Compagne des Indes, 67–68
competition, 195–96, 208–10, 219–26
computers, 20–25, 79–80, 83, 100, 122,
    126, 191, 198, 207–8
computer science, 191, 198
Confucianism, 60–61, 84, 85, 109–14,
    153
Congo, 19, 67
Congressional Record, 187
Congress Party (India), 140, 162, 163
Conrad, Joseph, 72
conservatives, 61–62, 125–26, 223,
    228–29
construction industry, 27, 28, 91
consumer demand, 19, 135–36, 201–2
contracts, 112–13, 134
Convention on the Rights of the Child,
    206
Cooper, Richard, 200, 201
Copernicus, Nicolaus, 55
corporations:
    foreign investment by, 67–68,
        185–86
    multinational, 2, 45–48, 134, 234
    regulation of, 204, 206–7
    savings of, 200–201
    taxation of, 206
    see also specific corporations
corruption, 97, 101, 117–19, 141,
    146–47
Cortés, Hernán, 67
Coubertin, Pierre de, Baron, 170
Council on Foreign Relations, 213, 255
Counter-Reformation, 170
Courage Matters (McCain), 252
credit, 27, 136–37
credit cards, 136, 200
cricket, 138
crop yields, 30
Cultural Revolution, 104, 116
currency rates, 20, 23, 24, 26, 40, 92,
    183, 205, 217–18, 242–43
current-account deficits, 199, 200
czars, Russian, 60, 70–71, 174
Czechoslovakia, 168, 227

Dalai Lama, 125
Darfur crisis, 29, 39, 118, 248
Das, Gurcharan, 135

debt, national, 26, 124, 200–202,
        217–18, 247
Defense Department, U.S., 237–38
deflation, 27
Dell, Michael, 131
Deming Prizes, 137
democracy, 38, 43, 45, 47, 78, 95, 96,
        97, 99–104, 107, 121, 122, 125,
        129–30, 134, 136, 138, 140–46,
        150, 153, 156, 157, 160, 162–66,
        210–14, 218, 239, 249–59
Democratic Party, 47, 213, 231,
        254–55, 257
Deng Xiaoping, 89, 104, 105, 116,
        120–21
Denmark, 183
Depression, Great, 24
derivatives market, 205
Deshmukh, Vilasrao, 134
developing countries, 22–23, 26, 28,
        33–34, 43, 78, 84, 89, 93, 95, 98,
        105–6, 135–37, 141–46, 152–53,
        159, 161, 165–66, 192, 207
    see also specific countries
Diamond Jubilee (1897), 167–68, 169,
        171, 174
dictatorship, 63, 99–104, 250
Diderot, Denis, 110
Diplomacy (Kissinger), 221
disease, 57, 133
Dobbs, Lou, 256
dollar, value of, 23, 24, 40, 183, 217,
        242–43
Dominican Republic, 141
"Dream Team," 131
drug cartels, 4, 244–45
Dubai, 2, 8, 15, 29
Dutch East India Company, 67–68

East Asia, 22, 27, 30, 40, 42, 51n, 52,
        109, 120, 197, 217–18, 221
East Asian crisis (1997), 120, 217, 221
East Asian Summit, 120
East Germany, 22, 220
East Indies, 66
East Timor, 221
Eberstadt, Nicholas, 196, 197n
education, 46, 69–70, 95–96, 121, 139,
        142, 144, 145, 170, 184–95, 198,

        201–2, 208, 211
efficiency, 24–25, 30, 136, 195–96, 257
Egypt, 8, 11, 12, 22, 72
Eisenhower, Dwight D., 182, 230
ElBaradei, Mohamed, 158–59
elections, U.S.:
    of 1984, 227
    of 1992, 220–21
    of 2008, 251–55
electricity, 31
Emory-Georgia Tech Nanotechnology
        Center for Personalized and Pre-
        dictive Oncology, 184
energy resources, 27–31, 35, 115, 118,
        159, 210, 211
Engels, Friedrich, 72
engineers, 187–91
English language, 68, 72, 79–80, 86,
        135, 150, 152, 157, 170, 207
Enlightenment, 109–12
Enron Corp., 204
entitlements, government, 199, 202,
        217
entrance exams, 188–89, 193–95
entrepreneurship, 95, 176, 182
environmental issues, 30–31, 37, 72, 98
EP-3 plane incident (2001), 122
equities, 27, 185
Erickson, John, 35
Essai sur les moeurs (Voltaire), 110
Essay on the Principle of Population, An
        (Malthus), 57
Ethiopia, 117
"Eurabia," 14
Europe:
    agriculture in, 57
    balance of power in, 4, 233, 241–42
    colonialism of, 33, 35, 45, 47–48, 52,
        65–70, 116, 140, 146, 178
    cultural influence of, 1–5, 14, 36,
        38–39, 49–86, 113–14
    Eastern, 205, 235–36
    economies of, 30, 195–96, 204, 205,
        210, 221
    education in, 184–85, 190–91, 193
    fertility rate of, 196, 198
    foreign investment by, 67–68, 195
    foreign trade of, 65–66, 195
    geography of, 63, 64

global influence of, 42, 44, 210, 221, 228–29
health care in, 195–96
immigration to, 14, 207, 255
industrialization of, 74, 91, 237
military forces of, 13, 156, 221, 223, 226–27, 243
Muslim communities of, 14, 255
parliamentary system of, 212
Pershing missiles in, 226–27
population of, 53, 67
postwar, 19, 34–36, 40, 41
poverty in, 67
privatization in, 205
productivity of, 183, 195
religious attitudes in, 109–11
Roman rule of, 64–65
technology sector of, 55–57, 110, 183–85, 190–91
unemployment rate of, 195
U.S. relations with, 220–21, 226–30, 248–49
see also specific countries
European Union, 4, 43, 80, 92, 98, 118, 123, 125, 207, 216
euros, 242–43
"Eurozone," 195–96, 204

Fallows, James, 186
Falun Gong, 100
family values, 79, 80
famine, 54, 57
fascism, 34, 178, 231, 251
fashion, 75–77
fatwas, 14
fengshui, 113
Ferguson, Niall, 68, 173
Ferris wheel, 3
fertility rates, 132, 196, 197–98
feudalism, 86, 176
Figaro, 171
film industry, 77–78, 81, 131, 137–39
financial markets, 7, 15–16, 27, 59–60, 97, 200, 202–10
Finland, 183
"five keys," 177–78
"flat world" concept, 25
Flynn, Stephen, 255
follow-on equity offerings, 185

food prices, 19, 28, 30, 54, 57
Forbidden City, 58, 90
Ford Motor Co., 91
Foreign Affairs, 101, 213
foreign aid, 116–19, 120, 121–22, 139
foreign exchange, 26, 92, 205, 217–18
foreign investment, 67–68, 91, 95, 137, 185–86, 195, 202
foreign trade, 19, 23, 40, 45–46, 56, 65–69, 89, 91–92, 116–19, 120, 183, 195, 199, 200, 257
Fortune, 187
Foster, Norman, 136
France:
    colonies of, 66, 67–68
    culture of, 78, 82
    democracy in, 103–4
    economy of, 23, 40, 103–4, 136, 174, 175
    foreign policy of, 112, 117
    global influence of, 104, 216
    infrastructure of, 136
    labor force of, 209
    Muslim population of, 254
    nuclear weapons of, 158
    technology sector of, 184–85
    U.S. relations with, 227, 228
Frederick II, King of Prussia, 110–11
French Revolution, 103, 110
Friedman, Thomas, 25, 40, 187
Fuchs, Thomas, 110
Fukuzawa, Yukichi, 71, 73
"Future of European Universities, The," 190

G-7 countries, 26
G-8 countries, 38
Galileo Galilei, 55
Gama, Vasco da, 49
Gandhi, Indira, 149, 151, 152–53, 164, 249
Gandhi, Mohandas K., 76, 131, 147, 157
Gandhi, Rajiv, 142
Gandhi, Sonia, 143
Gates, Bill, 96, 139, 187
General Electric, 87, 91, 234
General Motors, 91, 133, 208, 219–20
Genesis, Book of, 155

geography, 63–64
George III, King of England, 56
Georgia, 235
German Democratic Republic (East
      Germany), 22, 220
Germany:
      economy of, 18–19, 24, 35, 38, 40,
            105, 175
      global influence of, 10, 35–36, 43,
            104, 105, 108, 159, 232, 233,
            237, 241–42
      gross domestic product (GDP) of,
            46, 174
      Imperial, 169n, 175, 178, 233, 237,
            241–42
      industrialization of, 18–19, 176
      labor force of, 209
      military spending of, 217
      navy of, 169n, 178
      Nazi, 10, 24, 34–36, 127, 241, 251
      reunification of, 220–21
      taxation in, 206
      technology sector of, 184
      U.S. relations with, 220–21, 227
Gibraltar, 178
Gibraltar Strait, 215–19
Gilpin, Robert, 114
Giuliani, Rudy, 251–52
Glimpses of World History (Nehru), 147
globalization, 6–48
      agriculture and, 19, 28, 30, 52–54,
            57, 58–59, 87, 93–94, 99, 123,
            135, 144
      capital markets in, 19–20, 23, 27,
            183, 202–10
      competition in, 195–96, 208–10,
            219–26
      cultural impact of, 1–5, 14, 36,
            38–39, 49–86, 113–14
      demographics of, 195–99
      economic conditions of, 6–48,
            80–81, 84, 180–82, 200, 217–19,
            230
      energy resources and, 27–31
      environmental impact of, 30–31, 37,
            72, 98
      expansion of, 18–21, 26–31
      free markets in, 21–26, 45, 47–48,
            200, 202, 218, 234

future trends of, 1–5, 81–86, 182–86,
      187, 215–59
identity and, 38–39
international organizations and, 4,
      22, 38
labor markets in, 25, 189
language of, 79–80
mass media in, 9, 14–15, 24–25, 82,
      83, 192
military destabilization and, 6–10,
      124–27
modernization and, 14–15, 32–33,
      36, 73–77, 81–82
multinational focus of, 1–5
nationalism and, 31–40
nuclear proliferation in, 158–61
political impact of, 18, 21, 26–27,
      31–40, 42–44, 80–81, 86,
      114–15, 124–28, 216–26
in post-American world, see post-
      American world
poverty rate in, 3, 20, 21
regional powers in, 232–38
technology in, 24–25, 27, 183–85,
      202, 207–8
terrorism and, 10–18, 26, 31, 47,
      240
U.S. as superpower in, 4–5, 40–48,
      104, 107, 126–28, 166, 206–59
global warming, 30–31, 37, 72
God, 109–12, 153
gold, 23, 172, 180
Goldman Sachs, 26, 37, 132, 197
Goldsmith, Oliver, 80
gold standard, 23, 180
Good Earth, The (Buck), 87
Great Britain, 167–82
      agriculture in, 57, 58–59
      capitalism in, 170, 175–76
      culture of, 170, 237
      decline of, 167–82, 199, 213–14,
            236–38, 241, 243
      democracy in, 38, 107
      economy of, 22, 25, 84, 132, 169,
            174–80, 181, 199, 201, 213–14,
            237
      education in, 69–70, 170, 193
      Empire of, 33, 35, 45, 47–48, 52, 66,
            67–70, 71, 76, 81, 84–85, 135,

138, 140, 143, 145, 146–47, 148,
    154, 157, 163, 167–82, 213–14,
    236–38, 241, 243
financial markets of, 205, 206–7
foreign investment in, 137
foreign policy of, 112, 117, 177–80,
    213–14, 236–38, 241
global influence of, 104, 167–82, 241
gross domestic product (GDP) of,
    53, 174, 176, 179, 180
home ownership in, 208
industrialization of, 52, 53, 91, 174,
    175–76, 201, 237
infrastructure of, 136
manufacturing sector of, 25,
    175–76
military forces of, 92n, 158, 168–69,
    175, 178, 181, 217, 252
military spending of, 92n, 217
navy of, 169, 175, 178, 181
nuclear weapons of, 158
political system of, 38, 107, 169,
    177–80, 212
population of, 174
productivity in, 58–59
technology sector of, 184–85
terrorist attacks in, 15–16, 253–54,
    256
U.S. relations with, 151–52, 172,
    177–80, 217, 229–30, 236–37,
    249
in World War II, 33, 34, 178–80
Great Depression, 24
Great Exhibition (1851), 51
Great Leap Forward, 104, 116
Greece, 54, 135, 176
Greenspan, Alan, 22
gross domestic product (GDP), 17, 20,
    44–45, 46, 53, 91–92, 97, 98,
    105–6, 129, 132, 135, 136, 141,
    174, 176, 179, 180–82, 183,
    190–91, 198, 200, 201, 202n,
    225, 231
Grove, Andy, 40
"grow-the-denominator" strategy, 94
Guantánamo Bay, 253
Gujarat earthquake (2001), 139
Gulf War, 220
Gurr, Ted Robert, 8

Haass, Richard, 243
Haiti, 24, 247
Halloween, 79
Hamas, 6, 252
Hapsburg Empire, 104–5
Har Hui Peng, 194
"harmonious society," 98
Haussmann, Georges-Eugène, 90
Head & Shoulders shampoo, 92
health care, 95, 133, 139, 141, 142, 144,
    195–96, 208–9, 211, 213, 257
Heathrow Airport, 136
helium, 28
Henry, Prince of Prussia, 169n
Heritage Foundation, 213
Hezbollah, 6, 7, 244, 252
"hidden hand," 150
Hinduism, 61, 62, 84–85, 130, 152–58,
    163, 164
Hinduism (Monier-Williams), 154
Hira, Ron, 188
Hitler, Adolf, 34, 90
HIV, 133, 146
Hodges, William, 58
Holbrooke, Richard, 222
Hollywood, 77–78, 81
Holman, Michael, 184–85
Homeland Security Department, U.S.,
    252
home ownership, 27, 72, 136, 200,
    208
Hong Kong, 69, 137, 168, 192, 197,
    205
household savings, 200–201
Huang, Philip, 58–59
Huang, Yasheng, 137
Hu Jintao, 98, 105, 106, 116–17,
    120–21
human capital, 135, 201–2
human rights, 75–76, 81, 84, 108–14,
    141–42, 145, 157, 218, 232, 236,
    250
Humphrey, Hubert, 257
Huntington, Samuel P., 43, 74
Hussein, Saddam, 172–73, 223n,
    249
Hwa Chong Institution, 194
hyperinflation, 23–24
"hyperpower," 222

IBM, 91
Ignatius, David, 246
Ikenberry, John, 232
Immelt, Jeffrey, 187, 234
immigration, 14, 48, 74, 150–51,
        195–99, 207, 211, 247, 251, 254,
        257
Imperial China, 49–61, 63–64, 65, 71,
        73, 109–12
Imperial Germany, 169n, 175, 178, 233,
        237, 241–42
imperialism, 39, 234, 236–38
Imperial Japan, 34, 35–36, 71, 121–22,
        178–79
income levels, 21, 27, 54, 100–101, 132,
        189, 190, 195, 199, 200–201,
        202, 257
independent regulatory agencies, 77
India, 129–66
    agriculture in, 135, 144
    ancient civilization of, 51, 52, 54–55,
        57–58, 60, 65, 69–70
    as Asian country, 135–36, 140,
        156–57, 165
    author as native of, 188, 193,
        246–47, 257, 258–59
    automobiles in, 97, 98, 133
    banking industry of, 136–37, 141
    billionaires in, 133, 139
    British rule of, 33, 35, 47–48, 68, 71,
        76, 81, 84–85, 135, 138, 140,
        143, 145, 146–47, 148, 154, 157,
        163
    capitalism in, 61, 100–102, 136–37,
        141, 150
    caste system of, 61, 163, 164
    China compared with, 51, 95, 97,
        98, 100, 130, 131–34, 136, 141,
        143, 151, 152, 153, 159–61, 165,
        233
    Chinese relations with, 120, 127,
        148–49, 152, 156–57, 233
    coal power in, 31
    Communist Party of, 142
    Constituent Assembly of, 138
    Constitution of, 134
    consumerism in, 135–36
    corruption in, 141, 146–47
    credit in, 136–37

    culture of, 51, 52, 54–55, 57–58, 60,
        65, 69–70, 75–78, 80, 81, 82, 86,
        152–58
    as democracy, 38, 95, 96, 100, 104,
        129–30, 134, 136, 138, 140–46,
        150, 153, 156, 157, 160, 162–66
    demographics of, 132
    as developing country, 135–37,
        141–46, 152–53, 159, 161,
        165–66
    diversity of, 162–66
    economic reform in, 95, 143–46,
        152–53, 162
    economy of, 2, 21–22, 27, 38, 52,
        61, 74, 95, 100–102, 104,
        129–46, 149, 150, 152–53, 159,
        162, 165, 225
    education in, 69–70, 96, 139, 142,
        144, 145, 187–91, 193
    Election Commission of, 141
    as emerging market, 26, 37, 41, 43,
        234
    emigration from, 150–51
    energy needs of, 28, 31, 159
    engineers trained in, 187–91
    female literacy in, 141–42
    film industry of, 77–78, 81, 131,
        137–39
    foreign aid by, 139
    foreign investment in, 137
    foreign policy of, 146–61
    free markets in, 21–22, 26
    global influence of, 43, 130–32,
        146–61, 165–66, 232, 233, 244
    government of, 129–30, 134,
        140–51, 161, 162–66
    gross domestic product (GDP) of,
        53, 132, 135, 136, 141, 225
    growth rate for, 129–40, 142,
        143–46, 149, 152–53, 162, 165,
        225
    health care in, 133, 139, 141, 142,
        144
    Hinduism in, 61, 62, 84–85, 130,
        152–58, 163, 164
    HIV rate in, 133, 146
    human rights in, 75–76, 84, 141–42,
        145, 157
    income levels of, 132, 190

independence of, 138, 143, 146
industrialization of, 135
inflation in, 129
infrastructure of, 133–37, 143
languages of, 80, 135, 151, 152, 162–63, 164
legal system of, 134, 141
literacy rate in, 141–42
living standards in, 53–54
manufacturing sector of, 21, 132–33, 135, 137
mass media in, 138, 139, 157
middle class of, 144
military forces of, 148, 151, 158–61, 165–66, 225, 235, 252
modernization of, 61, 129–32, 135
multinational corporations in, 47–48
Muslim minority in, 12, 142–43, 156, 163, 164
nationalism in, 38, 129, 142–43, 163–66
nonalignment policy of, 147–50, 161
nuclear weapons of, 151, 158–61, 225, 235
oil needs of, 28
Pakistan's relations with, 129–30, 149, 156, 160
political parties in, 138, 140–46, 162, 163, 164
population of, 21, 53, 132, 162–66
poverty in, 3, 133, 134, 139–42, 146–47, 153, 161
private sector of, 132–37, 144–45
regional governments in, 129–30, 145–46, 162–66
service sector of, 132, 135
socialism in, 141, 145, 157, 162
technology sector of, 25, 40, 132–33, 145, 187–91, 193
as UN member, 38, 148n
urbanization of, 134, 137–39, 144, 150
U.S. compared with, 139–40
U.S. relations with, 128, 144, 150–52, 156, 158–61, 165, 225–26, 238, 239, 242, 244, 246–47, 249, 257
wage levels in, 190
Western influence in, 75–78, 81, 86

women in, 75–76, 141–42, 145
Indian Institutes of Technology, 129, 145, 188–89
Indonesia, 3, 11, 13, 16, 22, 73, 86, 97–98, 99, 119, 155, 253–54
industrialization, 2, 3, 18–19, 52, 53, 74, 91, 93–94, 97, 135, 174, 175–76, 183, 187, 200, 201, 237
industrial revolution, 91, 237
inflation, 23–24, 26, 27, 129, 133–37, 143, 200
information technology, 9, 191, 198, 202, 209–10
Infosys Technologies, 40, 132, 137, 139
infrastructure, 133–34, 136
initial public offerings (IPOs), 185, 203–5
intellectual property, 112–13
interest rates, 19, 62, 205
Intergovernmental Panel on Climate Change, 30–31
intermediate business expenses, 201
International Atomic Energy Agency (IAEA), 158–59, 160
International Herald Tribune, 83
International Monetary Fund (IMF), 22, 38, 217
Internet, 24–25, 80, 83, 100, 122, 126, 207–8
investment funds, 3, 29–30, 184–85
iPod, 131, 186
Iran, 6, 9, 15, 17, 29, 83, 112, 125, 151, 173, 235, 236, 248, 252–53, 258
Iranian hostage crisis, 258
Iran-Iraq War, 9
Iraq, 6, 7–8, 9, 11–12, 13, 14, 39, 42–43, 125, 146, 168–69, 172–73, 182, 213, 220, 222, 223–24, 252–53
Iraq War, 6, 7–8, 39, 42–43, 125, 168–69, 172–73, 182, 223–24, 226, 227–28, 235, 244, 248–49
iron, 118, 174
Islam, 2, 10–15, 61, 62, 76, 109, 112, 129–32, 135, 142–43, 156, 163, 164, 196, 217, 238, 247, 251, 252, 253–54, 255
Islamic fundamentalism, 10–15, 62, 76, 156, 217, 238, 247, 252, 253–55

Israel, 6–7, 83, 151–52, 183, 222, 235,
    244, 249, 258
Italy, 23, 84, 132, 165–66, 178
It's a Wonderful Life, 72
"Ivory Tower" nations, 184–85

Jakarta, 16
James, Lawrence, 172
Japan:
    Buddhism in, 155
    China compared with, 91–92
    Chinese relations of, 88, 107,
        121–22, 127
    culture of, 74, 76, 78–79, 85, 86,
        109, 195
    democracy in, 101, 103
    economy of, 19, 20, 22, 25, 35–36,
        38, 40–41, 74, 91–92, 105, 107,
        210, 221
    education in, 190–91, 192, 193, 195
    family values in, 79, 80
    fertility rate of, 197
    foreign aid by, 121–22
    foreign trade of, 65, 69
    global influence of, 20, 32, 34,
        35–36, 38, 43–44, 105, 107, 108,
        159, 210, 232
    gross domestic product (GDP) of,
        183, 190–91
    Imperial, 34, 35–36, 71, 121–22,
        178–79
    manufacturing sector of, 25
    Meiji Reformation in, 71
    military forces of, 121
    population of, 41, 197
    savings rate of, 91–92
    technology sector of, 74, 184,
        190–91, 192, 210
    trade balance of, 91–92
    U.S. relations with, 220, 242
    Western influence in, 69, 71, 85, 86
Jemaah Islamiah, 11
Jiang Zemin, 120–21
jihad, 10–15
Joffe, Josef, 227, 241
Jordan, 8, 254
Judaism, 11, 109, 155, 156

Kagan, Robert, 228–29

Kant, Immanuel, 110
Karnataka, 163–64
Kennedy, Paul, 61, 176
Kenya, 3, 38–39
Keynes, John Maynard, 179
kimonos, 76
Kissinger, Henry, 221, 240
Kitchener, H. H., 172
knowledge economy, 202, 209–10
Kohl, Helmut, 221
Korean War, 19
Kosovo, 32, 221, 247–48
Kotak, Uday, 137
Kreuz-Zeitung, 171
Krishnadevaraya, 54
Kursk, Battle of, 34
Kyoto accords (1997), 31, 37

labor market, 25, 56, 135, 185, 189,
    201–2, 208–10
labor-saving devices, 58–59
labor unions, 142, 195
Landes, David, 60
Las Vegas, 3
Latin America, 6, 17–18, 29, 38, 77, 82,
    221
Latin language, 79
law:
    common, 68
    contract, 112–13, 134
    divine, 110
    Islamic, 14–15
    natural, 110–11
    rule of, 101, 112–13, 134, 141, 208,
        253–54
Laxman, R. K., 150
League of Nations, 229
"Leaving Asia" (Fukuzawa), 71
Lebanon, 6, 12, 152, 258
Lee Kwan Yew, 80, 102, 103, 115–16
Leibniz, Gottfried Wilhelm, 110
Leila Island, 215–17
Lend-Lease Act (1941), 179–80
Lewis, Bernard, 15, 250
liberals, 61–62, 157
Liberia, 206
Libya, 178
Lincoln, Abraham, 106
liquidity, 19–20, 23, 27, 183, 202–10

literacy, 141–42
living standards, 23–24, 53–54, 57, 100–101
London, 15–16, 90, 205, 206–7
London bombings (2005), 15–16
Lux, 184–85
Luxemburg, Rosa, 72

Macao, 3, 85
McCain, John, 252
Machiavelli, Niccolò, 249–50
McKinsey and Co., 29–30, 205
McKinsey Global Institute (MGI), 31, 189
macroeconomics, 199–202
Maddison, Angus, 53n
Madison, James, 212
Madrid bombings (2004), 15
Magna Carta, 63
"magnetism," 107–8
Mahbubani, Kishore, 75–76, 226
Malaysia, 2, 217
Malthus, Thomas, 57
"Malthusian trap," 57n
"managerial imperialism," 234
manufacturing sector, 19, 20–21, 25, 89, 91–92, 132–33, 135, 137, 175–76, 185–86
Mao Zedong, 10, 88, 96, 104, 116, 122, 253
Marcos, Ferdinand, 96
markets:
    capital, 19–20, 23, 27, 52–54, 57n, 62, 63, 80–81, 135–36, 183, 198–99, 201, 202–10
    domestic, 91–92, 98, 105, 117, 123, 128, 207, 218, 242, 257
    emerging, 2, 19–21, 26, 37, 41, 43, 105, 234
    financial, 7, 15–16, 27, 59–60, 97, 202–10
    free, 21–26, 45, 47–48, 93–95, 102, 136, 200, 202, 218, 234, 256–57
    global, see globalization
    labor, 25, 56, 135, 185, 189, 201–2, 208–10
Marshall, George C., 230, 231
Marshall Plan, 229
Marx, Karl, 72, 101–2

mass media, 9, 14–15, 24–25, 82, 83, 138, 139, 157, 192
mathematics, 191–95
Mecca, 253, 254
Medicare, 202
Mediterranean Sea, 64, 215–19
Meiji Reformation, 71
memorization, 193–94
Menon, K. P. S., 147
Menon, V. K. Krishna, 148
meritocracies, 193–94
metric system, 206
Mexico, 2, 18, 26, 44, 228, 251
Microsoft, 91, 112–13
Middle Ages, 54, 63, 79
middle class, 21, 23–24, 102, 144, 254
Middle East:
    Arab population of, 65, 67
    colonialism in, 146, 178
    economies of, 61, 62–63
    political situation of, 6–8, 105, 183, 221, 222, 224n, 238, 258
    U.S. influence in, 7–8, 29, 42, 250
    see also specific countries
military spending, 17, 92, 126, 181–82, 217, 237–38
Ming dynasty, 49–50, 60, 64
"mixed" economic model, 141
"mixed" regimes, 101
Mobutu Sese Seko, 96
modernization, 14–15, 32–33, 36, 61, 73–77, 81–82, 89, 96–97, 101–2, 113–14, 129–32, 135
Mogul Empire, 61, 62, 84
Mohan, C. Raja, 149
monarchy, 63, 110–11
Mondale, Walter, 227
Monier-Williams, Monier, 153–54
Montgomery, Bernard Law, 230
Morocco, 16, 192, 215–17, 253–54
Morocco bombings (2003), 16
Morris, James, 167–68
mortgages, 27, 72, 136, 200, 208
Mountbatten, Louis, 33, 148
Moynihan, Daniel Patrick, 61–62
MRI machines, 28
Mugabe, Robert, 96, 118
multiculturalism, 52
multilateralism, 222–30, 240, 242–44

multipolar order, 1–5, 36–37, 42–43,
    210, 216–17, 218, 219–26, 240,
    241–44, 249–50
multi-spindle wheel, 59
Mumbai, 134, 157, 163, 193
Mumtaz Mahal, 58
Muslim Brotherhood, 252
Mussolini, Benito, 178
Mutual Assured Destruction, 124

Naím, Moisés, 117
Nanjing, 50
nanotechnology, 183–85, 198
Napoleon I, Emperor of France, 87–88
Nasser, Gamal Abdul, 72
National Academy of Sciences, 187
national debt, 117, 124, 200–202,
    217–18
nationalism, 4, 31–40, 63, 88, 121–22,
    127, 129, 142–43, 163–66,
    174–75, 249
nationalization, 180
national saving, 201
National Science Foundation, 188
nation-states, 31–40, 63
natural gas, 28, 116, 236
natural resources, 6, 27–30, 31, 35, 52,
    91, 102, 116–19, 210, 236
Nazism, 10, 24, 34–36, 127, 241, 251
Needham, Joseph, 109
Nehru, Jawaharlal, 71, 73, 138, 140,
    146–49, 152, 157, 161, 164
neoconservatives, 125–26, 223, 228–29
Netherlands, 54, 59–60, 66, 67–68,
    171–72, 192
New Delhi, India, 134
Newsweek, 83
New World, 49, 66, 67, 170
"new world order," 35–36
New York, N.Y., 203–4, 206–7
New York Times, 147, 171, 234
Nigeria, 48, 73, 85, 117, 133
Nixon, Richard M., 210, 258
Nobel Prize, 193, 198
nonaccelerating inflation rate of unem-
    ployment (NAIRU), 200
nonalignment policy, 147–50, 161
nongovernmental organizations (NGOs),
    4, 32, 37, 45, 152, 157, 247

North Africa, 12–13, 18, 67
North America, 66
North Atlantic Treaty Organization
    (NATO), 13, 156, 223, 243
North Korea, 6, 17, 19, 125, 159, 213,
    222, 235, 239
Nuclear Nonproliferation Treaty (1968),
    158–61, 240–41
nuclear weapons, 6, 16, 26, 31, 83, 124,
    126, 151, 158–61, 225, 226–27,
    232, 235–36, 240–41, 248, 251,
    253, 254
Nunn, Sam, 240
Nye, Joseph, 108

Obama, Barack, 255
Oglethorpe University, 251–52
oil, 6, 27–30, 35, 102, 210, 236
Olympic Games, 90, 92, 124, 170
Omdurman, Battle of, 171
one-child policy, 132, 197n
O'Neill, Thomas P. "Tip," 162, 258–59
Opium Wars, 68–69
Organization of American States
    (OAS), 243
Organization of Petroleum Exporting
    Countries (OPEC), 28
Orissa, 139
Ottoman Empire, 54, 55, 61, 62–63, 69,
    71, 72–73, 104–5
outsourcing, 25, 40, 132, 186

"Pacific Century," 221
Pakistan, 12, 13, 129–30, 143, 149, 156,
    160, 217, 235, 239, 246
Palestinians, 6–7, 222
Pampers diapers, 92
Parsley crisis (2002), 215–17
Patriots Alliance, 122
Patten, Christopher, 224–25
"peaceful rise," 106–7, 114–23
peasants, 52–53, 87, 93–94, 99
Pei, Minxin, 93, 97–98
pensions, 195–96, 211
Perejil Island, 215–17
Perry, William, 240
Pershing missiles, 226–27
Persian Gulf, 29
Peru, 24

Peter I, Emperor of Russia, 70–71
petrochemicals, 29–30
Pew Global Attitudes Survey, 47, 109, 150, 209
Philippines, 11, 25, 120
Philosophical Dictionary (Voltaire), 110
Pilhofer, Aron, 202–3
Pinker, Steven, 9
Pitt, William, 69
Pizarro, Francisco, 67
platinum, 118
plutonium, 160
polar ice caps, 31
political parties, 47, 138, 140–46, 162, 163, 164, 213, 231, 251–54, 255, 257
"political risk," 18
Poos, Jacques, 221
population growth, 21, 30, 41, 52–53, 67, 87, 97–98, 99, 128, 129, 132, 162–66, 174, 195–99
Portugal, 56, 66, 67, 103, 135
"positive supply shocks," 19
post-American world:
    anti-Americanism and, 13, 32, 36–37, 39–40, 47–48, 150, 217, 221, 226–30, 249–50, 257
    asymmetry in, 126–28, 244–47
    cultural change in, 1–5, 14, 36, 38–39, 49–86, 113–14
    economic conditions in, 6–48, 80, 81, 84, 180–82, 217–19, 230
    future trends for, 1–5, 81–86, 182–86, 187, 215–59
    legitimacy in, 219–26, 245–50
    multilateralism in, 222–30, 240, 242–44
    nationalism in, 4, 31–40, 88, 121–22, 127, 129, 142–43, 163–66, 174–75, 249
    power shift in, 18, 21, 26–27, 31–40, 42–44, 80–81, 86, 114–15, 124–28, 216–26, 241–42
    "rise of the rest" in, 1–5, 52, 83–84, 86, 88, 181–82, 202–10, 218, 232–34, 238–39, 242–44, 259
    strategic approach to, 126–28, 231–50

    unipolar vs. multipolar order of, 1–5, 36–37, 42–43, 210, 216–17, 218, 219–26, 240, 241–44, 249–50
    U.S. global role in, 4–5, 40–48, 104, 107, 126–28, 166, 206–10, 213–59
    see also globalization
postindustrial economies, 135, 183, 187
poverty, 3, 20, 21, 52–53, 87, 89, 93–94, 98, 100–101, 104, 108, 130, 133, 134, 139–42, 146–47, 153, 161
Powell, Colin, 216
Pratt School of Engineering, 188
Premji, Azim, 139
price levels, 19, 24–25, 28, 30, 54, 57, 115
private property, 60, 134
private sector, 132–37, 144–45
privatization, 94, 97, 134–35, 136, 137, 205
Procter & Gamble, 92, 135
product development, 185–86
productivity, 19, 28, 30, 41, 58–59, 144, 183, 195, 257
profit, 59–60, 67–68, 115, 186
Protestantism, 68, 84–85, 112, 237
Prussia, 110–11, 174
Pudong financial district, 90
Punjab, 163
purchasing power parity (PPP), 17n, 20, 53n, 100n, 132n, 181n

qi (energy), 113
Qienlong, Emperor of China, 56
Qing dynasty, 50–51, 68–69
quotas, 96

Raffles, Stamford, 168
Rajasthan, 163–64
Ramo, Joshua Cooper, 126–27
Ranbaxy, 137
Ratner, Ely, 36
Reagan, Ronald, 152, 227, 258
real estate, 27, 72, 136, 200, 201, 208
recessions, 23–24
regional governments, 129–30, 145–46, 162–66
regional powers, 232–38
Reliance Industries, 133, 137

religion, 14, 61, 63, 67, 68, 74, 85,
        109–12, 114, 129–32, 135, 153,
        155, 156, 196, 237, 255
Renaissance, 55
Report of Phibihu (Frederick II),
        110–11
Republican Party, 47, 213, 251–53, 254,
        256–57
reserve currency, 242–43
"responsible stakeholders," 232
retail sector, 186
Revolutionary War, U.S., 177
Rhine River, 64
Ricci, Matteo, 111
Rice, Condoleezza, 228
Richie, Donald, 79
Rig Veda, 155
Rise of the Great Nations, The, 106–7
Roberts, J. M., 61
rogue states, 17–18, 36, 173, 251
Roman Empire, 54–55, 64–65, 115,
        167, 171, 176, 217, 237
Romney, Mitt, 252–53
Roosevelt, Franklin D., 107, 152, 179,
        229–30, 251
Roosevelt, Theodore, 107, 166
Rousseau, Jean-Jacques, 110
Roy, Pranoy, 161
Roy, Raja Ram Mohan, 69–70, 73
Royal Navy, 169, 175, 178, 181
Rumsfeld, Donald, 47, 222–23
Russia:
    Chinese relations of, 120, 124, 126
    czarist rule of, 60, 70–71, 174
    economic reforms in, 94
    economy of, 2, 27, 35–36, 94, 174
    as emerging market, 26, 234
    foreign policy of, 6
    geography of, 63
    global influence of, 12, 43, 104, 232,
        244
    gross domestic product (GDP) of,
        174
    industrialization of, 2
    nuclear weapons of, 158, 159–60,
        235–36, 240–41
    oil resources of, 29
    poverty in, 3
    privatization in, 205

    taxation in, 71
    U.S. relations with, 173, 217, 223,
        235–36, 242, 244
    Western influence in, 70–71, 85
    see also Soviet Union
Russian Orthodox Church, 71

Sachs, Jeffrey, 22, 89
Sahney, Rajiv, 189
St. Mark's Square, 85
St. Petersburg, 70–71
Salafist Group for Call and Combat
        (GSPC), 12–13
salwar kurta, 75–76
samba, 82
Sarbanes-Oxley Act (2002), 204
saris, 75–76
Sarkozy, Nicolas, 228
Saudi Arabia, 8, 11, 13, 14, 29–30, 35,
        112, 151, 210, 224n, 239, 253–54
savings rate, 23–24, 40, 91–92, 135–36,
        199–202, 211, 257
Schumer, Chuck, 203–4
Schwab, Klaus, 131
Schwarz, Benjamin, 34–35
scientific research, 55–57, 85, 110, 175,
        181, 182, 183–85, 191–95, 201–2
Security Council, UN, 38, 88, 105, 118,
        148n, 230, 247–48
September 11th, 2001 terrorist attacks,
        6, 10–11, 14, 15, 16, 201,
        222–23, 240, 247, 248, 252, 253
service sector, 132, 135
Shah Jahan, 58
Shakespeare Wallah, 81
Shanghai, 32, 90, 97, 105, 134, 168, 194
Shanghai Stock Exchange, 97, 105
Shanmugaratnam, Tharman, 193–94
sharia, 14–15
Sharma, Ruchir, 163
Shia Muslims, 11–12, 238, 253
shopping malls, 3
Shultz, George, 240
Sicily, 34
Sikhs, 163
Silicon Valley, 198
Singapore, 3, 29, 102–3, 119, 137, 168,
        178–79, 192, 193–95
Singh, Manmohan, 143, 144, 153

Sino-African summit (2006), 116–17
Sky News, 83
Slaughter, Anne-Marie, 243
slavery, 66
Slovakia, 206
"smiley curve," 186
socialism, 22, 23, 107, 128, 141, 145, 157, 162, 180
Social Security, 213
Socrates, 110
"soft power," 108, 170, 234–35
Somalia, 168–69, 206
South Africa, 2, 3, 44, 85, 119, 171–73, 232, 234
South America, 66
South Asia, 19, 20n, 42, 47–48
South China Sea, 120, 243
South Korea, 2, 19, 38, 71, 80, 82, 85, 91–92, 99, 102, 103, 119, 141, 155, 197
Soviet Union:
    Afghanistan invaded by, 13, 88, 258
    Chinese relations of, 120, 124, 126
    collapse of, 8–9, 22, 35–36, 43, 219, 220–21, 258
    Communist regime of, 22, 23, 107
    Czechoslovakia invaded by (1968), 227
    expansionism of, 10, 156, 231, 258
    space program of, 58, 210
    as superpower, 10, 88, 107, 156, 231, 241, 258–59
    technology sector of, 58
    U.S. relations with, 4, 8–9, 19, 35–36, 125, 127, 128, 147–50, 179, 182, 220–21, 223, 227, 229–30, 231, 247, 250, 253, 258–59
    in World War II, 34–35
    see also Russia
space program, 58, 210
Spain, 15, 103, 170, 215–17, 253–54, 256
Spanish language, 83
special interests, 212, 213
Speer, Albert, 90
Speer, Albert, Jr., 90
Spence, Jonathan, 111
Spiegel, 227

Spielberg, Steven, 92
Sputnik launching (1957), 210
Sri Lanka, 141, 149
Stalin, Joseph, 35, 179, 229–30, 251, 253
state-directed capitalism, 29–30
state socialism, 128
"stealth reforms," 144
steel, 91
Steingart, Gabor, 40
stocks, 27, 97, 205
subprime mortgages, 27
sub-Saharan Africa, 67
Sudan, 29, 35, 39, 118, 171, 248
Suez Canal, 19, 152, 169, 178
Suez Canal crisis (1956), 19, 152
suicide bombings, 13–14, 254
Summers, Lawrence, 222
Sunni Muslims, 11–12, 238, 252–53
Sun Yat-sen, 71, 73
Sun Zi, 127
Sweden, 23, 103, 183
Syria, 6, 8, 141

Taiwan, 2, 19, 32, 99, 103, 105, 106, 119, 122–23, 124, 125, 126, 148n, 197, 239
Taiwan Strait, 19
Taj Mahal, 58
Talbot, Strobe, 94
Taliban, 13, 156, 217, 252
Tamil Nadu, 163
Tancredo, Tom, 253
tariffs, 38, 180
Tata Group, 132–33, 137
taxation, 38, 51, 59, 62, 71, 95, 206, 213, 238
Tay, Simon, 234
technology, 9, 20–25, 27, 40, 41, 46, 48, 74, 79–80, 100, 122, 126, 132–33, 145, 181, 182, 183–95, 198, 200, 201–2, 207–10, 211
Tehran Conference (1943), 229–30
telecommunications industry, 145
television, 82, 83, 157
tennis, 202–3
terrorism, 4, 6, 9, 10–18, 26–27, 31, 47, 201, 217, 222–23, 240, 245, 247, 248, 250–59

textile industry, 25
Thailand, 25, 119
Tharoor, Shashi, 148n
Thatcher, Margaret, 22, 180, 208, 220, 221
Third Plenum of the Eleventh Central Committee of the Communist Party (1978), 89
Third World, 10, 37, 89, 145, 161
Thirty Years' War, 110
Thornton, John, 101
Tiananmen Square massacre (1989), 24, 250
Tibet, 148–49
Time, 83
Times (London), 83
Times Higher Educational Supplement, 190
Tojo Hideki, 34
Tokyo, 78–79
totalitarianism, 63, 99–104, 250
Toynbee, Arnold, 168, 179–80
Toyota, 208
trade balance, 19, 40, 45–46, 91–92, 199
traditional culture, 77–86
"treasure ships," 49–51
Treasury Department, U.S., 11
Trends in International Mathematics and Science Study (TIMSS), 191–92
Truman, Harry S., 229, 231
Tsongas, Paul, 221
tsunami disaster (2004), 139
Tunisia, 192
Turkey, 3, 16, 26, 71, 102, 249, 253–54
Turkey bombings (2003), 16
Twain, Mark, 246

Ukraine, 2, 235
unemployment rate, 195, 200, 208–9, 258
unilateralism, 46–47, 222–30, 240, 242–44
"uni-multipolarity," 43
unipolar order, 1–5, 36–37, 42–43, 210, 216–17, 218, 219–26, 241–42, 249–50
United Arab Emirates, 3

United Nations, 38, 39, 88, 105, 118, 141, 148n, 196, 216, 220, 226, 229, 230, 239, 243, 247–48
United Nations Human Development Index, 141
United Nations Population Division, 196
United States, 215–59
    African policy of, 245–46, 248–49
    alliances of, 219–26, 245–50
    Asian policies of, 77, 217–18, 221, 234–35, 242, 243, 248–49
    automobile industry of, 175, 208–9, 219–20
    British Empire compared with, 168–69, 172–73, 180–82, 213–14, 236–38, 241, 243
    British relations of, 151–52, 172, 177–80, 217, 229–30, 236–37, 249
    budget deficits of, 202, 217–18, 220
    capitalism in, 21–22, 25, 48, 107, 183–85, 206–7, 209–10
    China compared with, 87, 90, 95, 176, 218, 239
    Chinese relations of, 87, 91, 92–93, 95, 105, 123–28, 160–61, 173, 213, 230, 235, 238, 239, 241, 242, 244
    colonial period of, 52, 177
    culture of, 1–5, 33–34, 77–78, 80, 81, 187, 195–99, 206–11, 246–47, 250–59
    democratic ideals of, 125, 150, 210–14, 239, 249–59
    demographics of, 195–99
    diversity of, 195–99, 254–55, 257, 258
    domestic market of, 207, 218, 242, 257
    economy of, 17, 19, 21, 27, 40–41, 44–45, 74, 105–6, 107, 124, 136, 166, 169, 174, 175, 180–82, 195–202, 210–12, 214, 217, 220, 221, 231, 251, 256–57
    education in, 46, 187–95, 198, 201–2, 208, 211
    elections in, 220–21, 227, 251–55
    energy needs of, 35, 210, 211
    engineers trained in, 187–91

European relations of, 220–21,
    226–30, 248–49
family values in, 80
film industry of, 77–78, 81
financial markets of, 200, 202–10
foreign investment in, 202
foreign policy of, 7–8, 39–40, 42,
    46–47, 112, 117, 118, 119,
    126–28, 151–52, 172–73, 206,
    213–59
foreign trade of, 19, 40, 45–46, 91,
    183, 199, 200, 257
French relations of, 227, 228
future development of, 1–5, 81–86,
    182–86, 187, 215–59
German relations of, 220–21, 227
global influence of *see* post-American
    world
gross domestic product (GDP) of,
    17, 44–45, 91, 105–6, 174, 179,
    180–82, 183, 190–91, 198, 200,
    201, 202n, 231
growth rate for, 195–99, 210–12, 220
health care in, 208–9, 211, 213, 257
immigration to, 48, 74, 150–51,
    195–99, 211, 247, 251, 254,
    256–57
income levels of, 195, 199, 200–201,
    202
India compared with, 139–40
Indian relations of, 128, 144,
    150–52, 156, 158–61, 165,
    225–26, 238, 239, 242, 244,
    246–47, 249, 257
industrialization of, 2, 18–19, 52,
    176, 183, 187, 200, 201
infrastructure of, 136
insularity of, 206–10, 250–59
Japanese relations of, 220, 242
labor force of, 208–10
legal system of, 208, 253–54
manufacturing sector of, 185–86
Middle East policies of, 7–8, 29, 42,
    250
military forces of, 124–27, 158–61,
    168–69, 181–82, 217, 230,
    235–38, 240–41, 243, 244–47
military spending of, 17, 92n, 126,
    181–82, 217, 237–38

Muslim population of, 247, 251, 254
national debt of, 124, 200–202,
    217–18
nationalism in, 33–37
nuclear weapons of, 124, 126,
    158–61, 235–36, 240–41, 253
oil needs of, 35
political system of, 169, 199–200,
    210–14, 250–59
population of, 21, 41, 87, 183,
    195–99
productivity of, 183, 257
religious attitudes in, 109
rhetoric of fear in, 250–59
Russian relations of, 173, 217, 223,
    235–36, 242, 244
savings rate of, 199–202, 211, 217,
    257
scientific research in, 181, 182,
    201–2
Soviet relations of, 4, 8–9, 19, 35–36,
    125, 127, 128, 147–50, 179, 182,
    220–21, 223, 227, 229–30, 231,
    247, 250, 253, 258–59
special interests in, 212, 213
as superpower, 4–5, 40–48, 104, 107,
    126–28, 166, 206–59
taxation in, 95, 206, 213, 238
technology sector of, 41, 46, 48, 181,
    182, 183–95, 198, 200, 201–2,
    207–8, 211
terrorist attacks against, 6, 10–11,
    13, 14, 15, 16, 26–27, 47, 201,
    217, 222–23, 240, 245, 247, 248,
    250–59
unemployment rate in, 200, 208–9,
    258
unilateralism of, 46–47, 222–30,
    240, 242–44
as UN member, 105, 230, 239,
    247–48
in World War II, 34–35
urbanization, 89–90, 93–94, 97, 134,
    137–39, 144, 150
U.S. Information Services, 246–47
Uttar Pradesh, 163

Valentine's Day, 75
Vedrine, Hubert, 222

Véliz, Claudio, 170
Venezuela, 6, 17, 29, 173, 177n
venture capital, 184–85
Vesalius, Andreas, 55
Victoria, Queen of England, 167–68
Vietnam, 19, 119, 120–21, 127, 141,
        182, 227, 258
Vietnam War, 19, 182, 227, 258
Vijayanagar, 54–55
visas, travel, 256
Voice of America, 83
Voltaire, 110

wage levels, 27, 54, 189, 190, 257
Wahhabism, 12
Wall Street Journal, 192
Wal-Mart, 91
warfare, 56, 60, 63–64, 72
War of 1812, 177
war on terror, 26–27, 217, 240, 245,
        248, 250–59
"Washington consensus," 94
Washington Post, 194
Watergate scandal, 258
water supplies, 30
wealth, 52–54, 57n, 62, 63, 80–81,
        135–36, 198–99, 201
weapons of mass destruction (WMDs),
        16, 226
Weber, Steven, 36
WEF Competitiveness Index, 195–96
Weller, Robert, 113
Wen Jiabao, 101, 106, 121, 122
Western culture, 1–5, 14, 36, 38–39,
        49–86, 113–14
wheat prices, 19, 54
Whelan, Theresa, 245

Wilhelm II, Emperor of Germany, 169n
Wilson, Woodrow, 166
Wohlforth, William, 232–33
Wolf, Martin, 210
women's rights, 75–76, 81, 141–42,
        145
working class, 198–99
World Bank, 22, 38, 117
World Economic Forum, 41, 130–31,
        183, 195–96
*World Economy: A Millennial Perspective,
        The* (Maddison), 53n
World Is Flat, The (Friedman), 187
World Trade Organization (WTO), 4,
        95, 124
World War I, 146, 173, 174, 178, 229
World War II, 19, 34–36, 38, 40, 41, 88,
        121–22, 178–80, 229–30, 232,
        258
Wu Jianmin, 105, 115

Xinghai Fang, 105–6

Yalta Conference (1945), 179, 229–30
Yangtze River, 58–59, 98
Yeltsin, Boris, 94
Youth (Conrad), 72
Yugoslavia, 10, 221
yutori kyoiku (relaxed education), 195

Zambezi, 67
Zarqawi, Abu Mussab al-, 12
Zawahiri, Ayman, 13
Zenawi, Meles, 117
Zheng Bijian, 106
Zheng He, 49–51, 57, 58, 64
Zimbabwe, 24, 118

PENGUIN POLITICS

FREE WORLD: WHY A CRISIS OF THE WEST REVEALS THE OPPORTUNITY OF OUR TIME
TIMOTHY GARTON ASH

'A compelling manifesto for the enlargement of freedom and a new era of world politics' Vaclav Havel

At the beginning of the twenty-first century, the world plunged into crisis. What began as an attack on the West by Osama bin Laden soon became a dramatic confrontation between Europe and America.

Britain has found itself painfully split, because it stands with one foot across the Atlantic and the other across the Channel. The English, in particular, are divided politically between a Right that argues our place is with America, not Europe, and a Left that claims the opposite. This is today's English civil war. Both sides tell us we must choose. In this powerful new work, Timothy Garton Ash, one of our leading political writers, explains why we cannot, need not and must not choose between Europe and America.

Drawing on an extraordinary range of sources, from unique conversations with leaders such as Bush, Blair and Schröder, to encounters with farmers in Kansas and soldiers in Aldershot, from history, memoir and opinion polls to personal observations based on a quarter-century of travelling in Europe and the US, he demolishes the popular claim that Americans are from Mars and Europeans are from Venus. He shows why Washington can never rule the world on its own, why the new, enlarged Europe can only realise its aspirations in a larger, transatlantic community, and why the torments of the Middle East and the developing world can only be addressed by working together. To remain true to itself, the West must go beyond itself.

In fact, this crisis reveals a historic opportunity for free people everywhere to advance together from the cold war West to a new international order of liberty. Defying conventional wisdom and eschewing easy answers, this timely, provocative book should be read not just by those who purport to lead and inform us, but by anyone who wishes to be a citizen of a free world.

PENGUIN HEALTH

FAST FOOD NATION: WHAT THE ALL-AMERICAN MEAL IS DOING TO THE WORLD
ERIC SCHLOSSER

'A shocking exposé ... *Fast Food Nation* could make a difference to the way we eat. For ever' *Evening Standard*

'*Fast Food Nation* has lifted the polystyrene lid on the global fast food industry ... and sparked a storm' *Observer*

Do you *really* know what you're eating when you tuck into that juicy burger?

Britain eats more fast food than any other country in Europe. It looks good, tastes good, and it's cheap. But the real cost never appears on the menu.

Eric Schlosser's explosive bestseller, by turns funny and terrifying, tells the story of our love affair with fast food. He visits the lab that re-creates the smell of strawberries; examines the safety records of abattoirs; reveals why fries taste so good and what really lurks between the sesame buns – and shows how fast food is transforming not only our diets but our world.

'Has wiped that smirk off the Happy Meal ... Thanks to this man, you'll never eat a burger again' *Evening Standard*

'Startling ... Junk food, we learn, is just that ... left this reader vowing never to set foot in one of these outlets again' *Daily Mail*

'This book tells you more than you really want to know when you're chomping that hamburger ... Have a nice day? Listen – you should live so long' *The Times*

PENGUIN POLITICS

GLOBALIZATION AND ITS DISCONTENTS
JOSEPH STIGLITZ

'A massively important political as well as economic document ... we should listen to him urgently' Will Hutton, *Guardian*

Our world is changing. Globalization is not working. It is hurting those it was meant to help. And now, the tide is turning ...

Explosive and shocking, *Globalization and Its Discontents* is the bestselling exposé of the all-powerful organizations that control our lives – from the man who has seen them at work first hand.

As Chief Economist at the World Bank, Nobel Prize-winner Joseph Stiglitz had a unique insider's view into the management of globalization. Now he speaks out against it: how the IMF and WTO preach fair trade yet impose crippling economic policies on developing nations; how free market 'shock therapy' made millions in East Asia and Russia worse off than they were before; and how the West has driven the global agenda to further its own financial interests.

Globalization *can* still be a force for good, Stiglitz argues. But the balance of power has to change. Here he offers real, tough solutions for the future.

'Compelling ... This book is everyone's guide to the misgovernment of globalization' J. K. Galbraith

'Stiglitz is a rare breed, an heretical economist who has ruffled the self-satisfied global establishment that once fed him. *Globalization and Its Discontents* declares war on the entire Washington financial and economic establishment' Ian Fraser, *Sunday Tribune*

'Gripping ... this landmark book ... shows him to be a worthy successor to Keynes' Robin Blackburn, *Independent*

PENGUIN ECONOMICS

THE RETURN OF DEPRESSION ECONOMICS
PAUL KRUGMAN

'Essential reading' *Economist*

At the end of the 1990s, seven economies experienced slumps eerily reminiscent of the Great Depression. A botched devaluation in Thailand set off ripples all the way from Indonesia to South Korea. Russian debt default triggered disaster in Brazil. Hedge funds seemingly unaccountable to any government nearly succeeded in their aim of forcing up interest rates in Hong Kong. And almost no one had predicted these developments. Perhaps, argues Paul Krugman in his dazzling polemic, that is because we are trapped by a cosy free-market orthodoxy which cannot accept that 'bad things happen to good economies'. Yet if we truly hope to confront the immense challenges which lie ahead, we had better start facing up to reality right now.

'A lucid and punchy analysis of the dangers posed by global financial markets and a wake-up call for complacent or economically ignorant policymakers' *Economist*

'One of the world's most talented economists…his combination of wit and clarity makes him a true heir to Keynes' *Independent*

'An account of the Asian crisis that is unlikely to be rivalled in its lucidity…a rattling good read' *Financial Times*

MICHAEL MOORE

DUDE, WHERE'S MY COUNTRY?

'Michael Moore is the sand in the underpants of the Bush administration'
Observer

'Washington's No.1 pain in the jacksie … *Dude* is a call to arms, a guide book on how to win the debate with right-wingers and generally a good laugh'
Daily Mirror

He's the man *everyone's* talking about. He's taken on gun freaks, stupid white men and corporate crooks. Now Michael Moore is on a new mission: to get us off our behinds and kicking out the corrupt political elites who rule our lives.

Dude gives *you* the ammunition: why it's time for regime change at Number Ten; the whoppers spun to wage war on Iraq and make a killing; the 'special relationship' between George of Arabia and the Bin Ladens; obscene tax breaks for the rich – and how Mike's going to get everybody together to get rid of Dubya. Not to mention how to stop terrorism (stop terrorizing Third World countries!), talk to your conservative brother-in-law and get non-voters voting. It's time to stop bitching, get reading – and get your country back.

'Furiously funny' *Evening Standard*

'Shocking, devastating, genuinely funny … What Moore has to say needs saying again and again. Having read this book, I would even vote for him' *Guardian*

'Rich with facts, gags, self-deprecation and righteous indignation … it will rouse readers here and in the US to timely revolt' *Independent*

PENGUIN ECONOMICS

THE ECONOMICS OF INNOCENT FRAUD: TRUTH FOR OUR TIME
JOHN KENNETH GALBRAITH

'A prophet whose warnings have come to pass ... Galbraith is an iconoclast'
Independent

John Kenneth Galbraith, lifelong critic of unbridled corporate power and one of
the most renowned economists of the twentieth century, delivers a scathing
polemic on today's economics, politics and public morality.

Sounding the alarm on the gap between 'conventional wisdom' and reality,
Galbraith distils years of expertise in this radical critique of our society. He shows
the danger of the private sector's unprecedented and unbridled control over public
life – from government to the military to the environment. And he reveals how
politicians and the media have colluded in the myths of a benign 'market': that
big business always knows best, that minimal intervention stimulates the
economy, that obscene pay gaps and unrestrained self-enrichment are an
inevitable by-product of the system. The result, he shows, is that we have given
ourselves over to a lie and come to accept legal, legitimate, innocent fraud.

Galbraith's taut, wry and incisive analysis shows that the gulf between truth and
illusion has never been wider. It is essential reading for anyone who cares about
the economic and political future of the world.

John Kenneth Galbraith is Paul M. Warburg Professor of Economics, Emeritus, at
Harvard University. He has worked in economics for over seventy years, and his
many books include *A History of Economics*, *The Great Crash, 1929*, *The Age of
Uncertainty* and *The Culture of Contentment*.

'The scourge of contemporary economics ... he has always been superb at
attacking "conventional wisdom" *Observer*

'America's leading public intellectual' *Guardian*

'The most widely read economist in the world' Amartya Sen, Nobel Prize-winner
for Economics

PENGUIN LETTERS

LETTER FROM AMERICA 1946–2004
ALISTAIR COOKE

'A chronicler of amazing times ... There is never going to be anyone like Cooke'
Daily Telegraph

'Cooke's Letters are more than mere journalism: they are a moving picture of
Anglo-American relations – a piece of history in their own right' *Daily Mail*

For over half a century Alistair Cooke entertained millions of listeners across the
globe with his weekly BBC radio programme *Letter from America*. An
outstanding observer of the American scene, he became one of the world's best-
loved broadcasters and achieved the longest running one-man show in radio
history.

Here, published for the first time, is a selection of the finest of Alistair Cooke's
2,869 broadcasts, which celebrates the inimitable style of this wise, witty and
acute reporter. Presented chronologically, these famous letters span Cooke's
extraordinary career, beginning with a powerful description of American GIs
returning home in 1946, and ending with his last broadcast in February 2004
discussing the US presidential campaign.

Imbued with Alistair Cooke's special brand of good humour, elegance and
understanding, *Letter from America 1946–2004* is a captivating insight into the
heart of a nation, and a fitting tribute to the man who was for so many the most
reassuring voice of our times.

'No one succeeded in explaining to the English-speaking world ... the
idiosyncrasies of a country at once so familiar, and yet so utterly foreign'
Independent

'An enchanting volume ... A remarkable, perhaps unique transatlantic diary ...
what stories he has to tell ... Cooke expressed a mutual affection between two
nations which radiates from these debonair pages' *Sunday Telegraph*

BUSINESS

THE WORLD IS FLAT
THOMAS FRIEDMAN

Winner of the *Financial Times*/Goldman Sachs Business Book of the Year 2005

Three-times winner of the Pulitzer Prize

> The world is changing, the future is flat.

Thomas Friedman's international bestseller is the most up-to-date and exciting view yet of today's new era of globalization. He draws on this travels to India, China and the Middle East, and on the explosion of new technologies including blogging, online encyclopedias and podcasting, to show how knowledge and resources are connecting all over the planet as never before. This 'flattening' of our world, he argues, can be a force for good – for business, the environment and people everywhere.

'Truly amazing ... an essential read' A. C. Grayling

'A great book ... makes you see things in a new way' Joseph Stiglitz

ECONOMICS

FREAKONOMICS

STEVEN D. LEVITT & STEPHEN J. DUBNER

'A sensation ... you'll be stimulated, provoked and entertained. Of how many books can that be said?' *Sunday Telegraph*

'The book is a delight; it educates, surprises and amuses ... dazzling' *Economist*

'Prepare to be dazzled' Malcolm Gladwell

What do estate agents and the Ku Klux Klan have in common?

Why do drug dealers live with their mothers?

How can your name affect how well you do in life?

The answer: Freakonomics. It's at the heart of everything we do and the things that affect us daily, from sex to crime, parenting to politics, fat to cheating, fear to traffic jams. And it's all about using information about the world around us to get to the heart of what's *really* happening under the surface of everyday life.

'If Indiana Jones were an economist he'd be Steven Levitt' *Wall Street Journal*

NASSIM NICHOLAS TALEB

THE BLACK SWAN
THE IMPACT OF THE HIGHLY IMPROBABLE

What have the invention of the wheel, Pompeii, the Wall Street Crash, Harry Potter and the internet got in common? Why should you never run for a train or read a newspaper? What can Catherine the Great's lovers tell us about probability?

This book is all about Black Swans: the random events that underlie our lives, from bestsellers to world disasters. Their impact is huge; they're nearly impossible to predict; yet after they happen we always try to rationalize them. A rallying cry to ignore the 'experts', *The Black Swan* shows us how to stop trying to predict everything and take advantage of uncertainty.

'An idiosyncratically brilliant new book' Niall Ferguson

'Great fun … brash, stubborn, entertaining, opinionated, curious, cajoling' Stephen J. Dubner, author of *Freakonomics*

FOOLED BY RANDOMNESS
THE HIDDEN ROLE OF CHANCE IN LIFE AND IN THE MARKETS

Everyone wants to succeed in life. But what causes some of us to be more successful than others? Is it really down to skill and strategy – or something altogether more unpredictable? This book is the word-of-mouth sensation that will change the way you think about business and the world. It is all about luck: more precisely, how we perceive luck in our personal and professional experiences. Nowhere is this more obvious than in the markets – we hear an entrepreneur has 'vision' or a trader is 'talented', but all too often their performance is down to chance rather than skill. It is only because we fail to understand probability that we continue to believe events are non-random, finding reasons where none exist. This irreverent bestseller has shattered the illusions of people around the world by teaching them how to recognize randomness. Now it can do the same for you.

'Brilliant' John Kay

He just wanted a decent book to read ...

Not too much to ask, is it? It was in 1935 when Allen Lane, Managing Director of Bodley Head Publishers, stood on a platform at Exeter railway station looking for something good to read on his journey back to London. His choice was limited to popular magazines and poor-quality paperbacks – the same choice faced every day by the vast majority of readers, few of whom could afford hardbacks. Lane's disappointment and subsequent anger at the range of books generally available led him to found a company – and change the world.

'We believed in the existence in this country of a vast reading public for intelligent books at a low price, and staked everything on it'
Sir Allen Lane, 1902–1970, founder of Penguin Books

The quality paperback had arrived – and not just in bookshops. Lane was adamant that his Penguins should appear in chain stores and tobacconists, and should cost no more than a packet of cigarettes.

Reading habits (and cigarette prices) have changed since 1935, but Penguin still believes in publishing the best books for everybody to enjoy. We still believe that good design costs no more than bad design, and we still believe that quality books published passionately and responsibly make the world a better place.

So wherever you see the little bird – whether it's on a piece of prize-winning literary fiction or a celebrity autobiography, political tour de force or historical masterpiece, a serial-killer thriller, reference book, world classic or a piece of pure escapism – you can bet that it represents the very best that the genre has to offer.

Whatever you like to read – trust Penguin.